D0070437

Chicago Public Library
C
P
L
REFERENCE
Form 178 rev. 1-94

More Advance Praise for *The Twelfth Commandment of Wildly Successful Women:*

"No one said success would be easy, but Pamela Gilberd's book shows you how to ride out the rocky road of life and turn it into your personal path to success. Her real-world scenarios and thought-provoking choices for dealing with daily life are a must-read for every woman (and some men) who think life will pass them by. Pam shares her insights, courage, and secrets on becoming the mistress of your own destiny."

—Lillian Vernon, Founder and CEO, Lillian Vernon Corporation

"Read this rich collection of adventures full of wisdom and honesty, then pass it on to the women AND men in your life."

—Rick Cronk, President, Dreyer's Grand Ice Cream, Inc.

"Gilberd hasn't written a book, she's created an interactive journey that injects the reader into the lives of women we all know—our best friends, our mothers, sisters, co-workers, and even ourselves. In each vignette, she shows us that life is a series of choices, and that no predicament is insurmountable. It all depends on what we choose to do."

—Jeanie M. Barnett, Editor-in-Chief, Women's Business Executive

"This book helps you turn your vision into reality—your problems into opportunities."

—Nancy Mueller, President, Nancy's Specialty Foods

"Provocative and practical, this book is a tool kit for turning career challenges into adventures. Women today are breathlessly balancing work and family and conquering new frontiers. Gilberd's 'adventure guide' framework provides helpful ideas about taking charge of our lives in a proactive way—whether facing career transitions, starting a business, or enhancing leadership skills."

—Gail Shaffer, CEO, Business and Professional Women/USA

"This book is a challenging and fun way to explore varieties of challenges and opportunities common to all of us as women in today's world. What I like most about it is the message that there is no one, easy, prescribed answer; in fact, there are many answers and we all need to pay attention to our own inner voice as we find our own solutions. It has taken me many years to learn this important message!"

—Joan Welsh, President and CEO, Hurricane Island Outward Bound School

"A must-read for all women in search of success."

—Brad Ytterberg, Principal, Edward Jones

"I had the pleasure of dealing with Pamela Gilberd in the mid-1980s when she changed her career and reentered the job market. Pam has definitely 'walked the walk.' In *The Twelfth Commandment*, Pam lays out the road map that will give all of its readers a chance for success. This book offers great vision and can be a valuable working tool for both men and women."

—William J. Markowitz, President, Brown Jordan

"With the sometimes confusing array of opportunities won by the women's rights movement, Pamela Gilberd provides some much-needed tools to help women decide what they really want and go for it! By turns entertaining, informative, and inspirational, Ms. Gilberd uses [fictional and] real-life stories, including her own, to show women how to make good choices at turning points in their lives. *The Twelfth Commandment of Wildly Successful Women* will help all of us take control of our destinies."

—Patricia Ireland, President, National Organization for Women

The Twelfth Commandment of WILDLY Successful Women

Discover Your Own Best Answers to the Big Questions About Life, Work, and Love

Pamela Boucher Gilberd

Chandler House Press
Worcester, Massachusetts
1999

The Twelfth Commandment of Wildly Successful Women
Discover Your Own Best Answers to the Big Questions about Life, Work, and Love

ISBN 1-886284-34-2

Library of Congress Catalog Card Number 98-89739

First Edition

ABCDEFGHIJK

Published by
Chandler House Press
335 Chandler Street
Worcester, MA 01602
USA

President Lawrence J. Abramoff
Publisher/Editor-in-Chief Richard J. Staron
Director of Retail Sales and Marketing Claire Cousineau Smith
Editorial/Production Manager Jennifer J. Goguen
Book Design Bookmakers
Cover Design Bookmakers
Author Photo Fred Gilberd

Chandler House Press books are available at special discounts for bulk purchases. For more information about how to arrange such purchases, please contact Chandler House Press, 335 Chandler Street, Worcester, MA 01602, or call (800) 642-6657, or fax (508) 756-9425, or find us on the World Wide Web at www.tatnuck.com.

Chandler House Press books are distributed to the trade by

National Book Network, Inc.
4720 Boston Way
Lanham, MD 20706
(800) 462-6420

Dedication

To Tauni, with my love.

CONTENTS

Part II Work Adventures

ACKNOWLEDGMENTS

Many thanks to the hundreds of women from across the country who asked the "big questions" that sparked the idea for this book. The idea grew from inspiration to its final shape under the sharp eye (and dull #2 pencil) of Michael Snell, my agent-collaborator-editor and friend. Bless you.

I'm forever grateful for the continued support from Richard Staron, Editor-in-chief of Chandler House Press, who not only championed my previous book but also encouraged me to write this one. As always, it's a pleasure working with you. Thanks, too, to Jennifer Goguen and Claire Cousineau Smith, and the many talented people at Chandler House who have helped in the publishing process of this book.

Great thanks to my research experts and friends who have shared their knowledge and experiences with me to increase my understanding of the issues and develop the scenarios, strategies, and sound advice that fill this book. Thank you Jan Agnew, Betsy Bernard, Shirley Dennis, Sharleen Daugherty, Sally Edwards,

Carolyn Elman, Karen Fardelmann, Betsy Feichtmeir, Wendy Gilberd, Sharon Gillin, Judge Bonnie Crane Hellums, Candace Pratt Hoover, Arlene Inch, Elizabeth Jamison, Donnie Klingen, Michele McCormick, Nikki Martinez, Adrienne Nalley, Micki Napp, Myrna Nickelsen, Cyndi Nipkow, Cynthia Orr, Susan Passovoy, Julie Mower-Payne, Catherine Abby Rich, Margie Sborov, Maggie Smith, Sharon Smith, Linda Snively, Dr. Nancy Snyderman, Tauni Swenson, Glady Thacher, Cheryl Turpin, Diana Ullman, Claudette Weber, and Hollie Webster.

And my love and thanks to Fred, my best friend and partner in our "Two Year Plan" of retirement.

INTRODUCTION

The Twelfth Commandment: Discover Your Own Best Answers

Does your best friend seek your advice when she's stricken with a devastating illness, loses her job, or separates from her husband? Don't you always rise to the occasion with compassion, support, and practical advice? Of course you do, and so does she. So, why do we find it easier to help our best friend find solutions to her problems than to solve our own? As a friend we can offer her advice free of ego, free of the weight of past disappointments, and free of what others expect: her "woulda, coulda, shoulda's." While our friend feels stuck in a fog, we see her problems clearly and objectively, unburdened by self-doubt and self-criticism. Solutions seem obvious, from the outside in. But how do we find them from the inside out? Then where do we find the courage to follow them? In my own case, the answer came when I gave myself permission to feel like **The Great Impostor.**

Meet the Great Impostor

From my own experience and from hundreds of conversations with women across the country I have found that the happiest of us have faced tough problems in life, work, and love and have overcome them by listening to the little voice inside that says, "You can do it."

I know how difficult it is to find answers to the tough questions. In 1982, I held several part time jobs: I acted in television commercials, taught modeling out of my home, and worked as an inside sales representative in the Pan American World Airways San Francisco sales office. My son and daughter, ages four and nine, attended school most of the day. I needed to make more money, but I didn't know how I could do that with my English Literature degree. Although I held a teaching certificate, schools were shutting down and teachers were losing their jobs left and right. When I began to panic over the need to earn money I even thought of working for a temp agency cleaning houses, but when I found out that they charged clients fifteen dollars an hour and would pay me five, I gave up that idea.

Over Labor Day weekend my husband and I went water-skiing with one of the women in my modeling class and her boyfriend, Mike. Over lunch Mike told me about his factory, proudly explaining a new product they had manufactured, a large wood framed, canvas top patio umbrella. Then Mike surprised me by saying, "Pam, you meet a lot of people. If you run into anyone with a lot of energy who could market this, let me know."

Those words sparked the beginning of my career as The Great Impostor. Though I knew nothing about business or manufacturing or marketing, somehow I *knew* I could do it, that I could find out what I needed as I went along. I knew, too, that I could never become successful at anything totally new to me unless I was willing to endure the awkward stage of feeling like an impostor.

The following Tuesday I telephoned Mike and said, "You need *me*." And he believed it.

The next day I drove to the factory in Oakland, an hour from my home, and stood under the huge, fifteen-foot diameter umbrella, wondering what I'd gotten myself into. I tried to think of the skills from my previous jobs I could apply to the business world. Having majored in English Lit, I could certainly write a product brochure; as a Pan Am stewardess—we were "stewardesses" back then—I knew how to show up on time, to look well groomed, and to smile through adversity; as a third grade teacher I'd learned to prepare myself *before* I entered the classroom and to remain patient with those around me; and as a model I'd schooled myself in the art of handling rejection. That day standing under the umbrella launched my ten-year career developing and running a separate division of the company and growing it into a multi-million dollar operation. I imagined I could do it, and I did it. Much later, I realized that I had brought one other "skill" to the job: I knew what I *didn't* know and asked a million questions along the way. I found that people really want to share their expertise. Not only would people gladly offer advice, many expressed pride in seeing my business grow.

During that decade I faced a number of life-altering experiences. I suffered through the sadness of divorce from my college sweetheart after seventeen years of marriage. I became a single parent with two children. And, eventually, I married a bachelor father who had been raising his four sons alone for ten years. We weren't a "blended" family exactly, we were more like a Cuisinart family. Nevertheless, by toughing-out those downs and creating those ups, developing confidence from the success of my umbrella business, and embracing the lessons learned from all of the new people in my life, I grew tremendously during those years. I knew I could survive and believed I could do *anything*.

Yet, it's amazing how fast you can go back to square one when life throws you another curve ball. In 1992, the mother company hit rough times and reorganized. Despite the success of my division, I wasn't an owner and lost my job. The umbrella business had been "my baby," and I liked my identity as "The Umbrella Lady." Suddenly downsized, I didn't know who I could be, or what I could do next. But I did know it was time to put on The Great Impostor Hat again.

A few weeks later, having reached the manic stage of joblessness, that point where you would scrub floors just to keep busy, I searched the classifieds and almost took a job selling solvents to gas stations. That's when my husband said, "Whoa, Pam, don't do anything you can't love." I thought that was extremely generous of him because he had been downsized two years earlier and had busied himself with start-ups and odd jobs, none of which were his passion. With four kids in college and one more at home in eighth grade, I didn't know if I could afford a passion search that might not help pay the tuition bills. Even if I felt I could take my husband's advice, a major problem remained: I didn't know what I loved.

I thought to help me find the answers I sought I should learn how other women managed transitions, how they found something they loved doing, and how they became wildly successful. As I began researching and interviewing women on the process, I became fascinated by what they had to say, and almost addicted to finding more and more interesting stories. Sharing their stories, strategies, and advice to help others became my new passion. Hoping to impart what I learned by writing a book, I went to a bookstore, bought a book on how to write a book proposal, and, three and a half years, three book proposals, and twenty-four rejections later, published *The Eleven Commandments of Wildly Successful Women*. The Great Impostor strikes again!

As I look back on the last twenty years, I cherish each of the hats I created and wore: wife and mother, media host, the "Umbrella Lady," author, speaker and consultant on issues vital to women. It took a lot of work, and luck, to make those hats fit, but I wouldn't trade a minute of my life as The Great Impostor.

The last few years have brought so many rewarding experiences my way: articles and interviews in the *Wall Street Journal*, the *New York Post*, the *San Francisco Chronicle*, the *San Francisco Examiner*, the *Toronto Sun* and business journals across the country, plus *Mademoiselle*, *Cosmopolitan*, *Executive Female*, and *National Business Woman*.

I've enjoyed local and national call-in radio and television programs where I've heard the concerns of women and men across the country. I've been the guest expert in Internet on-line shows such as: @Watercooler Episodes produced by Hearst New Media & Technology for the Microsoft Network, and interviewed on ABC-news.com's business page by Bob Rosner, author of the syndicated column "Working Wounded."

I've lectured at gatherings around the country, from Governor Pete Wilson's Conference On Women in California to the New Women, New Leadership Conference in New York, and at many women's associations such as American Women In Radio And Television, Women In Science, the American Business Women's Association, the National Association of Women Business Owners, the Business and Professional Women USA, and the Women's Council of Realtors. As the featured guest for the Edward Jones' financial services company and the American Business Women's Association's Satellite Conference for Women, I felt that I had finally fulfilled my latest dream.

I mention all this, not to toot my own horn or pat myself on the back, but to emphasize a crucial point: "Dare to dream it, throw yourself into it, and it will come true."

Dream a Little Dream with Me

When I first started speaking professionally, a wildly successful lecturer warned me, "Never take questions. It ruins the flow of your talk and you might lose control of your audience." Although she had given me a lot of other good advice, I chose not to follow this particular suggestion because interacting with an audience is the part I love best. After all, I'm still a writer at heart, and a writer can't stifle her curiosity. When I'm standing in front of a group of 15 or 4,000, I'm dying to know *Who* are you? *What* concerns you? *Where* has your career led you? *Why* have you come to hear me talk? After interviewing and writing about successful women for six years, I can't help wanting to know all I can about the women (and men) around me. So, of course I invite questions. Those questions inspired this book.

As I traveled across the nation speaking to women's groups and conferences, colleges and businesses, and on call-in radio and television shows about the lessons in my book, *The Eleven Commandments of Wildly Successful Women*, I have been struck by the numbers of women who struggle through life affected with the "Woulda, Coulda, Shoulda Syndrome," grappling with chronic indecision, self-criticism, and self-doubt. Whether I speak in California, New York, Georgia, Oklahoma, Minnesota, or Arizona, I hear women ask the same questions over and over again: "How can I find my passion?" "Can I quit the profession I spent seven years mastering just because I hate it?" "How can I create life/work/love balance?" These well-educated, bright, capable women want more out of their lives, yet they feel somehow stalled—unable to follow their dream, live the life they desire, and enjoy the success they know they deserve. They come to my lectures because they're searching for a way out of their particular dilemmas and hope I can give them surefire answers.

I quickly learned that these women didn't really expect me to *give* them an answer, though certainly they would have liked me to wave my wand and make all their problems disappear. Instead, I came to realize that many of them instinctively knew the best answers to their questions and simply sought validation, *permission* to act on their intuition. So rather than offering quick-fixes, I tell stories about the wildly successful women I've met, hoping to stimulate these women to see themselves and their situations more objectively, to consider new ways of thinking "out of the box" to solve their problems, and, especially, to listen to their own inner voice. I learned to answer questions with parables.

But one of the problems about learning from others' experiences stems from the fact that it's too easy to sit back as armchair experts and think we know what others should have done, and how we would have done it better. But would we? It's an entirely different learning experience to force ourselves to walk in another woman's shoes, to think like her, and make decisions using her, perhaps limited, knowledge. While we all enjoy advising others, it's quite another experience to live that advice from the inside.

Select Your Own Adventure

I have written this book in an effort to help you find the best answers *for you* to the big questions about life, work, and love through 18 entertaining "select-your-own adventures." We all must make very difficult decisions at times, and each of us has developed our own way of dealing with issues based on our experiences and understanding of the world. Yet we can undermine our ability to make good decisions by trying to please others, putting others' needs before our own, fearing to "make waves," worrying about being misunderstood or disliked, and not knowing how to communicate clearly the reasoning behind our decisions. When we fall into such traps, we devalue ourselves, our passion, and our success. Wildly successful women know that expectations and obligations will always influence their decisions, but they don't let them control their thinking.

In this book you will walk the proverbial mile in other women's shoes, trying not so much to figure out what *they* should do, but what *you* would do if you found yourself in such a predicament. I have divided the book into three sections: Life Adventures (Money, Survival, and Personal Development), Work Adventures (Career Choices and Moves), and Love Adventures (Relationships, Family, and Balance). The 18 chapter titles represent the tough questions I've heard while lecturing. The short preface to each chapter sets the stage for your adventure, then a fictional scenario introduces a character wrestling with a true-to-life dilemma. As you immerse yourself in her adventure, you must slip on her shoes and then select one of four courses she might take to solve her dilemma. In this way you can test-drive different options and observe their outcomes, which may delight, frustrate, or surprise you. Regardless of your chosen option's outcome—good, bad, or indifferent—scan the other options to see how they might have turned out. You will then "experience" the affects of each choice and learn the benefits and downsides of your "actions." Also, take advantage of the factual information in the form of phone numbers, street and Internet addresses, and book titles that I insert throughout the adventures to assist you in furthering your own research should you want more information on a particular topic discussed in a chapter.

Every hard question about succeeding in life, work, and love lends itself to an endless number of possible answers, and each brings with it its own pluses and minuses. By analyzing several outcomes you may discover a pattern of effective thinking that will empower you to develop greater confidence in your own decision-making. By participating in the process of discovery, you will gain valuable tools for successful decision-making encompassed in the lead story and its four adventures with all their benefits and downsides, and in the "Exploring the Issue," "Expanding Your Thinking," and "Assessing Your Own Situation" sections at the end of each chapter. The eleven valuable commandments from *The Eleven Commandments of Wildly Successful Women* appear in this book as part of the "Affirmation" at the close of each chapter. The commandments are as follows:

Commandment 1:
One size does not fit all—create your definition of success.

Commandment 2:
Take responsibility for your career.

Commandment 3:
Change your thinking, change your life.

Commandment 4:
When the odds are against you, defy the odds.

Commandment 5:
Fantasize your future, but create your game plan.

Commandment 6:
Get ready, get set, risk!

Commandment 7:
When someone says you can't, say, "Watch me!"

Commandment 8:
Become financially savvy.

Commandment 9:
See mistakes as road signs, not roadblocks.

Commandment 10:
Enjoy your work and your life.

Commandment 11:
Give back to keep the cycle of success going.

Commandment 12:
Discover your own best answers.

While I fill the adventures with fictional women, I base them on composites of actual women dealing with real-life situations familiar to us all, either directly or through friends. Whether you share a similar problem, or you know someone who does, the adventures in this book let you practice thought processes and strategies that wildly successful women use to discover their own best answers to the big questions about life, work, and love. If you find yourself grappling with a problem unlike any in this book, try writing it up as a short story, then imagine how a few different choices might play themselves out. By the same token, if you think up an entirely different option than you find in the book for a certain problem, jot down how your own creative solution might turn out.

Think Like a Wildly Successful Woman

How do women who ask themselves tough questions sift through the possible answers to identify the right ones for them? More importantly, how do *you* discover the right answers for *you*? You begin by "unlimiting" your thinking. If you can't fit new or difficult ideas and experiences into your present view of "How I live my life," expand your thinking to account for the changes. Avoid the temptation to find *the* right answer or to force a solution based on your old habitual way of thinking. Dream up several answers.

All of us see the world subjectively, and each of us constructs a highly personal reality based on our own unique experiences. Educators call this Constructivism. When what happens to us fits snugly into our constructed framework, we feel secure and on track, but when an event shatters that framework, we feel threatened and out of control. Desperately wanting to understand what's going on, we often turn to others for help, hoping to find answers from the outside. Whatever the advice we get, we can do three things with it:

1. Reject it as invalid and stick our head in the sand.

2. Interpret the new information myopically and try to squeeze it into our old framework of how we interpret the world.
3. Expand and adapt our framework to embrace the new information.

Only the third choice "unlimits" our thinking. Adapting our thinking either comes in the form of an epiphany—"Oh, I really *can* do that"—or it more gradually influences our behavior. Regardless of how we incorporate new ideas, knowing that we can do it helps us grow more self-confident about looking inward for our own answers.

Let the Games Begin

Here's your chance to play the impostor yourself, imagining yourself in another woman's life, dreaming her dreams, suffering her setbacks, feeling her joys and pains, and solving her problems. Any of the women you'll meet could be you, your best friend, your daughter, your mother, or your colleague. By working through their stories as though they were your own, you'll discover many different ways to solve your own problems. You'll see that choosing the best solution can be as much fun as it is challenging.

I invite you to read through the entire book from front to back or to dip into it randomly for the questions that currently relate to you or someone you wish to help. Curl up on the couch with a hot cup of tea and read an adventure that intrigues you, or read it with a friend, each choosing different options, then comparing your outcomes. I hope you will laugh and cry with the characters in the stories. But most of all, I urge you to have fun deciding what you would do, or what you would advise your best friend to do, in each situation. In the process I think you will discover that the best answers always come from within!

part I

Life Adventures

Money, Survival, and Personal Development

ADVENTURE 1

HAVING LOST MY JOB, MY IDENTITY, AND MY SELF-CONFIDENCE, HOW DO I PICK MYSELF UP AND GET BACK ON TRACK?

Has life ever dealt you a wild card, leaving you shattered and trying to figure out how to pick up the pieces and get back in the game? If you've been downsized, right-sized, or pushed side-wise, you know the feeling. Like most of us in similar situations, you've probably filed your self-confidence in some "safe place" but can't remember where you put it now that you need it most. If this sounds familiar to you, read on, and think how you would emerge **From the Back Room to Full Bloom.**

From the Back Room to Full Bloom

Another long day has ended—this time with a bang. You've been pushed out the door after a hostile takeover of your employer, a mail-order kitchenware company. "No need for duplicate buyers," the new owners announced within days. Your boss seemed truly embarrassed when he presented you with your pink slip and a leaflet for the outplacement service the present company had retained. Before the commute home, you slump over the steering wheel of your sensible 1996 gray Ford Escort in the San Mateo suburb commuter parking lot and sob. The towering mercury light shining in the lot outside illuminates your reflection in the rear view mirror. Disgusted with your mascara streaked eyes, you think how pathetic you look.

"You're thirty-two, for Pete's sake," you scold the sallow stranger in the mirror, but she just sticks her tongue out at you. "You and your so-called career. Where has it gotten you? You idiot! All those late nights climbing up the ladder to the basement. 'Miss Dependable,' my foot. It's been 'Miss Expendable' all along."

Crippled by hopelessness, you sit there reluctant to return to the apartment you so meticulously decorated with Victoriana. Somehow, you've misplaced your sense of direction. You stare ahead, motionless, reflecting on your career path. Your art history major at the University of Southern California offered you no clue about what you could do in life to earn a satisfying living, so you job-jumped for a few years, trying to find your career footing. Right out of college you recorded and filed in the back room of a prestigious auction house, but you rarely saw and never got close to the art you loved. When you decided that working in an art gallery would satisfy that need, you landed a seemingly terrific job. A fascinating, passionate Russian couple owned a gallery on Union Street in San Francisco. Original Picassos and Monets hung on the gallery's white plaster walls. You could see them from your cubicle. Yet your knowledge and love of art languished at the gallery, too.

You filed, shipped, answered phones, and from time to time accepted platinum plastic in exchange for treasures by masters. You found the cold reality of art merchandising extremely upsetting to your aesthetic values and appreciation of art. Finally, after a year, you put practicality above passion and shelved your aspirations of a cosmopolitan career in the world of fine art.

During all that job-hopping, however, you discovered a talent for back room services, shipping and receiving, tracking, and filing. That talent helped to land a grunt job with a national tabletop and kitchenware mail-order company located near Fisherman's Wharf, a position from which, your boss promised, you might eventually rise to the position of buyer. You sacrificed much of your twenties in pursuit of that goal. Your salary paid you for a forty-hour week, but you arrived at seven in the morning and left late, commuting home to microwave a Weight Watcher's meal, brush your teeth, and watch the ten o'clock news alone in bed. Most of the other buyer wannabes kept a similar schedule. Young women like yourself, they had also put their personal lives on hold to get ahead.

Over time you zigzagged your way up, though most of your progress seemed sideways. There were fewer openings for buyers, of course, than for the detail brigade. Your social life also went sideways. After two years you moved from your San Francisco apartment in the trendy Marina district because your car had been broken into three times, but you found that living in San Mateo made you feel even more isolated from whatever young people did on weekends. Your career duties absorbed most weekends anyway. Finally, at age thirty-one, you reached your goal: you became a tableware buyer.

Now at thirty-two, slightly overweight, with a few unsatisfying relationships recorded in your diary under "time wasters," you're sitting in a parking lot feeling sorry for yourself. My God, you think, I wanted that job so much, but it gave me so little. You're surprised how the job you so diligently sought provided so few internal rewards. You look around the empty parking lot, crumple your pink slip and stuff it into the outside pocket of your backpack purse. You wonder which way to go.

You don't consciously realize this while you dry your eyes, but you have already begun to contemplate four distinct options. While you never write them down or approach them as actual plans, they materialize internally as follows:

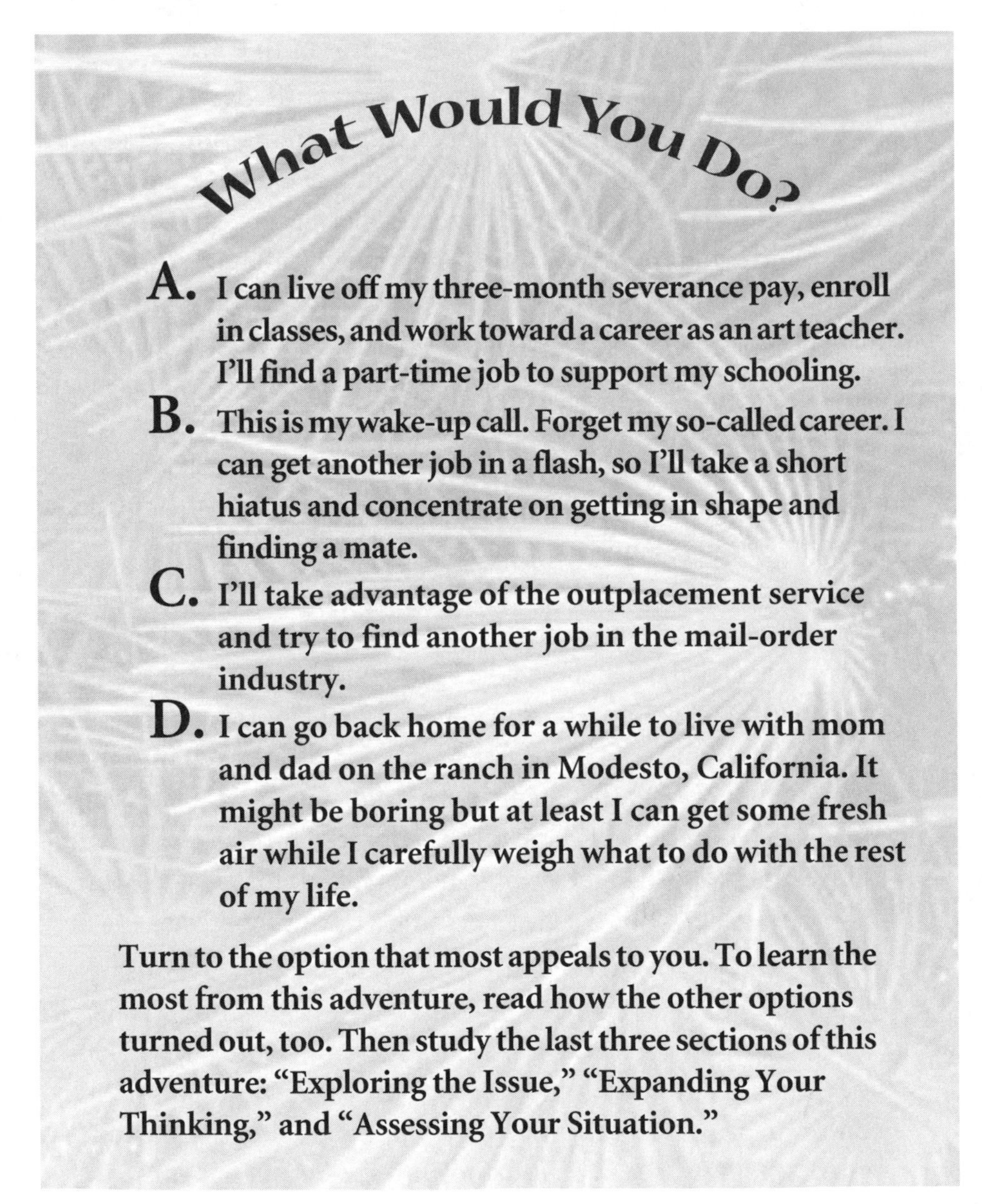

What Would You Do?

A. **I can live off my three-month severance pay, enroll in classes, and work toward a career as an art teacher. I'll find a part-time job to support my schooling.**

B. **This is my wake-up call. Forget my so-called career. I can get another job in a flash, so I'll take a short hiatus and concentrate on getting in shape and finding a mate.**

C. **I'll take advantage of the outplacement service and try to find another job in the mail-order industry.**

D. **I can go back home for a while to live with mom and dad on the ranch in Modesto, California. It might be boring but at least I can get some fresh air while I carefully weigh what to do with the rest of my life.**

Turn to the option that most appeals to you. To learn the most from this adventure, read how the other options turned out, too. Then study the last three sections of this adventure: "Exploring the Issue," "Expanding Your Thinking," and "Assessing Your Situation."

A. I can live off my three-month severance pay, enroll in classes, and work toward a career as an art teacher. I'll find a part-time job to support my schooling.

Despite your tear-blurred vision, you manage to arrive home safely. You feel physically sick that it's not only another Friday night without any social plans, but that you don't even have a boyfriend whose shoulder you could cry on. As you unlock the heavy beige-painted metal gate guarding your apartment complex, you vow to start a new life tomorrow. "They aren't going to keep me down," you declare with stubborn determination.

The next morning you pick up a Learning Annex class schedule from the stand in front of Papillon, your favorite Java shop. You've heard of the Learning Annex, a continuing adult education center which offers programs taught by everyone from famous authors such as Deepak Chopra to experts in Internet counter-intelligence, but you've never seen it as an option for you. Now, however, the catalog engrosses you. Scanning the pages, you discover titles of books you'd love to read, and you circle at least thirty classes you want to attend. One in particular catches your eye: "Art Study—Teaching With Passion."

The class, offered as a one-time, Sunday afternoon event, features an art historian and retired professor from Stanford University. You recognize his name, but more than that, you feel drawn to the class. When you phone the Learning Annex, you find, much to your delight, that you can register at the door the day of the class. Opening your backpack, you grab your weekly organizer, and scribble "My Day" across the "Sunday" page. You think of yourself as one of the "princesses" of Serendip, and laugh at your play on the words of Horace Walpole's fairy tale, "The Three Princes of Serendip," whose characters accidentally make fortunate and unexpected discoveries.

In class on Sunday you devour the retired professor's message: "Teach what you love. Love what you teach."

After class you approach the instructor to ask, "What can I do with a decade-old art history degree?"

"Teach, become a docent, go back and get your doctorate in art," he encourages. "But never, never stop sharing what you love."

"A doctorate?" you marvel as you feel something awaken in your soul.

For days afterward you fantasize, picturing yourself inspiring eager college students in your own classroom. Bouts of practicality interrupt your fantasy, "Costs too much. Takes too much time. Get real."

Luckily, you override your doubts, "What can I lose? I've wasted so much time already!"

Three years slip by while you attend night classes at UC Berkeley to earn your doctorate in art history, working days as an inventory control manager for a large Marina kitchenware store. You live in a rented a 1930's era bungalow on Hawthorne Terrace not far from the Berkeley campus. Your love life? Put it this way, doing what you love attracts men who just want to be near you, like your new husband, Perry, whom you met on campus. He's working toward his MBA at UC Berkeley's Haas School of Business. Your love nest Hawthorne Terrace rental suits the two of you just fine, but you're thinking of looking for a more permanent home, for three.

BENEFITS OF A:

- You waste no time feeling sorry for yourself.
- You have taken action to turn something awful into something positive, vowing to put something new in your life despite losing your job.
- You seek further information from the professor after class and listen with a cautious but open mind.

- You call on your purchasing skills from the mail-order business to land a decent paying job to fund your schooling.
- You invest in yourself and your future, set goals, and get admitted to UC Berkeley.
- You focus on learning to "teach what you love," and feel like the "old you" back studying art in a college setting.
- You don't expect change to happen overnight, realizing that the process brings as many rewards as the end product.
- You become a more "interested and interesting" person, which makes you more attractive to others. You meet and marry your husband, Perry.
- You rent a house in the area you love in Berkeley.

DOWNSIDES OF A:

- You've spent three years getting your degree without knowing if you can get a position as a college teacher.
- You did zero research on the availability of teaching positions.
- You live on less salary than before and must budget tightly to pay night school expenses.
- You spend many more years renting instead of building equity in a home of your own.

B. This is my wake-up call. Forget my so-called career. I can get another job in a flash, so I'll take a short hiatus and concentrate on getting in shape and finding a mate.

As you wipe the tears from your puffy eyes, you glare at your sorrowful face in the rear view mirror. You silently pledge, "This is the last Friday night I'm singing the 'Single Woman Blues.'"

Abandoning your urge to fill the void created by your pink slip, you immediately scour the classifieds, not in a job-replacement mode but as part of a larger personal plan: Lose flab and find a husband.

You join the Bay City Club north of the business district in San Francisco, a fitness facility famous as "the" place for singles to get in shape and to meet the opposite sex.

"No use joining the married-with-babies group out here in the gyms of suburbia," you reason. "I'm on a mission: Look good or else." You've been living the "or else" for too many years, and while you look okay, you don't look great, especially from behind. You blame your figure on all those pre-packaged meals and your sedentary office life.

Over the next six months you live off your savings and focus on creating the "new you." You eat plenty of fruits and vegetables, tone your body, and can leg press an amazing 300 pounds, more than twice your weight. To your great delight, your efforts at the gym pay off. You love working out. As a matter of fact, you've immersed yourself in exercise, weight lifting, and healthy living. You consume so much Evian that you've replaced your backpack with a double-bottle hip pack.

Every morning when you enter the gym's foyer and glance at the mirror, it salutes you with a visual "thumbs up." You feel exhilarated by the new you, but also slightly uncomfortable, even edgy, because you don't know what to do with your newfound purely physical focus. You wonder where it's taking you. Have you been exercising excessively to avoid searching for a job? Unfortunately, you don't know the answer and relegate the question to the back burner.

Three months later, on a particularly windy, gray afternoon, with the rain pounding against the opaque locker room windows, you overhear someone hidden from view refer to you as a self-centered, stand-offish, overly focused woman. You're shocked. You've found it difficult to make friends at the gym because *you* felt everyone else there seemed self-absorbed. Now they think that of you. You can't believe it. The pangs of having no job and no real direction resurface. No point in masking the issue, you have to do more with your life than work out.

That afternoon, after you pack up your gear to head home, you spot an "aerobics instructor position open" notice on the bulletin board. You stop by the reception desk to ask the lycra-suited, svelte-but-buff young woman behind the counter for more information. Despite her unapproachable looks, she happily takes time to explain that you will need a certificate of training. She rips out a sheet of yellow lined paper from a note pad and writes down the following places you can get more information about certification, guidelines, and workshops:

The American College of Sports Medicine (ACSM) 1-800-486-5643, www.wwilkins.com/acsmcrc.

The American Council on Exercise (ACE) 1-800-825-3636, www.acefitncss.org.

The Aerobic and Fitness Association of America (AFAA) 1-800-446-2322, www.afaa.com.

The International Association of Fitness Professionals (IDEA) 1-800-999-4332, www.ideafit.com.

You thank her profusely.

As you drive home the sky lightens and a clear image develops in your mind: You're leading a huge class in a cool gymnasium and everyone's stretching, dancing, and laughing. You're occupying center stage and loving every minute of it.

It's as though you've found the lost piece to the jigsaw puzzle to complete the picture of your new life. You diligently research information on the Internet from your list of sources, and, two months later, certificate in hand, you win the aerobics instructor position at the Bay City Club. You plan to further your education to become a personal trainer. And you move back to the Marina

District where you share a cheery apartment with another instructor whose lawyer and triathlete brother you're dating.

BENEFITS OF B:

- You set a goal to get fit and find a husband.
- You discover a new interest in working out.
- You become more fit and enjoy your looks.
- You budget your expenses carefully.
- You remain open to an entirely different career, notice a bulletin for a job and ask questions about how you could qualify.
- You visualize yourself happily teaching aerobics.
- You find where to get certified and take the appropriate steps to prepare yourself for the new career.
- You move into San Francisco to a place near work with a roommate and start dating.

DOWNSIDES OF B:

- You dig deeply into your savings, month after month, without a plan to look for work.
- You exercise excessively, to the exclusion of everything else, including looking for work.
- You become self-absorbed in your own fitness program.
- Your new career as an aerobics instructor provides less pay than your career as a buyer. It requires that you work as an independent contractor and pay for your own health and retirement packages.

C. I'll take advantage of the outplacement service and try to find another job in the mail-order industry.

You dry your eyes with an embroidered linen handkerchief, the kind your grandmother sent you for your birthday when you were a little girl. "Ladies always carry hankies," you remember her saying. You chide yourself for being a silly sentimentalist. "Nothing wrong with me," you reassure yourself. "This bad news just happened to come on a PMS day."

You turn the key in the ignition and drive to the bright lights of the shopping center not far from the dark commuter parking lot. Then you treat yourself to a pint of Dreyer's cookie dough ice cream and a Snickers bar. You can't resist picking up a copy of the *Inquirer* displayed at the Payless Drugstore checkout counter. Next door, at Take One Video, you rent *Out of Africa*, your favorite tear-jerker.

Before you slip the video into the VCR, you start thinking about your lost job. It's July, the most intense time of the year for buyers, when they must assure delivery of goods for the photography department to shoot the Christmas catalog. The products you bought last year sold sensationally well, almost too well because inventory dropped with no time to replenish. But you had weighed that against over-buying, which could have led to costly inventory overloads and huge markdowns after Christmas. You loved the balancing act, and you did your job well. Knowing that gives you negligible comfort, however. You can't help wondering if your replacement can gracefully keep so many balls in the air.

"It's so unfair," you say out loud to no one. "Why couldn't they see my total dedication?"

You bawl as you suffer through Karen Blixen's trials and heartaches in Africa, pausing only to lick the melting ice cream from your spoon.

The following Monday you locate the address on the leaflet for the outplacement office. Arriving at an office filled with files, books, tables, and counselors, you soon find yourself completing an extensive assessment of your skills. Organizing them into broad categories, you write down that you can manage effectively, spot new trends, and negotiate well. Armed with that list, you research other mail-order companies in the outplacement center files and on the Internet.

Joan, one of the counselors, stops by as you search the Internet and says, "How's it coming?"

You push back, remove your red rimmed glasses and rub the lenses with your embroidered handkerchief. "Not bad."

"Your handkerchief is beautiful. My grandmother used to carry one just like that," the counselor admits. "You don't see many people using them anymore. Where did you get it?"

"Well, I have a collection of them. I love them. People compliment me all the time on them. I really should find a source for them and sell them. I'd make a mint."

"Not a bad idea. Why don't you check out 'hankies' on the Internet," the counselor quips, only half in jest.

Staring at the hankie for a long time, you recall the many men and women who've complimented your handkerchiefs. You do love them, they're part of your "Victorian flair," as your grandmother once called it.

"Actually, that's not such a bad idea, Joan. Not hankies, per se, but to find a company that deals with soft, feminine Victoriana products."

For the first time in months, you feel enthusiastic. You know you're on the right track because you look forward to finding companies that carry Victorian furniture, clothing, even dolls. After pinpointing several firms, you contact the president of each. Over the next week, you send out a dozen résumés, enclosing a lovely lace handkerchief with each.

Three weeks later the Human Resources director of Victoria's Whispers, a mail-order lingerie, bedding, and accessory company, calls you and asks simply, "Are you willing to move to New York City?"

"Yes," you answer without taking a breath, feeling elated, apprehensive, and invigorated all at once.

"Then let's set up a date when we can fly you out for an interview," continues the HR director. "And, by the way, where did you find that beautiful handkerchief?"

BENEFITS OF C:

- You realize that the merger of your company doesn't mean something is wrong with you or how you did your work.
- You treat yourself well after a bad day.
- You allow yourself to cry and get it out of your system by watching your favorite sad movie.
- You give yourself credit for what you did well in your job.
- You know that losing your job doesn't change the fact tha you're a good and dedicated buyer.
- You take advantage of the outplacement services.
- You assess the skills you've developed.
- You pay attention to your core being, relishing the enjoyment you get from your Victorian style.
- You refuse to listen to naysayers.
- You research companies that will develop your interests—ones that suit you, rather than visa versa.
- You research the appropriate person to receive your résumé and send something with it to make a unique impression.
- You're willing to move in order to develop your career and add excitement to your life.

DOWNSIDES OF C:

- During your job search you focus only on the mail-order industry and a position as buyer without exploring other occupations.
- You assess the skills you learned over the years and repackage them rather than expand your skills to broaden your marketability.
- You're afraid to exit your comfort zone by looking into different types of jobs.
- You ignore your longing for a social life and a significant other.

D. I can go back home for a while to live with mom and dad on the ranch in Modesto, California. It might be boring but at least I can get some fresh air while I carefully weigh what to do with the rest of my life.

"Me and my so-called career," you repeat as you drive home on automatic pilot. You grumble under your breath about how becoming a buyer had consumed your entire life, and you vow to make it a blessing that you lost your job. "Now I can find a job somewhere that doesn't swallow up my every waking hour." You surprise yourself with your choice of words, but they ring true.

Over the weekend you thumb through trade magazines, looking at the listings in the back for positions available in your industry. You hope that one of the ads will jump out at you. "I'll know it when I see it," you assume. But none of them appeal to you. You throw down the magazines in disgust, uncork a bottle of Turning Leaf Chardonnay, and rummage through your kitchen drawers in hopes of finding a cigarette. You finally find one squished in the pocket of a jacket that you haven't worn for almost a year. When you light up, you feel dizzy because you haven't smoked for nearly eight months. You've been proud of that, but today you figure, "So what?"

When your lease expires next month, you promise yourself not to renew it. You've resisted the urge to call your parents to tell them that the ax has fallen, but it's Sunday afternoon, it's raining, and you need a shoulder to cry on. You hear yourself asking your mother if you could come home for a few months and "regroup." You hadn't expected to do that, consciously, but you also knew she wouldn't say no.

Even while you're unpacking your things in your old blue bedroom-turned-guest room you realize it's a mistake. There's really no going home, at least as an adult. You hardly reached "your" room before you fought the urge to say, "Shut up!" to all your parents' questions: "What do you plan to do next?" "Have you started looking for a job?" "Do you plan to stay in the San Joaquin Valley or go back to San Francisco?" You know your parents mean well, that they are only concerned for your happiness, but you just want them to leave you alone to vegetate for a while.

Three months later you've mastered the art of "vegging out." You feel lethargic and resentful. You can't seem to let go of the fact that you spent years building up a career only to get tossed aside like yesterday's garbage.

Your mother finally pulls you aside. "Dear, enough's enough. You came home to 'regroup' but you've done absolutely zero. You've been so lost in your own sorrowful soup that you've shown no interest in anyone except yourself. What did you expect when you came home? That your dad or I would have all the answers for you? That by crawling back into the womb you'd be safe? Sure, we want to provide a safe haven for you, we love you, but I can see now that it's not necessarily in your best interest. And it certainly hasn't been a picnic for us."

Gazing at your mother, you realize that she looks much older than her fifty-eight years and you calculate that your dad will turn sixty-five on his next birthday. Shaken, you realize that when you came home you regressed. You'd reverted to being a bratty teenager. You see now that you wanted to act out because you were mad about work and about your empty life, and you wanted nothing more than to wallow in self-pity. But you didn't really mean to take it out on your parents. It just happened that way.

"Oh, Mom, I'm so sorry..." you begin, but she puts her finger to your lips.

"Just be happy. That's all we want for you."

You feel sick inside.

BENEFITS OF D:

- You look for different positions in your industry listed in trade magazines.
- You decide to take a break from your normal setting to "regroup."
- You contact people who can support and comfort you.

DOWNSIDES OF D:

- You take out your anger about losing your job by doing harmful things to yourself.
- You approach finding a new job in an unrealistic manner hoping that something will suddenly "jump out" at you and you'll know it when you see it.
- You break the good habits that you started, like stopping smoking, and lose even more control over your life.
- You go home expecting to be treated as an adult, but you act like a child.
- You want your parents to take care of you and provide easy answers.

- You haven't developed sufficient support systems for yourself.
- You don't take responsibility to create your own happiness.

Exploring the Issue

The situation in this chapter, losing a job, has become so common that it will affect each of us, or someone we love, at some point in our lives. Feelings of loss, disappointment, denial, and anger occur after any life-altering event, be it the death of a loved one, a divorce, or even corporate downsizing. Losing a job devastates and demoralizes us because it can strip us of our identity and deflate our self-confidence. Keep in mind that we can justifiably express our anger and feel sorry for ourselves, but only up to a point. If we carry resentment and disappointment with us, always thinking of how life "should have been," we paralyze ourselves and shortchange our future.

After losing a job we usually feel vulnerable and depressed because we feel our old way of life, our identity, and our livelihood have been jerked out from under us. We lose our equilibrium. Even if we know we did a great job, and even if we know we could not control the events that eliminated our jobs, our self-confidence suffers. And it's embarrassing. Even in this day of mass downsizing, there remains a very real stigma attached to those who have lost their jobs.

At this point in our lives, we face many difficult emotional as well as practical issues. What to do? First, you must identify the emotions caused by the loss. What are you really mourning? Are you grieving over a lost job (or lifestyle or relationship) that you didn't really like, or that didn't fulfill your needs, but stayed with simply because nothing better presented itself? A friend of mine fell into a deep depression over the end of her three-year relationship with a man whom she had told me from the beginning of the romance, and throughout, that she would never marry. Although

I knew she really wanted to be married, I didn't understand why she got so upset over the loss of someone she "wouldn't consider marrying." She said she regrets that she filled the void in her love life with someone she wouldn't marry, but that she had always had a man in her life and couldn't stand the loneliness. She admits mourning over a lost dream, not a lost man.

Whether you did or didn't obtain what you really wanted in your lost job, identify what you do want from the next. What in the old job satisfied you, and, conversely, what kept you from developing something else in your life that you wanted? Classify your wants, such as: "Elements I need to enjoy my work," "My preferred work environment," and "My required salary level." Under these broad classifications list specifics, including whether you enjoy working with people, numbers, or computers; prefer working indoors or outdoors, in sales or on assignment; and whether you can live with the uncertainties of compensation on commission or would rather earn a steady salary. Take all of this information and write a paragraph describing the atmosphere of your ideal job. When you create a picture in your mind of the best work conditions for yourself, you will conduct a more effective job search. In this way, you are more apt to "know it when you see it."

Next, ask yourself, "What will I miss about my old work identity?" We create our work identity by how we relate to and what we bring to the industry. Some people laugh now when I tell them that I felt proud to be "The Umbrella Lady" in my previous work life. I know they don't understand what it meant to me or what it took to develop my business, myself, and that identity. I knew nothing about business nor anyone in the Casual Furniture industry. In the beginning, people told me no one would want a wooden patio umbrella and "Who would want a canvas top on an umbrella?" Because I knew we manufactured our umbrellas from the same materials used on fine yachts, I believed they would work great outdoors. However, I didn't know how to price the umbrellas, or where I should market them, so I asked everyone questions. My best resources were my manufacturer's representatives. As my umbrellas became known, and the business grew, even people that I never met had heard about our quality umbrellas and knew of "The Umbrella Lady." So, when I first lost my job, I suffered a major identity crisis, not to mention the loss of my livelihood. What could I do? Who could I be next? Since I didn't know the answers, I resented having to let go of what I had proudly created.

For me, that identity represented the growth, the challenges met, the track of my professional development, and the friendships that I never would have developed without that job. I believe that we're proud of our work identity because it represents personal, as well as professional, achievement. I also believe that we can create a fully satisfying new identity, if we choose to put forth the effort. I thought I'd really miss being "The Umbrella Lady," and I do on a certain level, but by losing my job I found the opportunity to develop an entirely new side of me and create two new identities as an author and a speaker. We're never just one thing, one identity, one personality; we're many. Once we embrace this idea and incorporate it into our conscious thinking, we don't need to cling to our former identity.

It's like saying, "My son is an Eagle Scout." Yes, that says a lot about your son, but it doesn't say everything about him. It's the same for you or whomever you know who feels she's lost her identity. You must emotionally disengage yourself from your old work identity in order to recreate yourself. The old identity becomes just part of the whole, another small scene in the unfolding tapestry of your life.

Expanding Your Thinking

Losing a job forces you to make changes because it crumbles the current framework of your world. You can look at it as the close of a chapter of your life and anticipate seizing the opportunity to write a new one, or you can agonize over the gut-wrenching event and let it paralyze you emotionally.

In this adventure "you" lost your job because of a takeover. You had worked diligently to create a career path for yourself and had reached your goal as a buyer. Yet, even then, you felt something missing. In this case, if you hadn't lost your job, you probably wouldn't have made a job change any time in the near future and would have remained chronically dissatisfied and habitually frustrated. So was the job loss a crushing blow to your self-confidence or "a blessing in disguise?"

The less desirous outcomes result from denial, blame, and running away from your problems. While Option B results in a positive outcome, (you get in shape, prepare for and win a job as an aerobics instructor, move to the city and start dating) at first you focused on looking good as the answer to your problems. Your mission to "look good" could have been beneficial as simply part of a plan to recreate yourself. However, in this scenario, you thought that changing how you looked on the outside would change how you felt on the inside. There is some truth to this, but it's only part of the puzzle. In order to feel fully alive, you need a purpose. When you decided you could teach aerobics to inspire others, you became directed and happier.

Option D, "The Great Escape," doesn't work at all. While a change of scene can help clear the mind, burying yourself, regressing to childish behavior, and simply running away solves nothing. Cynthia Orr, a "success coach" in Seattle, helps women identify and correct self-defeating behaviors. She says, "Something triggers us back. We feel and act a lot younger, like when we visit our parents and fall into old roles. What happens is that when beliefs you had about the world, say at age five, resurface, you start operating at a five-year-old level." You regressed emotionally in Option D, and couldn't "regroup" because you reverted to your old childish view of the world.

DON'T:

1. Waste time feeling sorry for yourself.
2. Expect positive change will happen with little effort.
3. Wait for the right job to jump out from the classifieds and land in your lap.
4. Oversimplify your problems.
5. Run from your problems.
6. Look to others for answers.
7. Replace an obsession with another obsession.
8. Set your sights too narrowly.
9. Simply repackage old skills.
10. Take out anger by doing harmful things to yourself.

Some of your choices work out surprisingly well, and one turned out disastrously. The positive aspects of your choices result in creating a more fulfilling future. You do this in Options A and B by visualizing yourself in a new career, teaching an art class or an aerobics class, and by investing your time and money to further your education and expand your skills. You take risks and eagerly defy the odds. In Option C you take advantage of outplacement services, research new jobs, and believe you should follow your gut instincts. In Option D you take time out to "regroup."

DO:

1. Believe you possess the power to turn something awful into something positive.
2. Make well-thought-out plans of action to prepare for a new career.
3. Take advantage of all transition services available.

4. Invest in your future through continued education.
5. Allow yourself sufficient time to create the change you want.
6. Appreciate change as an opportunity for growth.
7. Visualize yourself enjoying new, maybe totally different, careers.
8. Get physically fit.
9. Acknowledge what you do well and that you can continue doing things well.
10. Assess your skills and remain willing to expand them.

Assessing Your Own Situation

Think of what questions you would advise your best friend to ask herself if she lost her job, then ask yourself the same:

1. If you've suffered a loss, and think you've let go of it, ask yourself, "Am I still thinking about how things 'should have been?'"
2. Before you spend too much time grieving over your lost job, make sure that it was something you wanted to continue for a long time. "Did I really love that job, or just hold onto it for the security?"
3. If you truly enjoyed your job, identify what aspects of it you would like to recreate in your next job. "What do I really miss about my old job?"
4. "Can I envision the work environment most satisfying to me?" List the qualities, atmosphere, and salary you require for your future job; write a descriptive paragraph about it; and carry that picture in your mind.
5. Consider the true nature of an identity crisis caused by the loss of your job. "Will I die if I'm no longer known as the ______?"

6. If you're fearful about not knowing what you could do next, ask yourself, "What do I want to achieve?" not "What do I want to do?"
7. Have you looked at the bright side and asked, "Can I make a lemon meringue pie out of these lemons?"
8. Most importantly, ask yourself, "Can I learn and grow from this experience?"

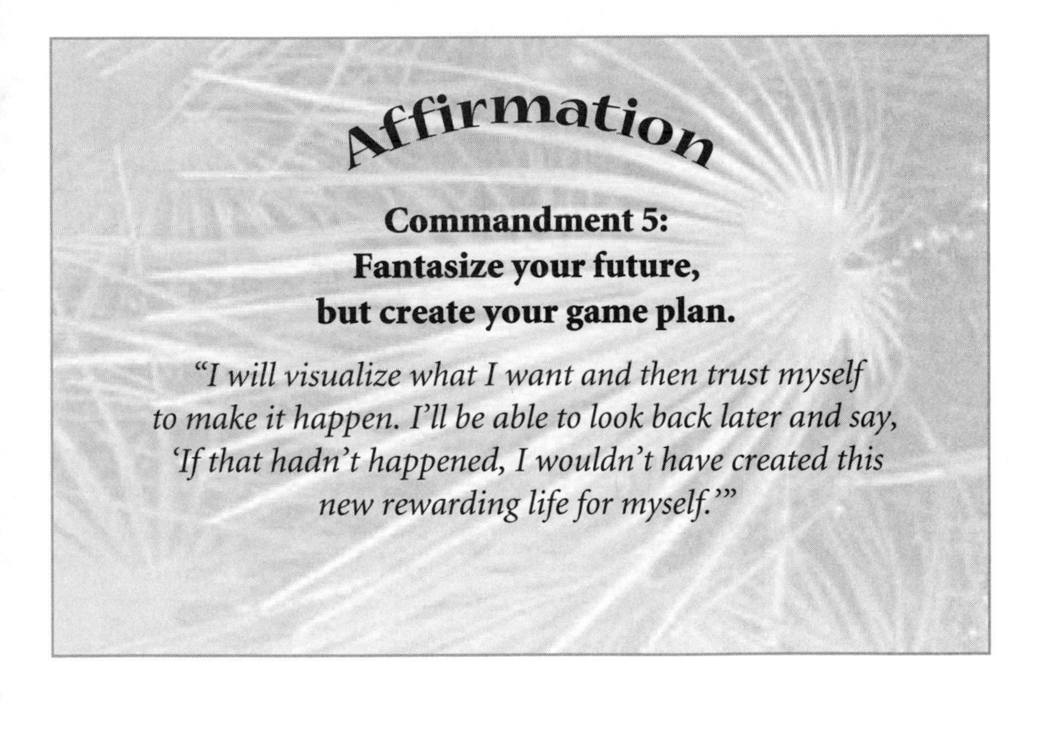

ADVENTURE 2

HOW CAN I QUIT THIS DEAD-END JOB WHEN I CAN'T LIVE WITHOUT THAT WEEKLY PAYCHECK?

Have you ever reached a point in your life when you felt that you had put a dream on hold? Perhaps you took a job as a stop-gap, expecting to move on to something better, only to find yourself unable to move on. Or maybe what you thought would provide a stepping stone to a dream career turned into a dead end with no chance of advancement. If you have ever felt frustrated, depressed, or stalled in such a situation, or if a friend in such a predicament has ever asked you for advice, think about how you would solve **A Case of Writer's Block.**

A Case of Writer's Block

You've been working at the same job for three years, and though you love certain parts of it, you can see that you'll qualify for early retirement before you move up to the position you really want. When you landed your job as an editorial assistant at Edgerton House, you went in with your eyes open, knowing that only one out of a hundred "secretaries with fancy titles" ever gets promoted to a real editorial job, but you committed yourself to proving your worth by coming in early to complete reports, staying late to assemble paperwork for book contracts, and taking manuscripts home on weekends to review them for your disorganized boss, the doyenne of romantic suspense fiction, Harriet Rubin. Now, three years later, not only hasn't all that extra effort paid off in a promotion, but you're feeling unappreciated, burned-out, frustrated, and depressed.

You've begun silently criticizing yourself, especially your decision to come to New York with the belief you could ever become an editor. Edgerton House meant "the big time" to you, a small town girl from Montpelier, Vermont, but now you're thinking if you stay you will not get any closer to what you really want to do, write books. Ms. Willis, your creative writing teacher at Radcliffe, had encouraged you to pursue a literary career, the one in New York City that she had wanted for herself. "New York is the only place for an aspiring editor and writer!" she enthused when you headed off to the Big Apple two weeks after graduation. Now you realize that life in Manhattan on $500 a week means living hand to mouth, month after month, slaving away in a job with no future.

"There's got to be a way out," you tell yourself. You wonder what's keeping you fettered to your cramped windowless cubicle on the eighteenth floor of Edgerton House. You wonder how you can get out of this mess. Where would you go? How could you afford to make a change? You look out of the perpetually dirty window of your Soho apartment where you live alone and decide you now simply must find the answers to those questions.

You shove the weekend paperwork you brought home from the office off your old oak bedside table onto the floor, then you pull open the tiny drawer where you store the journal you've kept ever since college. Studying it you realize you've filled it with entries not about the adventures you expected to experience in the New York publishing world or notes for the mystery series you plan to one day write but with a lot of bitching and moaning about your measly $22,000 a year income, the outrageous cost of your studio apartment, and the uselessness of your 3.8 grade point average—other than helping you land this dead-end job. The attention you got from good grades and hard work in college seems a distant memory, and they don't impress your boss at all.

You put down your journal in astonishment. You've never given yourself credit for anything you've accomplished, not even the fact that you've survived for three years in New York in an industry you love. Something else becomes painfully clear: you have lost sight of your original dream of writing mystery novels and find yourself mired in a dead-end job you don't think you can quit because you can't live without that weekly paycheck from Edgerton. Then you feel something stirring in your heart, a small beat of your old passion. "Damn it," you scold yourself, "I can sit around the apartment feeling stuck and sorry for myself, or I can *do* something right now to get a life—a life with enough excitement to fill dozens of dazzling journals."

Suddenly energized in a way you haven't felt for a long time, you leap out of bed and pound out on your word processor a list of possible ways to change your life.

Feeling relieved that you have pinpointed four viable, yet quite different, courses of action to get some adventure back in your life, you take the rest of the weekend off and treat yourself to a binge of suspense thriller movies with a friend. When Monday morning rolls around, however, you wake up determined to make the right choice. What will you do?

What Would You Do?

A. I can stay at Edgerton for one more year, working sensible hours and devoting evenings and weekends to writing magazine articles that will earn some extra money and help set me up as a freelancer or pave the way to a better paying job at a major magazine.

B. I can start an austerity savings program to add to my $3,000 graduation gift in my savings account until I have enough money to quit my job and spend up to three months finding a better one.

C. I can take that job my friend Carl Brady offered me as a writer with his new multimedia company. Though that job pays only $20,000 to start, Carl will give me equity shares in his fast-growing business.

D. I can kiss New York good-bye and head out to Aspen where I can ski all day and work tables at night. In my spare time I'll work on my novel.

Turn to the option that most appeals to you. To learn the most from this adventure, read how the other options turned out, too. Then study the last three sections of this adventure: "Exploring the Issue," "Expanding Your Thinking," and "Assessing Your Situation."

A. I can stay at Edgerton for one more year, working sensible hours and devoting evenings and weekends to writing magazine articles that will earn some extra money and help set me up as a freelancer or pave the way to a better paying job at a major magazine.

During your lunch hour you pay a visit to the Barnes & Noble Bookstore on the ground floor of the Edgerton Building. You enter via the stairs, descending from the sidewalk facing Broadway with your plan and a time frame in mind. "No more than another year," you promise yourself. "In the year 2000 I'm a new woman, earning good money as a freelancer."

You set your plan in action by purchasing the *1999 Writers' Market, Where and How to Sell What You Write*, where you look up the names of editors, their phone numbers and addresses, and the specifications and type of articles they require for their magazines. You note payment schedules also, though you don't expect to live on the fees at first. You believe you will attract the attention of magazine editors through your proposals and hope to get offered a full-time position.

Every evening and weekend you write and submit article proposals to magazines. The topics include profiles of women in business and pieces about women's health and fitness, topics that fascinate you. Four months and forty-five submissions later, you receive your first form rejection letter: "Thank you for your submission. Unfortunately it does not meet our editorial requirements at this time...." After six months, the bottom drawer of your dresser overflows with similar rejections.

In a fit of frustration-turned-inspiration you write an actual article, not a proposal for one, but an entire article about handling rejection, what you call your "daily dose of depression." In it you list how rejection letters can actually brighten your day: your mailbox always contains something for you, something small that doesn't take up too much room; your growing collection of interesting letterhead stationery allows you to decorate your apartment walls to coordinate with your black and white color scheme; and the vast scope of places to submit ideas narrows to a more manageable few, thus saving you money on postage. You submit your manuscript to *Writers' Digest* magazine. Two months later they accept it. Along with your acceptance letter you receive a $300 check, payment based on ten cents per word for your 3,000-word manuscript. You feel vindicated, but not elated, that you can sell your writing. However, the months you collected your "daily dose of depression" have taken their toll. You now feel more stuck than ever. Three hundred dollars isn't going to get you out of Edgerton. Then a friend calls who read your article. "It's the funniest thing I ever read. You're great."

Feeling heartened, you realize that perhaps you can make a mark for yourself with humor pieces. You decide to extend your one-year plan at Edgerton because it pays the bills and to focus on a new style of writing. Nine months later you're still collecting rejections and you haven't sold one other article. You wonder what went wrong.

BENEFITS OF A:

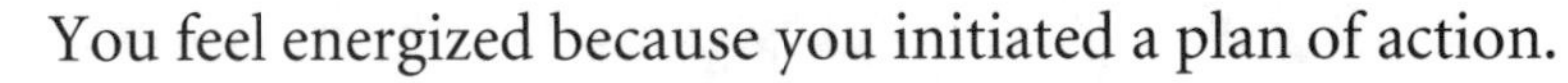

- You feel energized because you initiated a plan of action.
- You develop your writing skills even though they aren't needed at work, and you learn through trial and error that shot-gunning topics doesn't pay off. You realize you need to find your niche.
- You give yourself a time limit to pursue your plan.
- You cut back your office hours and make time to follow your passion and your plan of action.
- You keep an open mind. The phone call from your friend helped you begin to see yourself differently, perhaps as a humor writer rather than a mystery writer.

DOWNSIDES OF A:

- You design a long-term method to solve your problem, but you want a short-term solution.
- Even though you keep yourself busy, your approach is still pretty passive. If you want to be hired by a magazine, you need to contact the editors directly with sample articles rather than waiting to be "discovered."
- Your plan is ill-conceived. You don't attempt to contact editors personally. Meeting editors personally establishes a rapport with them that promotes greater understanding of what they want in an article or an employee.
- You set yourself up for failure. You're pursuing another job that fewer than one in a hundred succeed in landing, a poorer percentage than in your present job. Long shots are worth playing but you need time to play them out.
- You limit your thinking. You research just one way to get your writing published. While it's good to be focused, you need to think of other means to bring in extra cash if you plan to leave Edgerton.
- You lose sight of your ultimate goal to become a famous mystery writer.

B. I can start an austerity savings program to add to my $3,000 graduation gift in my savings account until I have enough money to quit my job and spend up to three months finding a better one.

When your lunch break rolls around on Monday and you automatically cross the street to Starbuck's for a latte, you feel a pang of anxiety over the humiliation you experienced at your neighborhood coffee place last weekend. On Saturday afternoon you returned the two movies you had rented on Tuesday, Blockbuster's two-for-one day, and paid eighteen dollars in late fees. Then you picked up your laundry at the dry cleaners and forked out another twenty-two dollars. When you ordered a latte at Mama's Café on your way home you found only a wrinkled dollar bill in your wallet. "I can't believe I left this morning with forty dollars and don't have enough money left for a cup of coffee!" you explained to the unimpressed young Jamaican woman holding your steaming cup at the register. You still see her smileless face when she told you, "There's an ATM machine around the counter." No, you decide, you won't be needing coffee this noon hour. Instead, you sit on the low wall surrounding the Edgerton Plaza, eating a tuna fish sandwich in the semi-sunshine, while you devise your austerity program.

The two small cost-of-living raises you received in the past three years have gotten swallowed up with rent increases, and your weekly expenses have somehow begun to eat into your savings. When you first hit the Big Apple, you rarely used dry cleaners and never for washable clothes, nor had you become a latte addict. You mentally calculate the money you waste every month on nonessentials like lattes, late fees, and credit card interest. If you wiped out those expenses, you could save almost $250 a month. It would take a year to save $3,000. Could that amount, added to your $3,000 in savings, fund a three-month search for a better paying job? More importantly, could you stick to your austerity program for an entire year?

You recall a conversation with a school friend who had become a securities broker and had encouraged you two years ago to start making your money grow. "You need to set aside money each month," she had suggested, "money that you would fritter away otherwise. Invest in mutual funds and make your money work for you. Call it your 'Freedom Fund.'"

Three months later, you've made major efforts to adhere to your austerity plan, you've arranged with your broker friend to invest $250 a month plus $1,000 of your savings in Fidelity Mutual funds, and you've started watching CNN's evening financial programs to educate yourself about money. A financial planner on one show says that if you only pay the minimum on a credit card balance of $4,000, it would take approximately thirty years to pay off the debt. That scares you so much, you decide to pay off your $2,000 MasterCard debt from your remaining savings, since that money has been earning only 4.3 percent in the bank, while you've been paying 18 percent in credit card interest fees.

At the end of the year you take stock of your financial situation. The $250 each month that you added to the $1,000 initial investment has earned an 8 percent overall average, a good return on your investment, and totals $4,300 in savings. A larger than usual raise at work has boosted your salary to $24,000 a year, which allows you to invest an extra $50 a month. You calculate in another year at 8 percent annually, compounded monthly, your "Freedom Fund" will have grown to around $8,300 at the end of two years.

You're not happy that you'll have to wait a year or more to quit your job with four months survival funds, but at twenty-five you're beginning to realize how fast a year goes by. However, you're proud of yourself for taking the initiative to put your plan in action, and begin seriously searching for a new job by contacting friends to develop leads at prospective companies. With your plan underway, your debt in control, and your "Freedom Fund" established, you feel more in control of your destiny and more confident than you've felt in months.

BENEFITS OF B:

- You've taken your head out of the sand and discovered you're spending a lot of money foolishly.
- You take responsibility for "frittering away" your cash and decide you can change bad spending habits.
- You realize, too, that by living hand to mouth you will continue to feel stuck, but instead of seeing yourself as a victim of circumstances you choose to take charge of your situation.

- You now define investing and saving as part of your monthly expenditures.
- You educate yourself about finances. You've paid off your credit card debt and invest your otherwise "hollow dollars," converting them into working capital. You really enjoy watching your money work for you.
- You gain a new sense of control which negates your self-criticism and makes you feel happier at work knowing you won't be stuck there forever.
- You got started on your job search by calling people to get leads.
- You admit it will take time, but you're willing to trade that inconvenience for the sake of reaching your goal.

DOWNSIDES OF B:

- You have to learn completely new spending habits that don't come naturally.
- You feel you're losing time while others get ahead. You feel that it will take forever for you to leave Edgerton and move on to something else with more career opportunities.
- You don't know if you can maintain the financial self-discipline long enough to reach your goal.
- You can easily feel sorry for yourself when others seem to have money to burn.
- You look at only one side of your situation, saving money. You've done little to find other ways to bring in extra money to speed up the process and perhaps expose yourself to other career opportunities.

C. I can take that job my friend Carl Brady offered me as a writer with his new multimedia company. Though that job pays only $20,000 to start, Carl will give me equity shares in his fast-growing business.

Bright and early Monday morning you call Carl to find out more about his offer.

"No, the position hasn't been filled," Carl answers in his deep, resonant voice. "Why don't you come by this evening, and we'll talk?"

You've known Carl for five years, but you had forgotten how much his energy, enthusiasm, and self-confidence had always rubbed off on you. Startled at your own reaction to the sound of his voice, you set up a time to meet him at his office. A rush of apprehension envelopes you. You never act on impulse.

At 7:00 P.M. you reach Carl's loft office in the Village. Carl's Brad Pitt smile greets you. "Please excuse the mess," he says, pointing to the piles of papers, computer peripherals, and components you've never seen before. As he shows you around the spacious loft, his infectious enthusiasm for his new multimedia equipment, his one major client, and life in general excite you. Carl believes your three years at Edgerton and your English Literature degree would serve you well in this environment, even though you lack experience in the field. Carl introduces you to the other employee, Tom, a self-professed computer nerd, and explains that the low pay will be overshadowed by equity opportunities. Carl adds, "You'll be getting in on the ground floor." When he flashes that old smile at you again, you're sold.

Eight months later you discover that leaving Edgerton has been tougher financially than you had anticipated. Your bills are strewn on your bedside table unopened and unpaid. The descriptive product copy Carl originally hired you to write has been put on hold because Carl and Tom have decided to redesign the software. Instead, you spend countless hours at the computer learning all about multimedia packaging and playing with small business management and operations programs. Carl's so preoccupied with his work, he seldom leaves the office, which disappoints you because you secretly hope he'll invite you out on a date. But a more urgent problem has arisen. It appears that Carl's main client, The National Education Association, plans to open a major new project to competitive bids. You're requested to make cold calls to potential new clients in an effort to generate more business, something you dread every time you pick up the phone. You feel completely foolish, and you begin to lay awake at night, wondering how you got yourself into such a mess. What if Carl's business fails? Of course 25 percent equity of zero is zero. You realize too late that you took this job for the wrong reasons. But now what?

BENEFITS OF C:

- You acknowledge that you must make changes to get ahead. You take a risk to terminate a dead-end job for something new with opportunities to grow.
- You keep an open mind to new opportunities, visualizing yourself in a different industry.
- You learn new skills. You make the best of an awkward situation and teach yourself new computer skills. You make cold calls that you never believed you could do.
- You wanted to work in a high-energy, positive atmosphere and, for a while, Carl's business provided just that.

DOWNSIDES OF C:

- You do not research the new company. You don't even ask pertinent questions about the company's financial health, the overall direction, or Carl's plan to make it successful.

- You ignore your gut feelings of apprehension and let a charming smile override your concerns.
- You let personal feelings rather than business judgment make your decision to join the company. You not only want to draw on Carl's energy and enthusiasm, you secretly hope he will take you out.
- The appeal of a long-term payoff caused you to ignore the need for monthly income to pay your bills.
- Your decision to leave Edgerton did not occur as an element of a well-thought-out plan. You acted on impulse.

D. I can kiss New York good-bye and head out to Aspen where I can ski all day and work tables at night. In my spare time I'll work on my novel.

Rushing into your apartment after work on Monday, you manage to grab the ringing phone and answer with a breathless "Hello?"

A familiar voice bursts out laughing at you.

"Oh, My God! Kristie!" you shout. "Where are you?"

Kristie, your super energetic college roommate, who always put excitement ahead of school work, confides that she has decided to move to Lake Tahoe, California. "Why don't you join me?"

"I can't believe you called. I was actually thinking about bagging New York and moving to Aspen, but I'm open to any place where I don't have to look at skyscrapers."

"Great! Come to Tahoe with me. We're only young once. It'll be really fun. I've got a job tending bar, and I've lined up a great condo we can share."

Kristie could always drag you away from your homework for a night on the town, and this phone call poses no exception. You go for it. Through the Human Resources department at Squaw Valley Resort you commit to a waitress job for the winter season. You can share the condo with Kristie. Three weeks later, you resign your job at Edgerton, pack up your belongings, and catch the 1:15 P.M. plane to Reno where Kristie picks you up and drives you the fifty miles to Squaw Valley.

That night you apprehensively explain to your parents over the phone that you've made a major move. New York had become a drag, and what the heck, you've never taken time out for fun. You had put your graduation trip to Europe on hold indefinitely when you took the Edgerton job, and now it's time to go a little crazy while you're still young with no commitments. "Besides," you conclude, "living in New York took every cent I earned. And Edgerton was a big, fat dead end." You deliberately avoid mentioning the health and retirement benefits you gave up at Edgerton in exchange for free ski passes, free ski lessons, and discounts on food and other items at Squaw Valley Resort retail stores. You did sign up for individual health insurance before you left your job, but you don't want your parents to know how much that cost, either. You feel you have made a gutsy decision. Naturally, your parents voice great concern about your sanity and pointedly let you know how disappointed they feel that you're wasting your expensive education. You feel really let down when you get off the phone, even though you never did expect them to understand.

Over the next few months you and Kristie snowshoe in the fresh mountain air, learn to snowboard, and meet all sorts of gorgeous people from all over the world. Waitressing in the Broken Ski Pole Tavern turns out to be more fun than you expected. It turns out you have a knack for the work, given the patience and organizational skills you've developed over the years. You especially like living as a member of the resort "family." One local man comes in often, always orders bread pudding with brandy-caramel sauce heated with extra whipped cream, and chats with you about the local scene. He loves hearing your views of the people, the weather, the sports, and the politics. One day he says, "You know, you're a walking gossip column." That's when you confess that you love to write and have actually been working on a mystery novel set in Tahoe.

"Mr. 'Bread Pudding' owns several regional newspapers," you tell Kristie after work. "He's asked me to 'write what I talk about every day.' He'll pay me for it! He wants to broaden his readership and hasn't found the right angle to attract younger people."

"Don't quit your day job," advises Kristie.

Three months later your column "Addicted to Fun" has won fans among the younger crowd. Readership increases. At the end of the winter season, you accept a full-time job at *Tahoe Times* as an assistant editor. Later that year, a national syndication group picks up your column. You've nearly finished writing the first draft of your mystery novel about a serial killer loose on the cross-country trails. You feel as alive and vibrant as that day you first set eyes on the Empire State Building.

BENEFITS OF D:

- You seize an opportunity to set your plan in motion.
- You try something out of the mainstream.
- You're timing is exquisite. You are young, have no restricting relationships or family responsibilities.
- You decide to do what you always envied other people doing but always thought too irresponsible. You act your age.
- By working at a resort, you save money on lift tickets, equipment rentals, lessons, food, and other necessities.
- You keep sight of your original dream of becoming a mystery writer.
- You "think small," realizing that a small town weekly paper gives you the growth opportunities you had originally sought in New York.
- You write the column for the local newspaper and get to know the company before you accept a full-time position.

DOWNSIDES OF D:

- Waiting tables doesn't develop technical skills for future jobs.
- You give up health and retirement 401(k) benefits at Edgerton and must purchase costly private health insurance.
- You leave Edgerton with no clear vision of how your new experience might fit into a career path.
- You still don't make much money.
- You get grief from your parents who don't support your decision. That creates a nagging sense of self-doubt.

Exploring the Issue

We all reach points in our lives and careers when we feel frustrated, depressed, or stalled. It's natural. But we don't have to stay that way. We can always step back and take a look at the big picture, put our problems in perspective, and try to see ourselves objectively. When we do this, and plot out several alternatives, we can free ourselves of the confines of our self-imposed prisons. If we get rid of the "I can'ts" and the "I shouldn'ts," we find we have many choices.

Thinking through a situation like the one we've been exploring in this adventure can help us forecast different solutions and thereby expand our decision making, especially if we focus on treating the disease rather than the symptoms. Before we can apply the problem solving tools, we must first become good diagnosticians. That means asking ourselves the hard questions: "Am I dissatisfied or bored?" "Is this a dead-end job because it truly offers no advancement, or have I failed to do everything that will lead to advancement?" "Did I thoughtfully choose my career or did I take the first available job?" What really causes your dissatisfaction? Is it the job, or is it *you*?

The root issue in this adventure boils down to this: Are you going somewhere in a chosen career, learning, growing, and rising to challenges along the way, or are you letting a troublesome situation control your life? Who's in charge, you or the job? Only you can make certain that you muster the resources and the willingness to change jobs if that's what it takes to move forward. Career counselors call this career self-reliance, which means that you take responsibility for your own happiness at work, that you create the financial resources to sustain yourself during a transition, and that you constantly build skills to increase your opportunities and your worth.

But how do you know when the time has come to change your situation? Certainly, as in this scenario, you can determine when the chance to advance to the position you desire falls to zero, though you've worked hard to prove yourself, and you feel you've learned everything you can in the position you hold. If you can't determine that for sure, don't jump ship just because you're bored. Take responsibility to create interesting work for yourself.

Take, for example, a young successful woman named Wendy, who, during summer recesses from high school, worked in her father's light fixture manufacturing company. A few weeks after she started, she complained to her father that she found all the filing and stapling boring. To this day she remembers his stern look when he said. "*You* make it interesting. When you attach the bill of lading to the order forms, look at them to see who's ordering what fixtures. Think what other products that customer might use. Talk to the inside sales representatives and ask what other information they might need. You never need to be bored at work if you pay attention to the big picture, looking for how you can help even if it seems insignificant at the time. Do every job as if you owned the company." Wendy says she not only followed her father's suggestions, but she also researched old orders to assess which customers might want to upgrade their lighting. The following summers she worked as an inside sales assistant and today at twenty-nine works as an operations manager for an insurance company. She says she always remembers her father's words and makes every job "her own."

If lack of advancement, rather than boredom, concerns you, first take a good look at your current career path. Consider whether you want to work for another company in the same field. Would it offer something you really *want* to do or merely something you know *how* to do? It's very easy to move along a career path in a certain industry because you're a capable person, but unless you want a long-term relationship with that industry, you might want to think about changing careers rather than companies.

Two years ago a forty-five-year-old woman I met at a conference for aspiring women entrepreneurs told me she had been downsized and hoped to start her own business because she didn't want to work for anyone else again. She seemed angrier at herself than at her old company. When I asked her why, she said that she never thought she'd lose her job because she was the only woman in upper management in the entire company, but when her company eliminated her whole division, she found herself on the street. What upset her even more than losing her job was the realization that she had spent fifteen years in an industry she didn't even philosophically agree with. Her company made munitions. She asked, "How do you explain that to your kids?" I think she's still trying to explain it to herself.

Take time to ask yourself the hard questions and listen to the answers that come from deep within your heart. Make certain you want what you wish for, because most likely you'll get it.

Expanding Your Thinking

In this adventure you chose a big "name" company, Edgerton House, expecting that only then would you gain the recognition you had always won in your small college classrooms. You knew up front that the firm offered you little hope of advancement to an editorial position, but you nevertheless became disappointed in yourself when you didn't move ahead despite your all-out efforts to prove yourself. When you wanted out, you felt financially strapped because you live paycheck to paycheck.

What type of thinking should you avoid if you want to create successful outcomes? Self-criticizing, passive, irresponsible thinking, such as the following:

In Option A, you design an ill-conceived plan expecting a short-term solution to a long-term problem. You set yourself up for failure and wonder what happened. You lose sight of your ultimate goal to become a mystery writer.

In Option B, you design new spending habits, but don't know if you have the courage or self-discipline to maintain them. You feel sorry for yourself as you try to save money and resent others who seem to have money to burn. You've tried to find only one answer—saving money—to a more complicated problem.

You do zero research about the new company in Option C, and ignore your gut feelings of apprehension. Working for someone you have a crush on doesn't work out in any fashion. You've become disillusioned and disappointed.

In Option D, you set your worries about your future on the back burner by taking a job in Tahoe, but in so doing you take a cut in pay and lose your health and retirement benefits. You upset your parents and doubt yourself.

If you find yourself in a situation that you don't like and that makes you feel stuck, don't feel guilty about it. What are some other don'ts to remember?

DON'T:

1. Wait to get noticed in your job, wasting time waiting for others to help you.
2. Undermine your self-confidence by criticizing yourself.
3. Overlook doing research on a prospective company.

4. Ignore your gut feelings.
5. Let your heart overrule your head, and vice versa.
6. Kid yourself about your real reasons for joining a company.
7. Act on impulse.
8. Plan to live off of future earnings.
9. Disregard benefit packages when seeking new employment.
10. Discount fun opportunities as simply frivolous.

What kind of thinking provided the most successful outcomes in this situation? Positive, action-oriented, risk-taking thinking. In this adventure, examples of a take-charge attitude include your taking your head out of the sand, confronting your problem, *and* assuming the responsibility to fix it. You weigh options, keep an open mind, make several plans, set time frames, and take action.

In Option A, you work on your writing skills, learn to focus on a niche, and give yourself time to develop your plan into reality. And, you remain flexible.

You analyze your spending patterns in Option B and plan to save money that you would otherwise spend on nonessentials. You no longer see yourself as a victim, but take full responsibility to make the changes you need to get "unstuck." You do this by learning more about managing your personal finances.

In Option C, you visualize yourself in an entirely different industry and take the leap. You develop new computer skills and learn to make sales calls.

In Option D, you're willing to take a cut in pay, move across the country, and work part-time in a company before accepting full-time employment. You learn the value of "thinking small" rather than expecting great rewards quickly. Who would have thought that moving to Tahoe would turn out so well? Sometimes a totally different environment allows you to take life less seriously. Having *fun* can and should be part of your work ethic. In Option D, getting out of the high-powered structure of business in a large city allowed you to have fun, get involved in a new life, and, not surprisingly, find the right atmosphere to write your mystery novel.

DO:

1. Take responsibility for your choices.
2. Make plans and set a time frame to begin and end them.
3. Analyze your spending patterns.
4. Save and invest money that you would spend on nonessentials.
5. Exchange a dead-end job for one with perceived opportunity.
6. Follow up on every phone number and resource you uncover.
7. Remain flexible, maintaining an open mind to unusual opportunities.
8. Know how much money you need to survive during a six-month transition.
9. Prepare to "think small," stepping down before you move up.
10. Consider working part-time for a company before accepting full-time employment.

Assessing Your Own Situation

The following questions can help you assess your own situation or one in which a friend or family member finds herself.

1. Before you go to all the trouble of planning to change jobs, make certain you really are in a dead-end job. Ask yourself, "Does my company offer little advancement, or am I creating a dead-end job for myself by assuming I have no future and making that a self-fulfilling prophecy?" Ask your boss what advancement opportunities may arise in the near future and what you can do to qualify for them.

2. If you find yourself in a situation with no growth opportunities, calculate your current financial status. "Can I afford to make changes?" If you haven't started your own "Freedom Fund" as in Option B, do it. Seek financial advice. Educate yourself on how to grow your money.
3. Pay attention to your own spending habits to make certain you aren't undermining your future. "Do I spend my money frivolously or frugally?"
4. Search your soul to make sure your desire to change jobs moves you toward a career goal and your passion. "Have I pulled back to see the big picture?"
5. Make room for ideas that aren't part of your current thinking. "Can I see myself in a completely different industry?" The multimedia start-up in this case offered an excellent opportunity to learn new skills in computer technology as well as to continue developing writing skills.
6. "Am I enjoying my work and my life? Or do I take everything very seriously? Have work and life become overwhelming?" If so, mentally "get outta Dodge" by reading a good book or going to a movie. While many things can happen in your life that make you feel a loss of control, avoid thinking like a victim. "Am I suffering from a 'victim mentality?'" You can control how you react to situations and take responsibility to change your thinking if you feel stuck.
7. "Do I undermine my outlook and self-confidence by criticizing myself?" Acknowledge what you've learned and accomplished. Find the good in every day.

Affirmation

Commandment 3:
Change your thinking, change your life.

"This may be a dead-end job, but I don't have to live a dead-end life. I can and will make the changes I need."

ADVENTURE 3

WHAT DO I DO WHEN MY ONCE-SHINY DREAM JOB TURNS INTO A NIGHTMARE?

Have you ever felt terribly alone, sick in the unfortunate reality that once the cheers have faded into silence and the roses have lost their fragrance, you've been left standing on the naked stage, hating the job you thought you'd love? It could happen to anyone in any job or profession, but when it strikes your life, it can feel like the end of the world. Will the nightmare ever end? If you or someone you know and care about feel trapped in a career that imprisons the soul, you'll want to set about **Unmasking the Phantom.**

Unmasking the Phantom

As you sit near the front window of Lucia's Restaurant in Uptown Minneapolis, you contemplate the pressed tin ceiling, the huge fragrant floral arrangements adorning the sparsely decorated but bright room, and wonder what caused the urgency in Allison's voice when she telephoned you for lunch. The last time you saw her, the two of you celebrated her receiving her MBA and your passing the bar exam at this very restaurant. That was five years ago. In the intervening years, you stayed put in Minneapolis, while Allison had moved to Boston.

"Five years," you muse, "The years have just flown by."

Your anticipation heightens when you see a familiar figure rushing across the street to the restaurant door. You recognize Allison's 5'2" tense body, her familiar short, staccato steps and her straight shiny black hair which perfectly frames her round face and accentuates her almond eyes, which are magnified by wire rimmed oval glasses. You smile when you notice her gray Clothes Rack perfunctory "plainclothesman" suit and sensible flats.

"Same old Allison," you think as you stand up and wave to her as she enters the restaurant.

After clutching each other in a hug reserved for long lost sisters, the two of you stand there, smiling wordlessly at each other: You with your six-foot frame, long blond hair fashioned into a sophisticated French twist, wearing a black Armani silk suit with red silk wrap-around blouse, your gold knot earrings punctuating your high cheek bones and chiseled Norwegian jaw.

You take your seats, but before you can catch the waitress's attention to order two glasses of chenin blanc, Allison grabs a piece of Lucia's famous homemade bread, breaks it in half, and blurts out, "I'm living a nightmare, Em."

No "hello's," no "how are you's," no "you look great's." Despite your long term, if sporadic, friendship, Allison has just cut to the chase.

"What's going on, Allison?"

"I know I should be thrilled with my position at Anderson Accounting. After all, only the top of the MBA classes get hired. My parents brag about me all the time. But even though I'm really good at it, I don't like accounting. No, I *hate* accounting. Does that sound really stupid to you?"

You startle Allison with a nervous laugh. "Ditto," you almost shout. Puzzlement knits her brow as she slowly shakes her head.

The waitress interrupts the tension to take your order. When she departs for the kitchen, you push aside the cobalt blue bottle with fresh cut flowers, lean across the table and say emphatically, "I hate law."

"You're kidding!"

"Shhh," you whisper. "We're in the same soup."

Allison smiles then frowns. "Tell me about it," she murmurs.

"My dad primed me to become an attorney ever since I was six years old. 'Daddy's little lawyer' he'd call me. Mom and Dad took turns driving my debate team in high school. Remember? You'd have thought I'd won a presidential appointment when our team won the Minnesota State Championship."

"I didn't realize your parents pressured you. I thought only Chinese parents did that," Allison interjects jokingly.

"Oh, I never looked at it as pressure then. I got lots of attention. Lots of approval. Only, now I realize that they never allowed me to think for myself. In their eyes, my destiny lay in the halls of the Justice Department."

Allison nods. "Just five years ago we met right here at Lucia's, sitting on top of the world, having completed what our families expected of us. Did you have any doubts then?"

"I think so, but I never would have admitted it, especially to myself." You pause to gather your thoughts, and continue, "I don't like the law office atmosphere. I hate being chained to billable hours, which, by the way, has put so much pressure on my relationship with Jim that our engagement limps along in limbo. Clients distrust my ability because I'm a woman. My looks actually work against me or get me in untenable and uncalled-for situations. And," you lean really close to Allison and whisper, "I've become bulimic. I really don't know what I'm going to do about my job, everything. I don't know where to turn."

"Wow, I can't believe it. You, of all people. You've always seemed so 'together.' Look, you can do anything in the world with your brains and your looks. You'll find a way to get over it, all of it. I've got an idea, Em. Let's brainstorm right now and plan out ways for each of us to get out of our messes. I'll go back to Boston, then we'll meet here the same time next year, compare notes, and exchange our new business cards. Okay?"

"Great! You're on." You reach across the table and shake hands to confirm the deal.

You feel heartened as you leave the restaurant and wave a last good-bye to Allison. "What timing," you think, "Would I ever have admitted or confronted my situation without Allison confiding in me first?" You suppose you eventually would have done so, but the list of options you hold in your hand certainly would not have come so easily. You're grateful for having a friend like Allison.

What Would You Do?

A. I'll research other ways I can use my education that don't involve a law office or billable hours.
B. I'll seek advice from other women ex-lawyers to learn what they did to transform their legal careers.
C. I'll seek professional advice from a counselor.
D. I'll take a month's leave-of-absence to collect my thoughts.

Turn to the option that most appeals to you. To learn the most from this adventure, read how the other options turned out, too. Then study the last three sections of this adventure: "Exploring the Issue," "Expanding Your Thinking," and "Assessing Your Situation."

A. I'll research other ways I can use my education that don't involve a law office or billable hours.

At home later that day, you flip on the Channel 5 evening news and become momentarily mesmerized by a special report on female depression by Dr. Nancy Snyderman, the medical consultant for ABC. The topic interests you, but what catches your attention is the comfortable yet authoritative manner with which Dr. Snyderman gives her report. You hear a small voice inside say, "I could do that." After all, debating in front of an audience had been one of the great joys of your life.

Startled, you begin to laugh it off, but then you reconsider. You remember reading in *People* magazine a few years ago that Dr. Snyderman started her TV consulting by accident. She'd been an intern at a hospital when a news crew arrived to cover a multi-car accident; they ended up interviewing her about the condition of the patients. Her concise, informative but friendly account of the situation prompted the reporter to tell her that she was a natural in front of the camera. That comment stuck in her mind. Months later when she moved to another city as a resident doctor, she stopped by the local TV stations and offered herself as a medical advisor. This was a new concept for most stations, but one news producer tried her out. Viewers called in liking what they saw, and the rest, as they say, was history.

"I certainly have expertise in the legal field, and what I don't know I can research," you tell yourself. You pick up the phone book and scan the yellow pages for local TV stations in the Twin City area, discovering nine possibilities.

You phone Andie, your friend from Edina High School days whose husband, George, works as a television cameraman at Channel 5. "Hi, Andie. I've had a rather bizarre brainstorm about becoming a television legal consultant and want to see if George can give me some background about the different stations in the area."

"Gee, Em, don't stations have their own legal departments? Why would they need to hire a lawyer?"

"Oh, I don't mean handling legal issues *for* a station. I want to become the *on camera* consultant, sort of the Dr. Nancy Snyderman of the legal world," you clarify.

"No kidding? That's a *great* idea. You'd be wonderful at that. I'll have George give you a call later. He's on assignment right now. So how'd you come up with this idea...."

Ten weeks later you've followed every newsworthy trial, even corporate takeovers, and have written a brief "lay person" explanation of the legal ramifications of each. Taking George's advice, you capsulate them into one-, two-, and three-minute segments. You've spent hours practicing in front of your video camera set on a tripod. You've perfected your presentations, prepared them for videotaping, and have worked with George to assemble a demo tape for news directors and producers.

Nine and a half months after sending out your demo tape, and five days before your lunch date with Allison, your new business cards, embossed with "Newsnight Minnesota, Channel 2" across the top and your title "Legal Consultant" under your name, arrive in the mail. "Just in time to show Allison," you smile, although they'll not surprise her because she called to congratulate you months ago when she saw one of your segments picked up by a Boston station.

Your professional personality and clear explanations of the law have attracted the attention of others as well. You're considering an offer with a state supreme court judge who would like you to work in his office while you continue your television consulting. This offer, complete with a handsome salary, relieves you of working under the billable hours yoke of your old law firm. You're excited about the opportunity to develop the aspects of law you enjoy, primarily legal analysis, with such a well-respected judge. Meanwhile, your glimpse of fame has energized you even more than the state debating title.

BENEFITS OF A:

- You pay attention to your gut feeling that says, "I can do that."
- You recall reading an article which gives you encouragement to follow your own instincts.
- You recognize your qualifications as an on-camera TV legal consultant.
- You research prospective stations.

- You call a friend in the TV world for information and guidance.
- You follow the news and prepare written sample segments, sharpening your new skills.
- You practice in front of a video camera.
- You prepare a demo tape and win a job at a local station.
- Your efforts to try something new pay off in unexpected and lucrative ways.

DOWNSIDES OF A:

- You explore only one other avenue to use your legal education.
- You don't seek professional training from a speech coach.
- You must keep working for your old law firm and produce billable hours while you make the transition to TV legal consultant.
- Your restrict your efforts to the Minneapolis/St. Paul area, a tough market in which to begin a TV career.

B. I'll seek advice from other women ex-lawyers to learn what they did to transform their legal careers.

Two weeks ago at a luncheon given by the Women's Bar Association, Queen's Bench, a friend told you about Jane Byron, a successful woman who uses her law background in her management consulting business. You've kept her name tucked in your wallet and finally decide to call. When you call to introduce yourself to her secretary over the phone, you explain that you'd like to take Ms. Byron to lunch in hopes of receiving suggestions for a career change. To your surprise and delight, the secretary calls you back and sets up an appointment in Jane's office for the following Thursday at eleven o'clock.

"So you're looking to re-pot yourself," Jane Byron smiles as she stands and offers her hand to welcome you into her taupe office, warmed with Jane's personal touches: a characteristically uneven Kilim rug, a collection of delft pottery, and two ficus trees towering from tooled brass containers.

"Yes, thank you for seeing me," you say, conscious of her firm yet feminine handshake.

Jane gestures for you to sit in one of the facing wing chairs to the right of her Danish modern desk. Within an hour you've bared your soul and listened to Jane's frank and unadorned rendition of her escape from law into business. In the end, you confide personal interests and discover possible directions.

"One of the projects I'm working on involves a group that may interest you, Em," Jane surmises. "Environmental Law Alliance Worldwide known as E-Law."

"I haven't heard about that association. Tell me more," you urge as you lean forward to adjust your black pinching Ferragamo pump.

"It's a network of 'Amigos,' comprised of public interest attorneys, scientists, and other advocates in more than forty countries around the world. They exchange legal and scientific information to support each others' work and assist environmental groups in each country to build local expertise through international knowledge."

"Wow," you exclaim as you mentally slip into comfortable Espadrilles. "How do I find out more about it?"

"Here, I'll give you the e-mail address, elawus@igc.apc.org. However, that's just one of many organizations that can use your knowledge of the law. Have you done a search on the Internet? Contacted professional associations that may find mentors for you?"

You shake your head and explain your search has just begun in Jane's office. "Well, that's a good start. But next you need to write down where your interests lay and then see what else is out there. You have a variety of interests, as you've told me, but write them down, explore those areas, and see what develops." Jane gets up, reaches over to her brass business card holder on her desk and hands you a card.

"How can I thank you enough for your time?" you ask, giving her your own card on your way out.

"Call me in six months and let me know what you're doing. I'd really appreciate that."

When you return to your apartment, ideas swirl in your head. You feel excited and overwhelmed at the same time. You think, "I could do anything. There are so many choices." You wonder why you still feel depressed, then realize that you had hoped Jane would give you *the* answer, not merely suggestions. Now your future remains in your lap and it's darned uncomfortable carrying around that burden.

You telephone Greenhouse Florists and order a large spring bouquet sent to Jane's office with a note of thanks.

BENEFITS OF B:

- You attend a professional luncheon and obtain Jane Byron's name.
- You call and set up an appointment to met Jane, an ex-lawyer, for advice and guidance.
- You get information about E-Law and suggestions on researching other ideas.
- Jane encourages you to report your progress to her in six months, which makes you feel accountable to continue your research.

DOWNSIDES OF B:

- You expect others to give you *the* answer so you don't have to decide for yourself.
- You waffle when it comes time to follow up on the advice because you're not certain they will appeal to you.
- You continue to feel depressed.

C. I'll seek professional advice from a counselor.

Five months have passed while you mulled over seeking out a psychiatrist, but you have not actually approached one. Since you've basically decided not to do anything "for the moment," you continue feeling stalled, unmotivated, and uninspired. Completing your workload at the office has become a Sisyphean task, made more complicated by your struggle with bulimia. Since you've confided in Allison, you have had to admit your problem to yourself. Bulimia plagues your mind. You fear dental and gastrointestinal problems among other horrible consequences of bulimia, but you put off seeking help because you feel too embarrassed. You have withdrawn from associates, friends, and even poor faithful Jim, and have come to loathe yourself.

Last Friday when you left your office around 7:00 P.M., lost in your customary daze of depression, you didn't notice the white Mazda coming around the corner as you entered the crosswalk.

"I can't remember much," you told Jim later that night, as you laid on the taught antiseptic hospital sheets with your leg in a cast and harnessed to a jungle gym contraption above your bed.

"The guy in the Mazda said you didn't even look before you stepped out in front of him. He felt terrible that he couldn't swerve fast enough. The doctor says it's a multiple fracture, but you'll heal with time and lots of fun physical therapy," Jim informed you.

"What a way to get time off from work, huh?" you tried to grin, but tears belied your feelings.

Later that night you feel a strange sensation as if you were free-falling into an ever narrowing canyon, but instead of feeling afraid, you know you'll bounce back like a rubber ball high into a wide open grassy field. Though a fever has sent your mind reeling, you feel strangely calm. The next morning you believe the worst has passed, even though you haven't begun making efforts toward your recovery.

For several weeks following the accident, the staff psychiatrist, Dr. Judith Aker, visits you in your private room. The unexpected infection after your surgery has kept you in the hospital longer than planned. You begin to trust Dr. Aker and confide in her about your problems with bulimia, your frustrations over work, and your disappointment that your relationship with Jim has deteriorated. You realize during your sessions with Dr. Aker that only you hold the key to your own happiness, and that you need to take responsibility to create changes rather than wait for change to happen to you.

You continue meeting Dr. Aker monthly after your release from the hospital and, on her suggestion, you join a support group. To educate yourself about eating disorders, you contact all of the services Dr. Aker has recommended: American Anorexia/Bulimia Association, (212) 501-8351; The Program for Managing Eating Disorders, (212) 580-3332; the National Eating Disorders Organization, (614) 436-1112; and Overeaters Anonymous, (212) 206-7859.

A full year after your lunch with Allison at Lucia's Restaurant, you meet her there as promised. You share with her your journey toward self-control and self-respect, explaining that your counseling has helped you discover that you can establish control over all areas of your life, but that when you stifle your inner voice and shut out your intuition to solve the main problem, you may seek control in distorted ways. After you got out of the hospital, you had to cut back your time in the law office, which gave you time to look around. Eventually, you found a satisfying position as legal advisor to a well-respected nonprofit enterprise. You were drawn to the organization to focus on helping others, and feel that your legal training serves a greater purpose than before.

You explain to Allison, "When I couldn't make changes in my life myself, I let things go from bad to worse. Looking back now, I don't know why I didn't just follow my gut, quit my job, find a different career, and marry Jim. I thought I was imprisoned, but it turned out that no one but me held the key. Boy, did I learn the hard way."

BENEFITS OF C:

- You finally receive psychiatric counseling at the hospital.
- You realize that your decision to do nothing was an active yet ineffective decision.
- You accept the responsibility for making changes in your life and career.
- You continue therapy and educate yourself about eating disorders.
- You know that your eating disorder is a symptom of your frustrations and that you must face them before you can regain control of your life.

DOWNSIDES OF C:

- You put off seeking the counseling that you believed you needed because you felt embarrassed about the truth of your situation.
- Work and eating problems didn't go away with your "I won't deal with this now" attitude.
- You withdrew from everyone and loathed yourself.
- You avoided taking responsibility until the car accident forced you to change your life.

D. I'll take a month's leave-of-absence to collect my thoughts.

Your emotional turning point comes the following week when an insanely irate client—furious over a settlement that fortunately wasn't your case—stormed the office knocking over plants, sweeping papers off desks, and threatening bodily harm to the lawyer in the office next to yours. The building security guards wrestled the berserk man to the floor, news photographers sprung up in the hallways like mushrooms, and you hid for what seemed like hours under your desk to avoid getting inadvertently involved in the frightening imbroglio.

"I'm out of here," you promised yourself as you reached your apartment feeling physically sick from fear.

"Jim, it was so awful," you whimpered over the phone to your on-again, off-again fiancé. "I can't think. I've got to get away for a while."

"Best news I've heard coming from your mouth since you said, "Yes, maybe," to my proposal six months ago," Jim said soothingly.

"I didn't say, 'Yes, maybe,'" you countered defensively, already distracted from the day's events.

"You're right. You *said* yes, but *acted* maybe."

"You know it was the pressure from the office to produce, and..."

Jim cut you off mid-sentence, "Hey, it's okay. But I'm not taking no for an answer this time. Tell them tomorrow you're taking a month's leave. Clean up whatever cases you can and let's go trekking in Nepal like we've talked about a million times."

The plan sounded perfect to you. The following day you started the gears turning by receiving the okay for a leave. Five weeks later you and Jim arrived in Katmandu, and you were totally unprepared for the experience that awaited you.

The three extra days you and Jim stayed in the Katmandu Guest House changed your life. The monsoon rains delayed the beginning of your trek to the Buddhist area, the Solo Kumbu. One afternoon as you toured the Pashupati temple complex in Katmandu, you were struck by the innocent face of a six-year-old girl begging. She wasn't alone, you noticed. There were many little bedraggled children looking helpless, groping with outstretched hands for whatever they could get. Back at the hotel you learned that many of these young beggars earn food money by collecting used plastic bags for recycling.

"What's being done for these children?" you asked the dark-haired, wide-grinned man behind the desk.

"There are programs. Ah, but you should meet with Miss Ursula. She's from America. She helps many children," he advised. "She's here in Katmandu now."

Despite the rudimentary telephone system, communications in Katmandu operated along the lines of tribal drums. Within hours you received a note and hand-drawn map to come to the "keti" orphanage. "Keti" means "girl" in Nepalese. There you met Ursula Cochran.

"I'm very glad you came, Emily and Jim," she said as she pressed her warm small hand to yours.

"You can call me 'Em,' all my friends do," you said, cementing your instant connection with the diminutive but determined sixty-ish woman.

Ursula explained that she started supporting four children in the late eighties, and now has helped establish an orphanage for thirty-five. "We provide total support for most of them, their living expenses, school costs, clothes, medical care, and other needs," she added. Ursula showed you pictures of the adorable children.

"They're enchanting," you whispered.

"It's hard to imagine work more satisfying, Em," Ursula confirmed.

After your ten-day trek along breathtakingly beautiful trails decorated with empty plastic water bottles and international trash, you and Jim visited another orphanage in the Jawalakhel District of Katmandu. That experience convinced you to change your plans to tour Greece and Turkey during the remaining two weeks of your vacation and spend them in long conversations with Ursula and others in charge of caring for orphaned Nepalese children.

Upon your return to Minneapolis, you approach your law career with a new purpose. With your contacts, you and Jim form a foundation to help the orphans of Nepal. While you know there are many needy children in the U.S., you saw firsthand how little money it took to make a huge difference in children's lives in Nepal. You feel the U.S. hinders such help by manacling efforts with shackles of red tape. It takes three years for the foundation to get up and running before you quit your job. During that time you marry Jim and are now expecting your first child in June.

BENEFITS OF D:

- You decide to get away to collect your thoughts.
- You confide in Jim, who encourages you to go trekking with him as you two had planned but always put off.
- You tidy up loose ends at the office so you won't worry about them while you're gone.
- On your trip, you meet interesting people who are making a difference in the world.
- Your focus away from your own work and problems enables you to discover new interests and a new direction.
- Your time with Jim makes you appreciate him more and decide not to put off your wedding any longer.

DOWNSIDES OF D:

- You wait for a crisis at work to serve as the catalyst for change rather than instigating it yourself.
- You get swept up in the moment and the emotional impact of the child beggars, letting your heart overrule your head.
- For three years you take on the added responsibilities of starting a foundation and marrying Jim along with the pressures of working for billable hours.
- You have not fully considered the financial needs of your growing family.

Exploring the Issue

Many well-educated women, and men, with years of specialized schooling, such as lawyers, CPAs with MBAs, and doctors, discover to their surprise and dismay that once they get out in the workforce they don't like their chosen career. Yet, they feel they would be disloyal to their degree, the time and money they spent to earn it, and perhaps even to their parents and family, if they changed careers.

Though the character in this adventure is bright and well-educated, the type who appears capable of doing anything, she feels stymied in a profession she's grown to hate. The real person who inspired this character attended a continuing education night class I conducted in Boston. The tall, sophisticated Natalie Wood look-alike in an elegant black suit with red lapels stood up and introduced herself, "My name is.... I'm running from the law." The entire room gasped, then laughed as the look on this woman's face revealed her sense of humor. Yet, her angst proved no laughing matter. She felt caged in a career she desperately hated. For most of her life, pleasing others gave her direction and validation, but in the last few years, she realized her mistake and her dilemma.

She's not alone in wanting to find happiness but feeling hog-tied by guilt over others' expectations, over the money spent, or owed, on education, and over the years "wasted." Often people who feel trapped in a lucrative job suffer from the "hand caught in the cookie jar" syndrome. "What else could I do to make as much money?" they lament all the way to the bank. The reasons not to change careers pile on in sticky layers like baklava constructed of fly paper. The sweeter the paycheck, the bigger the title, the more they feel stuck. So what to do?

First, don't blame your parents, or anyone else who expects great things of you. Be thankful that others encourage you to further your training and career, and want the best for you and from you. Count the blessings brought about by their belief in you and their expectations of you.

Second, release yourself from the grip of well-intentioned expectations. Thank everyone who has ever pushed you, telling each of them you understand and appreciate their concern, then politely let them know that you now need to follow your own path.

Third, start your search for that path. Susan, an attorney in San Francisco, leads her own exploration of life after law. She attends seminars, participates in focus groups, and talks to women all over the country, primarily fellow members of the international women's group she has joined. Her efforts have both exhilarated and frustrated her. She feels charged by the interest and support of other women, and has found that she's not alone in her search. She feels frustrated because there's no easy, apparent answer to her dilemma. Susan will tell you, however, that after all of her searching, reading, and her "seminaring," she's found that the answer will come from "Listening to my own guidance."

Fourth, let go. To make the changes Susan, or any woman, wants in her life, she must be *willing* to let go of her title, her high income, her expertise in her field, and the expectations of others, while risking the disappointment of others by starting at the bottom to create the new excitement she desires. That willingness will give her the freedom to open her mind to new opportunities and challenges. Her new income may surpass even that of the law. She may develop a more satisfying identity for herself and gain expertise in a new field and new respect from those who put her down for daring to break the mold. But she'll never know if that will happen without releasing herself from the mental hold on her past accomplishments. They aren't who she is. They are merely markers, indicating that she can do it again in another field, if she's willing to make the effort and if she can decide what she wants to do. The effort and the decision will come after she lets go of defining herself in terms of her past accomplishments and listens carefully to her own guidance.

If you find yourself in a chosen career you dislike, have you determined why you're still in it? What keeps you there? Have you released the need for that title? Have you sought career counseling? Have you discussed the issue with your peers, parents, life-partner? If you feel trapped in a career because your parents paid for your training, do you think your parents want you to be unhappy for the rest of your life? Does your life-partner? If they do, you must confront another set of issues. Rather than exploring that now, let's stay focused on the tarnished dream job at this point.

Career problems, like airplanes, rarely vanish from the radar screen without some sort of intervening catastrophe. Often people wait to make the decision to change careers until something drastic occurs, like an illness, accident, or a crisis involving a loved one. Then their perspective changes immediately. One woman who left her hated high-powered corporate career to start a chocolate candy business after winning a battle with breast cancer laughs at her "past self" who never felt she could accomplish enough, earn enough, or win enough recognition. Now she earns less money, suffers less guilt and stress, and sees the fruit of her labors enjoyed daily. She wouldn't return to her old corporate job for the world, but it took a personal health issue to force her to make the necessary changes.

The trick is to change your perspective by letting go of old habits and identities if they no longer work for you. Free yourself from restricting thoughts, jobs, and people. Freedom comes from seeing alternatives and believing you're never stuck, and from realizing that change will probably require time, money, and some discomfort for a while. Weigh that prospect against continually feeling unhappy and frustrated in your current career.

Expanding Your Thinking

This adventure offers one underlying message: *give yourself permission* to be happy, whether that means getting out of an unsatisfying career, allowing yourself time to develop a lasting relationship, or championing a cause in which you believe. In this adventure "you" feel stuck in the wrong career for the wrong reasons.

Most of what you do in this adventure proves beneficial to transforming your situation from terrible to pretty terrific. But you could have avoided a few pitfalls had you known or thought about them beforehand. For example, in Option B, you seek Jane's advice but feel disappointed when she doesn't outline the exact plan of action or bestow a new career title upon your eager head. She offers what you sought, concrete advice and some specific suggestions, but you hesitate acting on them because you wanted her to provide the answer. You could have avoided this disappointment by maintaining realistic expectations and claiming responsibility for your career.

In Options C and D, you again could have avoided catastrophe by taking control of your own future. You eventually create change, but not in the most advantageous manner. The outcome turns out well in both, but you could have fended off much of the pain induced by getting there had you rejected your "I won't deal with this now" attitude. Also in C, you withdraw from the very people who could assist you, and you shelve your decision to seek the professional help that could have kept you from loathing your situation and yourself.

DON'T:

1. Delay making important career and personal decisions.
2. Undervalue your training, rather find new ways to use it.
3. Berate yourself when you can't easily find new direction.
4. Assume you will follow other people's paths to success; use their paths as markers, not maps.
5. Ignore the value of professional coaching to develop presentation skills.
6. Expect others to give you the answers you need to discover yourself.
7. Abandon the joy of research and discovery.
8. Act on suggestions without following them long enough to determine their value to you.
9. Wait to seek help when you feel low, out of control, or powerless.
10. Withdraw from others as a protective mechanism.

Examples of the positive actions you took include developing an "on camera" personality to share your gift for legal analysis, asking others who've successfully transformed their careers for their advice and suggestions, seeking professional counseling, and getting away from it all to discover new interests. In Option A, you seize the spark that leads to your becoming a television law consultant. You recognize and pay attention to your flash of recognition, "I can do that," then proceed to develop the needed skills. Your research and practice pays off, catapulting you far from the billable hours that swallowed your days and overshadowed your creativity.

You seek Jane Byron's advice in Option B, discovering the vast opportunities that could incorporate your knowledge of law. It took a catastrophe in Option C to lead you to psychiatric counseling, but you developed a rapport with your counselor and took responsibility for your own recovery.

Though your time in Nepal described in Option D could have ended with your gaining little more than the appreciation of high altitude trekking, you show an interest in the well-being of the child beggars. This distracts you from your own personal issues and expands your view of the world and your role in it. You develop future plans based on this new perspective.

DO:

1. Listen when your gut says, "I can do that."
2. If you admire someone else's achievements, think, "If she can do it, so can I." Then find out just how she did it.
3. Call on the qualifications you possess, but develop new skills to expand your options.
4. If you plan to follow something new, practice playing the role to see if you'd really feel comfortable in it.
5. As you develop new skills, keep an eye open for spin-offs for new career opportunities.
6. Attend luncheons, seminars, and conferences in your chosen field, paying attention to the variety of careers represented there.
7. Seek advice from others who have accomplished what you wish to do.
8. Find a caring person to whom you can report your progress as an impetus to continue when you might otherwise relax your efforts.
9. Understand that deciding to "do nothing for the moment" does not put your problems on hold.
10. Take yourself away from your everyday surroundings to refocus on the rest of the world.

Assessing Your Own Situation

In your search for answers, ask yourself the following questions and listen objectively to your answers as though you were listening to your best friend.

1. If you dislike your chosen career, and don't know what else you could do, ask yourself, "Have I ever described what I mean by happiness?" "What are the essentials I need in my career to be happy?"
2. Before you spend years and years digging yourself deeper in an inescapable hole, look in the mirror. "Do I like, or even recognize, who I see there?" "Is that the image of the confident person I know I could be, or that I was in the past?"
3. Ask yourself, "What are five things I like and respect about myself, my career, my choices." List them even if you aren't certain about them.
4. Redefine your dream job. "Can I paint a mental picture of the most rewarding job I can imagine?"
5. How important is your career image? "Am I part and parcel of my title?" "Can I live without it?" "When a stranger asks, 'What do you do?' can I look him in the eye and answer confidently, 'I live life to the fullest!'?"
6. Have you forgiven yourself for making the wrong career choice? "Can I admit that I goofed?" "Will my life fall apart if I recognize this isn't working and seek something better?"
7. Ask yourself, "Can I forgive others who pressured me either intentionally or otherwise to follow the course I now hate?"
8. Can you muster the courage of your convictions? "Do I have what it takes to re-pot myself?" "Do I look forward to recreating myself, or do I fear it?"

9. "Do I look at my career as a series of educational projects?" or "Am I attached to the belief a career must follow a path, and that I'll fall into oblivion if I stray from it?"

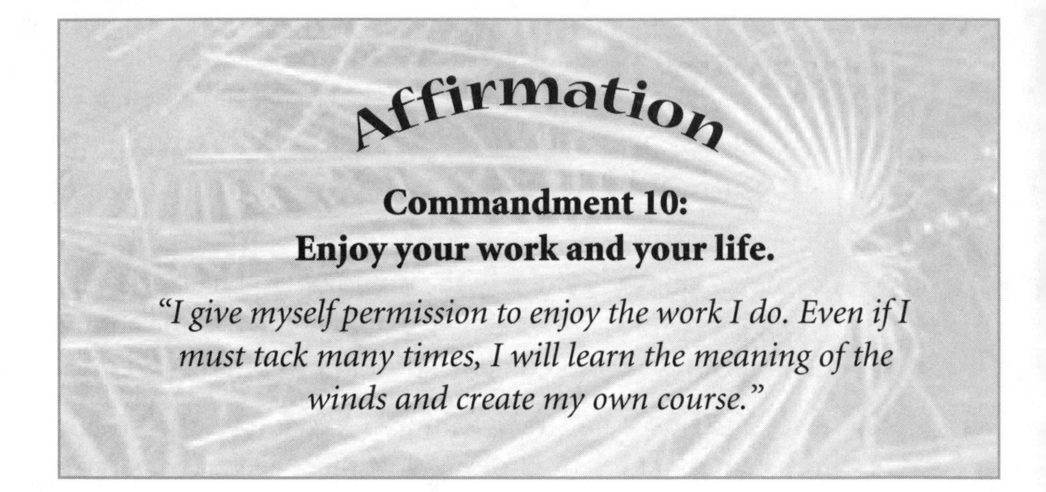

ADVENTURE 4

HOW CAN I REENTER THE WORKFORCE WHEN I'VE STAYED AT HOME RAISING KIDS FOR THE PAST EIGHTEEN YEARS?

When a "stay-at-home mom" has put her career on hold, even for a few years, in order to nurture her children full-time, she can find it hard to reenter the workforce. Imagine how much harder it can be for a woman who has stayed home for eighteen years and now faces an empty nest. Perhaps you're familiar with the fear and frustration of redefining yourself after a long hiatus from the career world. Maybe you, or one or more of your friends, feel out of sync with your husband whose job may have overshadowed you. Where do you begin to start over again? Read along and decide how you would recreate yourself like a ***Phoenix from the Ashes.***

Phoenix from the Ashes

When you married Roger during your junior year in college and moved with him to Miami for his residency in oncology, your life seemed heavenly. Roger was so handsome, with his wavy black hair, deep Mediterranean blue eyes, olive complexion and aquiline nose. Now, some eighteen years later, he still looks like a Greek god, but the trouble is, he acts like one, too. A prosperous and admired doctor, he's given you a good life and two beautiful children, but he's seldom home, and your kids will soon go off to college, leaving you with a big hole in your empty nest.

In the flush of newlywed euphoria you hadn't minded working to help support Roger's career. You felt lucky that National Airlines, a U.S. feeder airline for Pan Am and Braniff international flights, hired you because the job allowed you to be based in Miami, though you hated working when Roger managed a rare night off.

You never quite got around to decorating your small Miami Springs apartment. You barely hung even a picture on the wall, because you both spent so little time there together. It didn't feel like a permanent residence, let alone a home. You lived in limbo, zigzagging your way through the hungry years of your marriage. You took night classes for three years and earned your degree in social sciences, graduating with honors and a big, pregnant stomach. During that time Roger all but lived at Jackson Memorial Hospital. Your own loneliness then seemed like a small price to pay for what would surely evolve into a perfect life.

Yes, you and Roger weathered those times and somehow have held your marriage together raising your two children. Peter, eighteen, leaves for Boston College in the fall, and Amy, seventeen, busily collects college brochures for her great escape. Lately, you've noticed that you and Roger share few interests other than the children. This worries you. Roger keeps wrapped up in his busy office when he's not at the hospital. You've been a supportive wife, involved mother, and effective volunteer, and you feel proud of your accomplishments, but you doubt that Roger respects your efforts. He's the one with the important career. He's the god with the bedside manner. Thinking of the kids growing up and moving out, you fear the big gap between you and your husband will become a bridgeless chasm. You know you need to do something to make yourself more interesting, not only to rekindle Roger's attention, but to reestablish your own self-worth. Your self-esteem has depended almost completely on motherhood and being a doctor's wife. You wonder, "Who am I, if not a mom?" You need something that will make you feel useful when the children depart for college. This scares you. You have no idea what you can do, or if you have what it takes to reenter the workforce.

At dinner you announce, "I'm going to look for a job."

"Oh, sure, Mom. What can you do at your age?" quips Mr. Man-of-the-World, Peter.

"Out of the mouths of babes," you mutter, but you secretly agree.

"Now, Peter. That's unkind," Roger interjects.

"Yeah, Pete, don't be a brat," Amy chimes in.

"Mom knows I'm only kidding, huh, Mom?"

"Yes, Peter. I know. You're right. What can I do, old mom, at the ripe old age of forty-two? What do you guys think?"

"How about a brain surgeon or a rocket scientist," offers Peter, continuing his hilarious-to-himself humor.

"Why don't you open a shop and sell far-out fashions for teenage girls?" Amy suggests, striking a pose as a fashion model, fluffing her hair and batting her eyelashes.

"You can always work part-time in my office," offers Roger.

"You guys are useless," you laugh.

After dinner Roger retreats to his den to read his medical journals while the kids go to their rooms to work on their school assignments. As you sit alone at the kitchen table, pen in hand, you jot down four possible ways you can reenter the working world. You're on a mission to remake yourself. On top of the page, you scribble the words Stage Four. You always referred to Stage One as premarriage, Stage Two as marriage, Stage Three as marriage with children, and now you're about to begin the next stage, marriage with empty nest. Your options unfold like this:

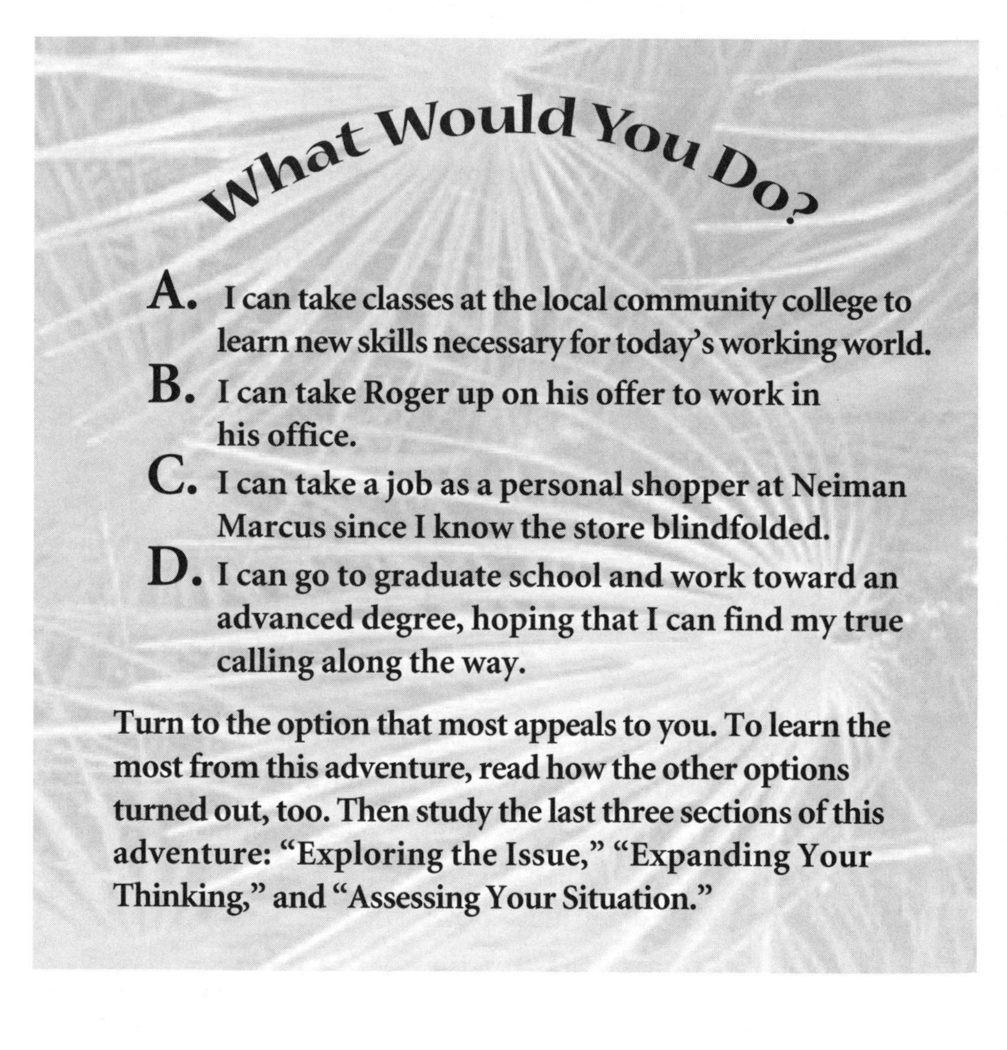

A. I can take classes at the local community college to learn new skills necessary for today's working world.

You call Miami Dade Community College, Kendall Campus, to order a class schedule. While you're on hold the taped message informs you about a Worker Solutions Program that sounds interesting. You research two-year associate degrees, and shorter, twenty-four credit "certificate" programs to become a legal secretary, a PC programmer, or a computer networking expert. You can't decide among the overwhelming array of choices, so you take basic computer classes thinking they will help you get a job.

Twelve months later you still lack any clear direction, even though you have learned Microsoft Word, Excel, Access, MeetingPro, Schedule Plus, and Lotus 1-2-3. Opting to study a specialized skill, you enroll in the legal secretary program and begin the courses necessary to earn your certificate. After only eighteen months, certificate in hand, you land a job in a distinguished, downtown Miami law office.

You were attracted to the firm because of its reputation for supporting women's rights issues. However, rather than getting involved with cutting edge cases, you find yourself buried alive in mind-numbing detail work. Your boss, a Clarence Darrow wannabe, is a young male litigator obsessed with making it to partner. He shows no respect for women, especially those who help him do his job. He wants his work done instantly, with zero mistakes. It's not unusual for him to hand you a forty-page brief to type after lunch, demanding that you finish it by five o'clock. Of course, the brief cites interminable references to past cases, so-and-so versus whosits—very boring and very convoluted. If you notice that a sentence doesn't make any sense and offer suggestions, your arrogant boss puts you down immediately, treating you as if you possess the brain of a gnat. The only hint of recognition or glimmer of appreciation for the role you play in making him a success is a perfunctory, paltry, grocery-store bouquet on Secretaries' Day. The office atmosphere steams with a constant tension that keeps you on edge, too. Egos rage and frustration rules. You become a major league grouch at home.

"Why don't you just quit?" Roger asks you one evening after a particularly rough day, picking a piece of your burnt pot roast dinner from between his teeth.

"Quit? I can't quit. I'd feel like a failure," you say, fighting back tears.

"Hey, Margie, you should enjoy what you do. You don't have to work, and you certainly don't have to prove anything to me or to anybody else."

The words smart. Your in-laws and even your children think you're nuts for working at all. They seem to think you're ready for early retirement and should enjoy your comfortable lifestyle. But deep inside you feel that you do need to prove your worth, if only to yourself. Unfortunately, whether you stay in this job or quit, you know you'll feel like a failure.

BENEFITS OF A:

- You research classes at the local community college.
- You take computer classes to update your skills.
- You earn a certificate to become a legal secretary.
- You work for a law firm that supports a cause you believe in.

DOWNSIDES OF A:

- You take computer classes without any sense of direction.
- You obtain your legal secretary certificate without researching or talking to others about what the job entails.
- The job bores you and you hate your boss.
- You dislike the office atmosphere.
- You feel like a failure.

B. I can take Roger up on his offer to work in his office.

Roger crawls in bed with you and mumbles through his yawn, "You know, Margie, my offer still stands for you to help out in my office."

You smile, happy that he brought up the topic, though you have mixed feelings about working for him. On the one hand, you feel that it's a cop-out to get a job with your husband. It's too easy, not really proving anything other than you can fill up each day. But on the other hand, you wonder if you can't make something more of it than busywork. Deep inside you know the issue isn't that you need to get a job *per se* to prove your self-worth. In fact, you fear accepting Roger's offer to work in his office because it doesn't present the kind of personal challenge you expect on reentering the workforce. So what will it prove? You want to prove to yourself that you can break from your comfortable yet cloistered life after raising your children and contribute something of value to the outside world. You don't know if you can do that working in Roger's office.

You confess your fears to Roger, "I really didn't give it much thought when you first suggested that a few months ago because I wasn't quite sure what I could accomplish. I didn't want to look like the stereotypical bored doctor's wife, wandering around the office with nothing of substance to do. But now I'd like to give it a try. What do you think?"

"Sounds fine. When do you want to start?"

"Tomorrow," you whisper in Roger's ear as you nibble a quick kiss good night. You roll over feeling surprisingly apprehensive. You truly don't want to appear unprofessional. You decide that, in order to define your role in the office, you will ask the patients what they need. You'll become a patient representative. Satisfied with your plan of action, you shut your eyes and imagine what you'll wear tomorrow, settling eventually on simple slacks and a sweater. You don't want to look too formal or unapproachable.

You arrive at Roger's office at ten o'clock, a half hour before he starts seeing patients after rounds at the hospital.

"Hi, Jackie. Did Roger mention to you that I would be coming in?" you ask Roger's office manager, a striking Cuban woman in her mid-forties with a glorious smile.

"Oh, yes. He called from the hospital. Welcome, Margie."

"Who's coming in today? Could you tell me about the patients, what they're here for, what stage of treatment they're in?"

"Why don't I brief you on the morning patients first. We can have lunch together and discuss the afternoon patients then. Sound good?" Jackie asks, as she scans the roster of today's patients.

You like Jackie and all of the office staff. They project a warm welcoming sincerity that reflects Roger's bedside manner. He may think of himself as a god, but he treats his patients like saints. You've been in many professional settings where the entire office seems aloof, hiding behind masks of authority, from the high and mighty doctor down to the smug receptionist. Whenever you make an appointment, you know by the tone of the receptionist's voice over the phone exactly what the rest of the office will be like. You're pleased that Roger's office atmosphere respects patients. Knowing that people usually feel vulnerable and apprehensive, especially in an oncologist's office, you set yourself the goal of finding out how to ease their fears. More than anything else, you vow to treat them as people rather than patients.

Within four months your presence in the office proves invaluable. "What did we ever do without you?" Jackie wondered out loud. "The patients love you. Your response to their questions and personal needs has helped them immensely. Our staff has never had the time to sit and talk at length with our patients to uncover their hidden fears."

It's true, by talking with each person informally, you discovered that many of their concerns centered around how to function in life while fighting their illnesses. To answer their questions you developed resource files that include everything from the best place to buy prostheses, to where to find home care, to how to start support groups; but the patients ask harder questions than where to buy a bra after a mastectomy. They each express individual and special needs. They want to know how to help their children cope, how to talk to their husband and rekindle intimacy, why they no longer feel feminine, and how they can continue their role as the mainstay of their families when they feel powerless. To meet some of these deeply personal needs, you've created a patient support group to assist, advise, and comfort other patients.

The success of your in-house counseling program attracts other patients and even doctors who want you to set up similar programs in their practices. This inspires you to organize your massive resource base and develop a prototype program that you can install as a paid consultant. Within two years, you manage a large resource center for doctors, nurses, patients and their families in Roger's hospital and create other centers across Florida.

At the opening of the tenth center in Boca Raton, Roger wraps his arm around you and whispers, "I'm so proud of you."

You look into his adoring eyes and see him less as the god and more the man you married. You smile back at him warmed in the glow of his pride, but feel more comforted knowing that you have created your own happiness through helping others overcome their fears.

BENEFITS OF B:

- You recognize your fears about working in Roger's office.
- You work with the office staff without trying to pull spousal rank on them.
- You define your role by asking patients what they need.
- You use your organizational skills to provide resources and develop patient support groups.

- Your understanding of the daily functions of your husband's business gives you more to share with him at home.
- Your efforts help the patients and attract the attention of others.
- You develop a program and sell your services as a consultant.
- Your interest in helping others turns into a real business.
- You win your own and Roger's respect.
- You discover you are responsible for your own happiness.

DOWNSIDES OF B:

- You feel like you're reentering the workforce through the back door.
- You ignore other more difficult, yet possibly more rewarding, paths to greater self-respect.
- Immersing yourself in your husband's world of work could set you up for clashes at home if he disagrees with any aspect of your program.
- Working together closely with a spouse always runs the risk of jealousy or resentment.

C. I can take a job as a personal shopper at Neiman Marcus since I know the store blindfolded.

Two months ago you had laughed when your friend Jessica, a high-powered investment banker at Goldman Sachs on Biscayne Boulevard, suggested you become a personal shopper. "I don't have time to shop, Margie. I would love someone I trusted to keep an eye out for stunning outfits, on sale of course," Jessica explained. "You've been involved in so many charity fashion shows with

Neiman's, you'd be a natural, and, after all, you know every inch of the store."

Now, as you consider what you could do to reenter the world of work, you think, "Why not?" Everyone has been advising you to do what you really enjoy. Well, that's easy. You love shopping, especially at Neiman's. You even relish the smell of the catch-them-as-they-come-in cosmetic counters and the piped-in music, though you much prefer the live music played by the tuxedoed pianist seated at the grand piano.

You've set up an interview with the Human Resources director at Neiman Marcus for Wednesday at ten o'clock, an appointment that worries you because you haven't worked since your National Airlines days. You're afraid she'll ask, "What are your weaknesses?"

On Tuesday night you corner Roger in his den after dinner. "Darling, what should I say in the interview? I mean, should I tell them I haven't worked in eighteen years?"

"Sure, tell the truth. But stress the positive aspects of your experiences as a flight attendant as well as a wife and mother, your organizational skills as a volunteer, and your observations as a world-class shopper."

Mulling over Roger's advice, you list your positive experiences first:

1. As a flight attendant I learned to show up on time, present an attractive appearance, and smile in adversity.
2. As a volunteer I gained organizational expertise and I developed a knack for writing effective thank-you notes after an event to win repeat contributors.
3. As an avid shopper, I know where to find anything in this store. As a customer I expect first-class service, and I can deliver that to other customers, too.

Next you think about how you would answer "What are your weaknesses?" You write:

1. My clerical skills need sharpening, but I believe that handwritten notes to customers work better than word processed ones. I certainly must learn to use the store computer programs as quickly as possible.
2. My Spanish needs work, but I do understand more than I can speak.

You rehearse your answers and go to bed dreaming of working miracles for working women who can afford to look great, but can't afford the time to shop.

Your efforts pay off the following day. You feel comfortable in the interview, having practiced beforehand. You even challenge the woman conducting the interview to give you a test: to gather a complete outfit for her. After discussing her tastes and budget, you win her over after you whip through the task with flying colors, silks, and shoes. She offers you the job on the spot. You can't wait to tell Jessica about the great Anne Klein suit you saw on sale in her size.

Weeks flash by, with you eagerly punching in and punching out every day. You enjoy helping customers, mostly men who are looking for something for their wives or girlfriends. Jessica has bought two outfits, including the Anne Klein suit. You realize, however, that you need a big holiday to boost your earnings. Ironically, the smells from the cosmetics counters that once tantalized you now simply stimulate you to wonder if a particular fragrance would work for a particular client. Shopping for a living, it turns out, has become a rather boring activity. Why hadn't you considered shopping for a life rather than for dresses and handbags and shoes? Working nights and weekends has pushed time with Roger aside, and you know he finds your work frivolous. You hate to admit it, but this choice is just not working out. You feel embarrassed that your foray into the workforce turned into such a disappointment.

BENEFITS OF C:

- You listen to a friend who recognizes your tastes and skills in shopping.
- You see the benefits of working in a setting you enjoy.
- You set up an interview and prepare answers to the probable questions the interviewer will ask.
- You tell the truth in the interview but present weaknesses in such a way that they do not jeopardize your qualifications as a personal shopper.
- You offer to prove your ensemble gathering skills.

DOWNSIDES OF C:

- You don't meet with a personal shopper at Neiman's to learn what she does or ask her what she likes about the job.
- You find that shopping for yourself is fun but working as a personal shopper is just plain old work.
- You followed a path of least resistance rather than considering other perhaps more difficult but more satisfying possibilities.
- You dislike working nights and weekends and should have anticipated the effects on your marriage.
- You're self-confidence declines rather than builds when you discover that you chose the wrong job.

D. I can go to graduate school and work toward an advanced degree, hoping that I can find my true calling along the way.

You begin your search of local graduate schools over the phone. "Hello, I'd like to receive some information about your graduate programs," you ask the first admissions assistant you reach.

"In what field?" the young Hispanic woman's voice asks.

You hesitate. "I'm not sure."

"Why don't you come in and talk to one of our counselors? Would you like me to set up an appointment?"

"Sure, great."

The following week you sit in the counseling office with Ms. Carter, a woman about your age, discussing options and programs in a variety of fields. At the outset she asks, "What do you think you'd like to pursue, Margie?"

"It's not crystal clear to me, but, actually, I think I'd like to do what you do, counseling. It's something I could see myself enjoying. It's not all that different from being a mom, is it?"

She laughs at that then turns serious, saying that it takes a lot of time and money to gather the necessary credentials. Plus, you'd have to work as an intern for the required 3,000 supervised hours. That doesn't bother you. You can afford the time and money, but your problem is the program accepts only thirty-five people a year, and this year's program started during the summer. However, since you don't give up easily, you don't see this as a closed door. You'll just take a few relevant classes for credit, hoping you'll win admittance to the program the following summer. What have you got to lose?

"You'll have to apply for next semester," the registrar tells you. "And you'll have to take the graduate record exam (GRE)."

Months later, you became an official student in the graduate program even though you didn't score phenomenally well on the entrance exam. The acceptance committee based its decision on the three classes you took, which proved your abilities and sincerity. You continue earning credentials over the next two years and win the honor of carrying the flag in the graduation ceremonies because you are graduating at the top of your class.

Then you face the next challenge, internship. You want to do it in a corporation, but you discover that's never been done before.

"Our people have always interned in schools," the course counselor informs you. "If you really want to intern in industry, we'll have to create a whole new approach. Can you research the possibility and come back with a proposal?"

Taking the initiative, you contact ten different companies. Most turn you down flat, but one start-up in the managed care industry likes the idea a lot. They say they will get back to you. When you don't hear from them after two weeks, you send them a letter suggesting that if they are so busy that they couldn't get back to you, they probably really need you. The next day they call and agree to participate in this pilot program. Your counselor agrees to sponsor it on a trial basis.

On your first day in the new position, the office personnel manager asks you, "Do you type?"

"No," you lie. Disappointed, she says she needs you to do more than just counsel people. If you'll do some clerical work, however, she'll arrange for you to counsel people in the afternoons with the required supervision. However, the personnel manager quickly sees that you're more valuable as a counselor than a clerical worker. From that day forward you see eight people a day. You're thrilled that you didn't believe that your internship should follow the norm: volunteering your time in a school setting. Not only did you intern where you wanted, but you got paid the entire time.

Roger advises you to contact insurance companies to get on their list of preferred providers. That good advice gives you a leg up on starting your business, which prospers from day one.

Today, you love running your own practice. You and Roger have much more in common than ever before, igniting a new spark in your married life.

BENEFITS OF D:

- You gather information about graduate schools.
- You seek assistance from the graduate school counseling office and recognize your interest in counseling.
- You enter the graduate program through the back door by taking classes without the guarantee of getting accepted to the program.
- Though you didn't score well on the GRE, you proved your interest and abilities through the three classes you took.
- You set your sights on and create a corporate internship, even though it had never been done.
- You earn an income during your entire internship.
- You refuse to get stuck as a typist.
- You set up your own lucrative business.
- Roger and you share more interests.

DOWNSIDES OF D:

- It takes years of study and a considerable amount of money to earn your credentials.
- You ended up in health care simply because Roger could pave that path for you.
- You did not explore the possibility that your school's traditional program might have turned out as well as or better than your innovative one.

Exploring the Issue

Returning to the working world after a long hiatus is like competing in a long jump competition, when you must jump from a standing position while your competition enjoys a running start. At least that's how you feel. It's an endeavor fraught with many misconceptions, mostly your own. Once you can convince yourself of your abilities and value you can compete for the gold, if you know which contest you want to enter.

The character in this adventure wants to reenter the workplace for many valid reasons. She's sincere in her efforts, but she finds the task daunting. You may have found walking a mile in her shoes a truly rewarding experience, or you may have felt quite frustrated. However, if you want to reenter the workforce yourself, you should consider the following.

The first stage of reentry requires self knowledge. With that you can set goals. Though reentering the workplace requires much more than goal setting, without identified goals you can easily end up wasting your time. Goal planning includes asking yourself the following questions: "What is my goal?" "Why do I want it?" "What new skills do I need to get there?" "How long will it take?" "Do I see myself 'there'?" and "What is my reward?"

But what if you don't know what you want to do? Research, talk to people, volunteer, experiment, take classes to pique your interest as well as hone your skills. Allow yourself some time to flounder while you're searching. Your first choice doesn't have to be *the* one and only. I modeled the doctor's wife in Option B on Margie Sborov, Patient Representative of the Minnesota Oncology Hematology Professional Association of Minneapolis. Margie found that taking a year-long class for women in transition that focused on all of life's situations (aging, divorce, etc.) became her turning point. Though she's the first to admit that it's a sometimes painful experience to try to find something meaningful to do, you can't accomplish anything if you don't build your self-confidence first. Classes, volunteering, and supportive friends and family helped her through the difficult transition. Today, her programs based on her original research positively affect the lives of all involved, including herself.

Ask yourself why you want to work again. Do you need the money? Are you bored and want to expand your interests? Do you want to try something you've never had the opportunity to do before, sort of a "now or never" undertaking? Your own special reasons will make a huge difference in what you finally choose, how long you're willing to work to get there, what amount of money you're willing to invest to attain that goal, and how seriously you'll go after it. Imagine yourself ten years from now looking back over the decade. What do you wish to have accomplished? What do you want to be known for?

Finally, assess your "hunger quotient." How badly do you want it? Are you willing to return to school for years to earn a new degree? Can you sacrifice your comfortable lifestyle for the struggle to reach new goals? I've met many women who mistakenly believe that since they earned a degree in college—who knows when, maybe twenty-five years ago—they simply should not have to start at the bottom of the ladder. Wrong. Every time you reenter or change to completely new fields, you must be *willing* to start at the bottom, to earn your stripes, to pay your dues. Part of the joy lies in the learning, the growing, the developing. Enjoy it, don't negate it.

When you can answer the above goal-oriented questions, proceed to stage two: strategic planning and goal implementation. In other words, plan out a program to reach your goal. What can you apply to today's workplace that you learned from the college degree you earned umpteen years ago? If a long list doesn't jump to mind, figure out what new skills you'll need. Research where to get them and enroll. Stockpile abilities. Prepare a résumé. Identify possible employers and contact them.

Stage three is your booster rocket: enthusiasm. Harness your fear of the unknown with the thrill of the adrenaline rush. Trying something new, learning, forcing yourself to grasp new concepts and to excel in something totally different from what you've done in the past makes you feel alive. Certainly, you may feel like an impostor for a while until you gain experience and know as much, if not more, than those around you.

You're cruising along in stage four when you've broken the invisible barrier into the working world and you feel not only part of it, but charged by it. You appreciate your abilities and your value in the workplace. You've completed a successful reentry.

Women who have successfully completed the reentry process stress the importance of keeping in mind that to accomplish a satisfying reentry, you may need to work on boosting your self-esteem first. This part takes time and energy, but the rewards far outweigh the effort.

Expanding Your Thinking

In this adventure "you" wanted to return to the job market primarily to boost your own self-worth. You didn't need the money. You needed much more than that. That's why just taking any job, and studying "marketable" skills, wasn't enough to satisfy your goals. Only when you found "a calling," your passion, could you fight the odds and win the recognition you sought.

What thoughts and actions displayed in this adventure should you avoid in the future? Those that limit your thinking and your belief in what you can accomplish. In Option A, you begin by busying yourself with directionless pursuits. You become proficient at several computer programs, but then decide to study to become a legal secretary. You discover you hate the atmosphere of the law firm where you work, especially the personal put-downs. You feel like a failure.

Almost everything you do in Option B is effective. However, you fear people will think you're taking the "easy" way out by working in your husband's office.

In Option C, you believe your love of shopping will help you become a great personal shopper. While that does happen to a degree, you lose interest because night and weekend hours harm your marriage. You find, too, that working in the store has dampened your enjoyment of shopping. You feel that it wasn't a good plan and feel embarrassed that it didn't work out better.

You must devote a great deal of time and money to pursue your idea to become a counselor in Option D.

Things you may wish to watch out for in your own thinking include:

DON'T:

1. Follow a course of action without knowing why and what you want to accomplish.
2. Assume you want to work in a certain field without talking to people who do it already.
3. Set yourself up for frustration and failure in a job that you cannot enjoy.
4. Seek your identity solely through your work.
5. Think that turning a hobby into a business will always work out successfully.
6. Believe that you should automatically start at the middle or the top when changing careers.
7. Look for shortcuts to long-term goals.
8. Turn down possibilities without carefully looking into them.
9. Negate the importance of trying something that may seem beyond your current abilities.
10. Avoid identifying and facing your fears.

In this adventure, examples of positive actions abound. In Option A, you research classes at the local community college and enroll first in computer classes and then work toward your legal secretary certification. With your newly developed skills you land a job with a promising law firm.

In Option B, though Roger had asked you to help out in his office before, you hadn't felt ready. You feared being seen as the "bored doctor's wife hanging around the office." However, you overcome your fears by "getting out of yourself" and listening to the needs of the patients. You rally around their needs, research an extensive resource base, and call on your organizational skills developed over years of volunteering and motherhood to form patient support groups. Your inventiveness and "resourcefulness" attract attention from the medical community, which asks you to set up a resource center at the hospital. You build that into ten resource centers around the state. You've become well-known and well-respected in the community. Most of all, you create your own happiness.

In Option C, based on your friend Jessica's recommendation to do something you enjoy, you foray into the retail world. You set up an appointment with the HR department of Neiman Marcus and assess your strengths and weaknesses before the job interview. Your enthusiasm and knowledge of the store help you win a personal shopper position.

In Option D, you decide you want something substantial to do after the children leave and look into graduate programs. You're willing to go the long route to get what you want. Through research and counseling you discover an appealing path. When roadblocks get in your way, you never give up, but instead create effective detours. You achieve your ultimate goals, increase your own self-worth, gain Roger's respect, and find satisfying work in a profession that makes a difference in people's lives.

Consider the positive lessons you can glean from this adventure:

DO:

1. List what you enjoy doing and do well, then try to identify possible jobs based on this list.
2. Identify what you want to do and why.
3. Research many possibilities.
4. Assess your "hunger quotient" to reach your goal.
5. Learn new skills, especially ones that will apply to what you want to do.
6. Allay your fears of reentering the workplace by focusing on what you wish to accomplish and whom you wish to help.
7. Listen to friends and family when they compliment you because this helps you develop stronger self-esteem.
8. Assess your strengths and weaknesses for an interview and express them honestly but in a way that will not hinder your chances to win the position.
9. Look for the best solution for now and for ten years from now.
10. Don't take no for an answer as you push your way toward your goal.

Assessing Your Own Situation

If you're thinking about reentering the workforce, you may want to consider the following questions that can help you assess your own situation:

1. Before you try to figure out *what* you want to do, ask yourself *why* you want to work. "What do I wish to gain?" "Do I want something to fill up my time, or to fulfill a personal need?"

2. State your goals in clear, specific terms and write them down. "Do I want to earn *x* amount of money?" "Do I want to write that book, study law, ________ (fill in the blank) that I've always dreamed of doing?"
3. Consider the timing of your goals. "Is this a good time to undertake a new project?" "How long should I plan to strive toward this goal?" "Do I possess the patience and commitment to persist that long to attain my goals?"
4. Figure out what you will need to reach your goals. "What skills do I need to develop?" "Where can I acquire those skills?" "What will it cost me in time and money?" and "To whom can I turn for support?"
5. What barriers can you foresee? "What can keep me from reaching my goal?" "What's the worst thing that can happen, and what would I do about it?"
6. Assess your "hunger quotient" by asking yourself, "What would my life be like if I didn't go for this goal?" "Will I always regret not going for this?" "What does it mean to me personally to try for it?"
7. Can you overcome your self-doubts? "Do I tell myself I'm too old, too inexperienced, too lacking in the education or money to get the job I want?" "Do I have the attitude of 'If not now, when?' to keep me on track?" "Do I give myself credit for my present skills and my ability to learn new things?"
8. What is your approach to reentering the job market? "Am I taking this too seriously?" "Am I enjoying the ride as much as grabbing the brass ring?"
9. Do you spend all your time preparing and researching, or do you take action? "Do I see the goal as a series of small but interesting steps?" "Do I do something each day that will get me closer to my goals?" "If not, why not?"

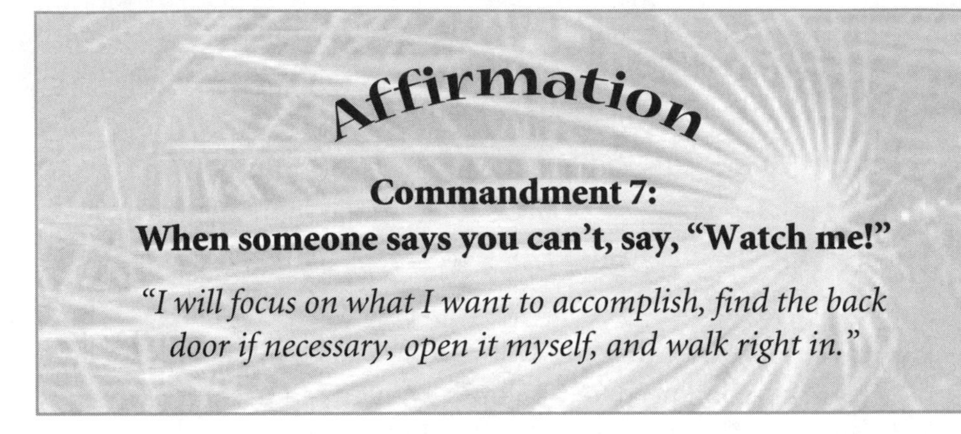
Affirmation
Commandment 7:
When someone says you can't, say, "Watch me!"
"I will focus on what I want to accomplish, find the back door if necessary, open it myself, and walk right in."

ADVENTURE 5

HOW CAN I START MY OWN BUSINESS WHEN I DON'T HAVE A CLUE ABOUT WHAT I REALLY WANT TO DO?

Are you itching to create a business of your own, but can't picture exactly what sort of business you'd be running? Do you want more control over your time, a new challenge, financial independence, and an outlet for your creativity? You may come up with a dozen reasons to start your own business and you may even know what you want to do, but lack the confidence to start the journey. If you're stuck in a Bermuda Triangle of indecision, fantasize for a few minutes how you would navigate safely to the shores of your desired destination: ***Me, Myself, Incorporated.***

Me, Myself, Incorporated

You sit behind your desk in room 301, barricaded behind stacks of textbooks and papers, your Delta Gamma sorority mug full of pencils, and your brown paper bag lunch awaiting the arrival of thirty-two seventh graders. You've taught at Herbert Hoover Junior High School in Merced, California for ten years. Once it was the perfect job for raising your girls through grammar school, but now you feel like a ship becalmed in a stifling sea of monotony. You itch for freedom, excitement, a business of your own.

"It's bor-ring," you confide to your friend and hairdresser, Jennifer, during your regular biweekly Saturday morning appointment. "Every day in that classroom I feel like I'm rowing through a sea of glue. Teaching has become such a drag. This just isn't what I'm supposed to be doing anymore."

"Well, what are you supposed to be doing?" Jennifer asks. She likes her job: hair stylist, confidante, preacher, and counselor. It satisfies her "curious streak," her euphemism for being just plain nosy. Today she's donned her counselor hat.

You're thirty-five with eight- and ten-year-old girls at home. Tom, your husband, works as a manager of the Central Valley Can Company. You enjoy a good relationship with him, founded while you both attended Merced High. You haven't told Tom about your frustrations at work. Not that he hasn't noticed, of course, you just haven't voiced them.

Today, you feel much older than Jennifer, who's ten years your senior. You're riled up over the new "let's-change-everything" principal at school, your recalcitrant students, and your own inability to decide what else you can do. You daydream about starting an exciting business, but all you see is a fuzzy picture of yourself sailing through a dense fog. After contemplating Jennifer's question, you blurt out, "I want do to something that makes me feel alive again. I want to work for myself, maybe run my own business, but I can't figure out what I really want to do."

"So, quit teaching," Jennifer agrees. "Go back to school."

"Yuck. That's just exchanging one classroom for another."

"I've thought about taking some cooking classes myself. Want to take one with me? You're a great cook already, but it could be fun," Jennifer muses, as she snips your streaked brown hair into your signature wedge cut, cropped in back, parted on the left side and jaw length in front. Before you can answer, Jennifer continues, "What do you like doing best?"

"Tennis," you quip.

"There you go. Start a tennis clinic. I can see your business card now: '10 S 4 Every 1.'"

"Cute, Jennifer." You rise from the mustard leatherette swivel chair and reach for your purse. "Well, I gotta run." You leave a twenty next to the natural bristle brush on the counter under the wicker framed mirror. "Talk to you later. Have fun with the cooking class."

"Maybe you should start a cooking school. Have you ever thought of that?"

"Well I love houses too, so should I build some?" you laugh.

"What about all the birdhouses you paint? I'm not kidding. You're talented. Turn your hobby into a business. I can see your company name now: 'Home Tweet Home.'"

"Right. Thanks for your words of wisdom, Jennifer. Talk to you later."

When you walk out into the blistering summer sunlight, you stand there in the parking lot on the corner of Bear Creek Road and M Street pondering what choices you might make about a business of your own.

"What do I know about business anyway?" you chide yourself as you unlock the door to your silver Ford Taurus. "I'm no captain of industry. 'Me, Myself, Incorporated'?! Right."

However, you're a confident person, good with people, and it's high time you expanded your horizons.

On your way home along shady Bear Creek Drive you think about Jennifer's half-serious suggestions and wonder if you could turn anything you really like doing into a business. Imagining four ways you can approach this dilemma, you hurry home and write them down.

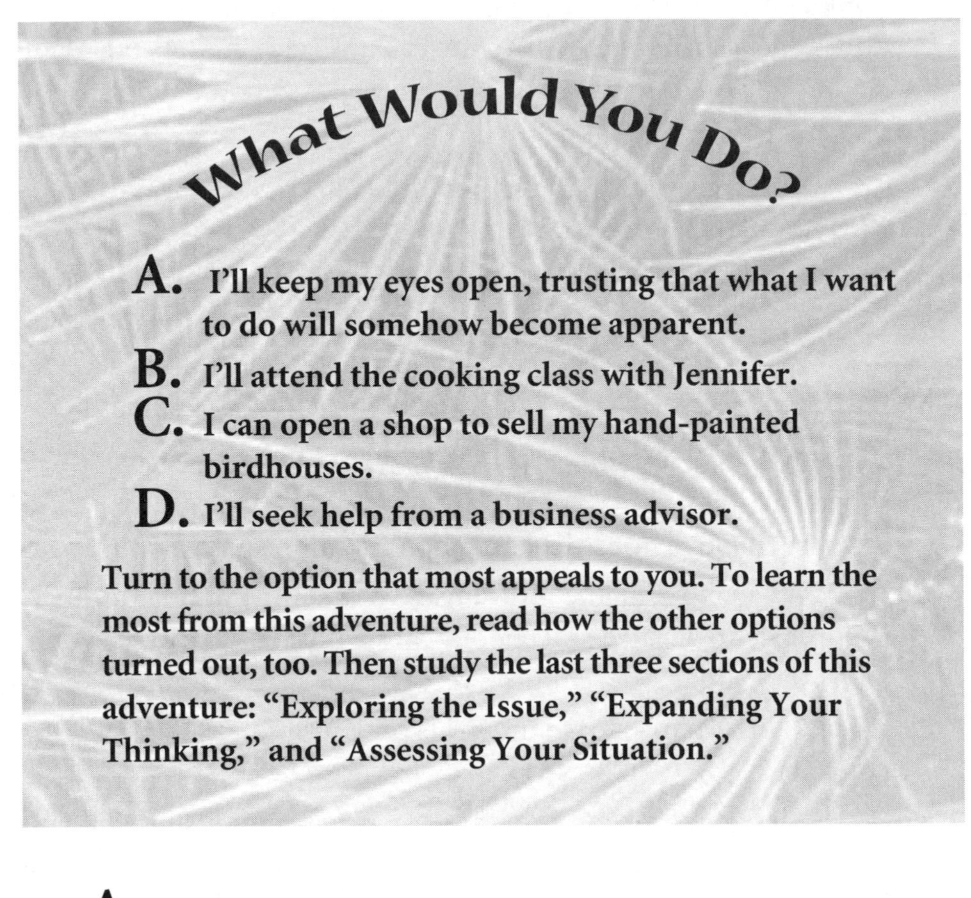

What Would You Do?

A. **I'll keep my eyes open, trusting that what I want to do will somehow become apparent.**
B. **I'll attend the cooking class with Jennifer.**
C. **I can open a shop to sell my hand-painted birdhouses.**
D. **I'll seek help from a business advisor.**

Turn to the option that most appeals to you. To learn the most from this adventure, read how the other options turned out, too. Then study the last three sections of this adventure: "Exploring the Issue," "Expanding Your Thinking," and "Assessing Your Situation."

A. I'll keep my eyes open, trusting that what I want to do will somehow become apparent.

The following month you join Tom on a weekend business trip to Dallas, where he must represent his company at a food processing conference. While he attends seminars, you meander through the maze of exhibits, gazing at the dizzying array of devices, equipment, preservatives, lighting, conveyers, and even insurance programs on display throughout the huge hall. Among all of the flashy, high-tech booths, a simple one catches your attention. A pleasant, well-dressed woman behind an antique oak spindle-leg desk sits under the "Convention Concierge" sign above the booth. You stop and ask the woman behind the desk what she offers.

"I help the convention-goers make dinner reservations, find theater tickets, arrange excursions for spouses, whatever. I'm like the concierge in a fine hotel," the cheerful woman replies. "Can I help you with something?"

"I think you just have," you reply. You start to walk away, but then you turn back to ask, "Does the convention bureau hire you, or is this your own booth? I mean, do you own this business?"

The woman glows with enthusiasm, "Yes, it's my own business. I rent the booth. It helps the convention center, but they don't hire me. They are, in effect, my client."

"Do you do this for other conferences that come to town?"

"Oh yes, quite a few now. It keeps me busy."

"May I have your card?"

"Certainly. And here's my brochure of services. Where are you from? What do *you* do?"

After you chat for a while, you linger around that aisle, pretending to look at other displays but studying the activity at the concierge booth. Something inside tells you that you could do that. It's a visceral feeling that sweeps from the soles of your feet upward. You know that you would be good at it. You decide to look into developing something like it when you return to Merced.

During your United flight on the way home, you tell Tom about your interest in becoming a convention concierge.

"I don't know, Cheryl. Why give up a secure job for something you don't know a thing about?"

"Because, as you may have noticed, my job is driving me crazy," you respond, hurt that he didn't understand immediately.

"Well, look into it, and we'll talk about it," Tom says, folding back the front section of his newspaper and adjusting his horn-rimmed bifocals.

"We'll talk about it," your mind echoes. You pick up a magazine and pretend to read, but your imagination is racing full steam ahead. You're determined to make it happen. "Talk about it, indeed," you mumble under your breath.

Every free period for the next two weeks you hog the phone in the teachers' lounge, as you contact the Fresno Convention Center and the Doubletree Hotel in Modesto, places within an hour's drive that you know host conventions. Each place gives you several other people to call, including catering managers, meeting planners, and restaurant owners. Your excitement grows each day. You describe to meeting planners and convention hall managers the value of your service. You develop your list of restaurants and tour companies for trips to Yosemite and other regional attractions that might appeal to convention goers and their families. You even contact the woman in the concierge business in Dallas and ask her for advice. She's delighted to help you.

You test the waters for your own business by booking booths at five conventions during your summer vacation. After your third very successful conference, you tell Tom, "Okay, it's time to seriously talk about my new business."

BENEFITS OF A:

- You consider new, unusual ideas.
- You notice the concierge booth at the conference and gather more information from the woman who owns the business.
- You pay attention to your positive gut reaction to that type of business.
- You research convention centers and call everyone referred to you.

- You ask the woman in Dallas for advice.
- You test the waters for your own concierge business at a few conventions before you consider quitting your teaching job.
- You discuss your business plans with Tom.

DOWNSIDES OF A:

- Your gut reaction may spring more from desperation than any real affinity for this business.
- You don't explore any other business opportunities, such as the ones Jennifer suggested.
- You get mad at Tom for not understanding your desire to run your own business, yet you've never discussed your unhappiness at work with him.
- You don't draft a business plan.

B. I'll attend the cooking class with Jennifer.

Jennifer calls you on Tuesday to tell you about the cooking class this coming Thursday night at Merced Junior College taught by the chef of the Sizzling Branding Iron Restaurant. Though you expect the class to feature nothing more than steak and potatoes, you agree to meet Jennifer there.

The first to arrive, you watch as Chef Bob sets up the demonstration table. You offer to help place his handouts on the chairs. He's grateful.

"How did you get into the food business?" you ask.

"I fell into it, literally," Bob laughs. "As a sales rep for Jumpin' Jane Sportswear Company, I was on the road all of the time. One night, after a few drinks with customers, we ordered dinner. I was so tired I fell asleep at the table and plopped my face square in a bowl of beef barley soup. I never lived it down. They started calling me Beef Barley Bob. All of my friends knew my hobby was cooking, but I surprised the heck out of them when I quit repping and opened my own restaurant."

You laugh at his ridiculous story. "Do you ever miss your old job?"

"Absolutely not. I love food and cooking," Bob brags. "You should come to my other classes, too. We're going to cover a lot of tasty items."

You and Jennifer thoroughly enjoy Bob's personality and his lesson on chunky soups. You especially like his recipe for his specialty, beef barley soup. You sign up for the rest of Bob's classes. In fact, you get so hooked on cooking classes in general, you attend every class you can find. You visit many Central Valley towns, comparing culinary teaching techniques. You feel you've become an unofficial expert on cooking classes in the area.

At your next hair appointment Jennifer surprises you with a flyer about a series of Paul Prudhomme cooking classes offered over one weekend in San Francisco three weeks from now. Since you know nothing about Louisiana cookery, you readily agree to sign up.

As you ride over the Altamont Pass to San Francisco in Jennifer's midnight blue Subaru Outback, you fantasize about teaching your own cooking classes. You've already started work on your own cookbook. You're looking forward to watching the master chef at work. In your mind, this weekend completes your self-styled education on learning the fine points of teaching cooking. After this, you're ready to go.

"His classes should be amazing," Jennifer says, interrupting your thoughts. "They're held at Moscone Convention Center auditorium, and I hear they rival rock star performances."

"Everything but lasers," you whisper to Jennifer, raising your right eyebrow.

"Just wait," she giggles.

You can't wait, wait to start your own cooking school, that is. You've been formulating your plan for months, and you know exactly what you want to do. Your school will offer a variety of ethnic foods courses, children's cooking classes, and a men's only class.

After the first day at Paul Prudhomme's show, back in your room at the Stewart Hotel off Union Square, you show Jennifer the layout for your cookbook you had described to her during your hair appointments.

"Wow, who's doing these drawings for you, Cheryl?"

"A graphic artist from Mill Valley named Donnie. She's incredibly talented, don't you think?"

"She's terrific. These illustrations make my mouth water. I had no idea you were this far along," Jennifer shakes her head in amazement. "You're really going to pull this off, aren't you?"

"I sure am."

After this climactic weekend, you return to Merced and spend six months looking at prospective locations for holding classes. Your best bet is the Presbyterian Church Community Hall with its new, modern kitchen. The rent is reasonable, and it's well-located. Your classes attract so many people that you expand the number of classes you give each week.

Two and a half years later, your cooking school receives national attention, which happily coincides with the release of your second cookbook, *Chef Cheryl's Culinary Creations.*

BENEFITS OF B:

- You pay attention to Jennifer's comment about your ability to teach a cooking class.
- You attend a cooking class with Jennifer.
- You ask how Chef Bob started his cooking business.
- You apply your existing teaching skills to business.

- You take all the cooking classes you can in order to compare and learn new techniques.
- You formulate your plan for the cooking school and cookbooks.
- You write the cookbooks, start the school, and win national acclaim.

DOWNSIDES OF B:

- You depend on Jennifer to encourage you to take cooking classes.
- You do not weigh other possibilities for a business of your own.
- You gravitate toward teaching, more out of habit than out of a genuine love of teaching.
- You don't write a business plan.

C. I can open a shop to sell my hand-painted birdhouses.

On your way to downtown Merced you drive down 21st Street and notice a "For Lease" sign in front of a stately robin's egg blue Victorian house. You know it previously housed an antique shop. You've always loved that building. You think, "This could be *the* home for my business." It reminds you of that wonderful shop in Fresno which offers an assortment of hand-made crafts, dolls, and *objets d'art*. It's the grand dame of gift shops. You want to recreate that here in Merced.

When you contact the Realtor indicated on the sign to discuss a lease agreement, you insist on a one-year lease, starting right after school lets out for the summer. You've already arranged a one-year leave of absence with the principal, who did not guarantee you a job at the end of your leave. That doesn't worry you too much, though, because they always need teachers, especially those who understand a couple of dialects of Vietnamese. Merced County became home to many Mings, Mungs, Cambodians, and Vietnamese in the eighties when refugees were flown to Castle Air Force Base in the neighboring town of Atwater. The extended families, whom the government planned to disperse throughout the country, refused to be separated. Coupled with the recent air force base closure, the influx of people needing welfare has put a tremendous strain on Merced's economy. Merced is hurting. Still, you can teach or at least tutor, should the need arise later on.

The day you sign your lease you incur heavy business expenses. You install an 800 number for your phone system, a fax machine, a postage machine, and a used cash register. You buy stunning stationery printed with your expensively designed rose and blue quilt pattern logo and matching business cards, and you hire a graphic artist to design a brochure/mailer for the corporate gift market you figure might exist in the law firms or real estate offices. Business taxes and licenses, planning department approved signage, and phone directory ads deplete your savings nest egg and make a sizable dent in your various credit cards.

You delight in decorating your shop. You create a crafts studio in the back room connected to the living room/showroom of your store, aptly named "Cheryl's Gift Shoppe." You paint the walls a deep rose, drape miles of white netting over mauve-painted wooden curtain rods above the tall double hung windows, and arrange lace tablecloths and silk flowers on display tables. You've spent months building your inventory of your signature birdhouses as well as hand-crafted cloth dolls, hand-painted glass vases, picture frames, and plates. You round out your selection with purchased decorative pieces and scented candles.

As the first few months go by with a mere trickle of customers, primarily comprised of family and friends, your excitement over your new business quickly wanes. Your heart sinks when the Christmas holiday season slips by with few shoppers even stopping by to see your festive decorations and array of hand-made ornaments. In January you must face the fact that the location of your lovely shop in the charming Victorian house stinks.

You begin to understand why the former tenant, the antique shop, couldn't make it. You thought you had a better idea, but now you realize that no idea could create the traffic you need to stay afloat, especially in Merced's lousy economy. You don't know what you're going to do to pay the rent for the remainder of the lease. Tom tries not to say anything, but you know he's upset. You feel foolish and sick.

BENEFITS OF C:

- You take a leave of absence from your teaching job.
- You turn something you love doing into a business.
- You find a charming store and enjoy decorating it.
- You set up shop, order stationery, and feel like a real businesswoman.

DOWNSIDES OF C:

- You expect to recreate a store you've seen elsewhere with little consideration of how long it takes to develop a business to that point.
- You do not investigate why the last tenant left the site.
- You do no market study to see if a store like yours would attract customers.
- You pay no attention to the possible effects of the sagging economy.

- You spend money on expensive stationery, buy new business machines, and hook up an 800 number, when you could have accumulated them more gradually and economically.
- You "play" business rather than create a business plan and follow it.
- You spend your savings nest egg and pile up expenses on your credit cards.
- You're stuck with a lease that you don't know how you'll pay off.
- You upset your husband and yourself.

D. I'll seek help from a business advisor.

Over dinner you explain to Tom that you want to do something other than teaching. "I feel stuck in a rut. I just can't muster the old enthusiasm. There's got to be something I can do that would make me feel creative and alive. I really want to start my own business, but I just don't know what it could be. Didn't you tell me about someone you knew who helps people start businesses?"

"You bet, Cher. There's a guy at work whose wife mentors entrepreneurs. I don't know much about it, but I could find out for you. Could be a smart move for you," Tom offers.

"I hope she's not expensive."

"So what? If she can get you on track, it's worth it."

"Thanks, Tom. I hope she has time to see me."

"You're really sick of teaching, aren't you?"

You roll your hazel eyes. Enough said.

Two weeks later you meet with Sara Kirkland, a certified professional personal coach, at your home after school. You ask her just what a personal coach does.

"Well, basically, Cheryl, I help my clients identify dreams and goals, live their vision, maintain momentum by working through obstacles, keep their balance, and increase their self-esteem."

"Do you wave a magic wand?" you quip.

"It's not as hard as it sounds. We start with clarifying your values, and we keep those in mind throughout. Clarifying your values greatly simplifies the decision making process." Sara hands you a sample list of values, which include: accomplishment, accuracy, acknowledgment, adventure, beauty, independence, peace, personal power, plus dozens more.

"Okay. I get it. How many can you choose?" you ask.

"However many fit you. The trick here is that you need to prioritize them. Next, we look at how you currently balance your life."

"Balance? Like a tightrope act?" you laugh.

"Well, there's prioritizing again. Think of your life as a pie chart. Divide the pie into sections representing career, money, health, family and friends, personal time, romance, and fun, and you'll see how you prioritize your time."

"But how do you help someone like me who wants to start a business but doesn't have a clue what it could be?"

"Cheryl, I act as a sounding board to your subconscious. There's a lot about what you want to do that you already know. We just have to bring those thoughts to the surface. We can do this through a series of questions about your passions, what you naturally do well, what you want to express, what you would do if you knew you wouldn't fail, that sort of thing. It's amazing what bubbles up, often from childhood dreams, to form a clear vision."

"Are you really a career counselor or consultant?"

"No, Cheryl, let me explain the difference. Personal coaching didn't exist before 1990. Think of me as a mind coach who helps people get unstuck, find out what they want to do, and helps them get there. I focus not only on careers but on life as a whole. A traditional career counselor usually helps people identify a field they want to enter or assists experienced workers changing careers. Consultants help executives find high-paying jobs."

"How long does this take, and what will it cost?"

"This first consultation, as I mentioned over the phone, costs you nothing. We can work together on initial goal planning, a one-hour session, or a longer two-hour strategic planning session. I would recommend that we enter into an ongoing coaching relationship which includes those sessions and weekly coaching phone calls. That way I can offer the best results and keep you accountable for reaching your goals. Normally sessions run from $100 to $125 per hour, but an ongoing coaching relationship costs from $200 to $500 a month. You can decide how long you'd like to participate in the program. That should give you a ballpark idea of costs and time. Why don't you think about it, then give me a call next week."

"Thank you, Sara."

Over dinner, you tell Tom about what you've learned. He has also done some research for you and found a list headed by two organizations: the International Coach Federation at (888) 423-3131, and the Professional and Personal Coaches Association in San Francisco at (415) 522-8789. He also discovered several training schools: New Ventures in West San Francisco at (800) 332-4618; The Coaches Training Institute in San Rafael, California at (415) 274-7551; Success Unlimited Network in Reston, Virginia, (703) 716-8374; and Coach University in Houston at (800) 482-6224. You plan to contact a few of them for more information.

Three years later, fortified by Sara's initial coaching, you totally enjoy running your successful tea house, open 11:00 till 4:00, five days a week in a lovely yellow Victorian home across from the old courthouse.

BENEFITS OF D:

- You discuss your dilemma with your husband.
- You seek professional advice to help you decide what you want to do.
- You ask about the distinction between personal coaches and counselors/consultants.
- You obtain the specifics about how coaches work and what they cost.
- You do further research into personal coaching by calling for information and referrals before making a decision.
- You decide to hire your coach and develop a business you love that doesn't consume your life.

DOWNSIDES OF D:

- You ignore any other suggestions and advice about business possibilities.
- You look to someone else for answers only you can ultimately provide.
- You pay someone to do what you know you could do yourself, if you took the time to think about it.
- You leave a salaried position for an entrepreneurial risk.

Exploring the Issue

A woman in one of my seminars came up to the microphone and asked my panel, composed of some of the women quoted in my book, *The Eleven Commandments*, "What do you do when you have only a vague idea of what you want to do, you want to flow with it, but you can't quite envision it? How do you get out of the fog? How do you get beyond the block?"

Working through that fog becomes the first priority. First, figure out what constitutes your fog. Is it expectations, yours or others'? Is it fear of failure, of success, or fear of feeling like an impostor? If it's not expectations or fear, then have you taken time to assess your true wants and needs?

Before you can become a master "fogbuster," you need to choose a direction. You can do this any number of ways. One, you can do it alone by writing out your ideas and exploring where you want to go. This involves asking yourself many questions, like the ones listed at the end of this chapter. Two, you can confide in a friend or a relative who can act as a sounding board for your ideas. Bear in mind, however, they may not be as open to your ideas because often they have their own agendas for your time and commitments. Three, you can seek professional advice through a career counselor or consultant, a professional personal coach, or even a psychoanalyst. In Option D, the character contacts a professional personal coach, but I'm not recommending a coach over a consultant, a counselor, or any other type of professional advisors. I meant only to illustrate a point and to let you know that coaching does offer a new option.

Once you develop a clue as to where you want to go, whether you do your own research or hire a consultant, you'll want to plan how to get there. However, watch out for two major barriers to success: self-doubt and lack of research.

Self-doubt, often disguised as anxiety attacks, keeps many great ideas from ever going beyond that stage. It's easy to question yourself, asking, "Am I fundamentally right?" "Can I sell this concept?" "Will I look stupid?" and "How can I counteract naysayers?" To overcome such attacks play "Name That Fear." Identify it. Challenge it. Weaken it by thinking, "What is the worst that can happen?" Once named, any fear can be conquered with research and knowledge. Learn details about the business you're thinking of starting, and learn where to get and manage money to make it successful.

Don't go into business blindly. That may sound obvious, but many women see a successful business and think, "Ah, yes, that's *exactly* what I want," without realizing the evolution of that business. Perhaps it started years ago in the owner's garage. Maybe it's been in three locations, or expanded twice. You may walk into a business and, with instant recognition, say, "This is it," but what you're seeing represents the end product of years of trial and error and eons of effort. Why should you assume you could duplicate that instantaneously? When it doesn't happen that way, you can easily lose your shirt. Take your blinders off by gathering all the knowledge you can from reading or talking to others. Join a support group, business association, or professional association. You'll find more than sounding boards, you'll find sound advice forged from experience. Through research, knowledge, and guidance you can create an effective plan of action.

Expanding Your Thinking

In this adventure "you" want to start your own business but you don't know what it should be. Most of the options in this adventure turn out well, with a few downsides. One option, however, created huge problems. Let's look at what caused the negative results.

While Option A turns out well, one of its weak points was not telling Tom about your frustrations with teaching at Herbert Hoover Junior High. You assume he knows, but you don't share with him what's going on in your mind. Naturally, he's ill-prepared to respond enthusiastically to your idea to start a business, plus he doubts your sincerity. His lack of understanding makes you mad, but you can only blame yourself if he doesn't understand you.

Option B includes few downsides, but what went wrong in Option C? Why couldn't you turn a passion into a business? In three words: lack of planning. You don't appreciate the fact that a business takes time to evolve, and that its success depends to some degree on the overall economic climate. In the highly successful store in Fresno, you saw the end product after years of development, and you expect to recreate that overnight without learning anything about what makes such a store successful. You neglect to inquire why the antique shop went out of business in your location. You don't look into leasing office equipment rather than buying new. You enjoy "playing" businesswoman, but you don't take any classes or contact the Small Business Administration for guidance. Many women new to the business world waste precious start-up money on expensive stationery, business cards, and brochures. Certainly you want to present a creative and professional appearance through your cards and literature, but the problem with this is that, in addition to spending a lot of money, you need time to learn just what image best fits your business. For instance, if your shop attracts mostly grandmothers, why print a brochure offering a corporate gift program?

In Option C, your overspending worries Tom, who tries to be a good guy and not say anything, but this puts a strain on your marriage, as well as your budget.

In Option D, you have to spend money on a coach after you leave a solid, salaried position at the junior high school, when you might have better invested that money in an actual business venture.

What should you watch out for when starting your own business?

DON'T:

1. Keep your frustrations about work and your desires to search for something new to yourself.
2. Ignore the possibility of doing something totally different from anything you've done before.
3. Think you'll discover what you want to do without actively searching for it.
4. Assume you'll "recognize it when you see it."

5. Talk yourself out of something when you sense, “Maybe I can do that.”
6. Get mad at others around you for not understanding your goals or supporting you, if you haven’t shared your goals with them.
7. Jeopardize your current job by using company time to develop your own business.
8. Simply play store.
9. Fall in love with a building and assume the location is perfect for your business.
10. Let your fears override your will to develop your business.

What works well? In Option A, you employ the “I’ll know it when I see it” approach. This approach doesn’t always work, but in this case it does because you remain open to ideas that are totally different from what you’ve done before. Going to the conference in Dallas helps you to focus beyond the boundaries of your home town. You see a bigger view of the world, of businesses, and your potential role in them. Also in this option, you pay attention to your gut feelings, research what a concierge business entails, and test the waters by renting booth space at several conventions before you quit teaching.

In Option B, you develop your passion for cooking into a business. When your friend, Jennifer, encourages you to attend classes, you adopt a “why not?” attitude. To your surprise you become fascinated with the art of teaching cooking. You attend class after class and take notes on how you would do it yourself. You realize that you can transfer many of your techniques from teaching junior high into teaching cooking. You also challenge your creative side by writing a cookbook and getting it published.

In Option C, you jump before you do any research, but the positive things you do include developing your love for making crafts into a business, finding a charming location for your business, and decorating it. Plus, you maintain a fall-back plan. You take a leave of absence from teaching but know there is always room for a teacher with your particular language skills.

It's always worth researching where to find professional advice. In Option D, you explore one form of counseling. You research it well, get quotes, referrals, and information from every possible resource. You choose to pay for coaching and develop a successful business that you enjoy but that doesn't take over your life.

What positive ideas from this chapter can you apply in your own life?

DO:

1. Stay open to new ideas.
2. Believe you can turn a passion into a business.
3. Pay attention to your gut reaction to new ideas.
4. Formulate ideas for a business and then talk to people in that field, attend classes, research it, and test it out before you take the plunge.
5. If you have a family, discuss your business plans with them.
6. Turn something you love into a business, but treat it like a business and not a hobby.
7. Use family and friends as sounding boards, but keep alert to their own agendas.
8. Seek professional advice.
9. Research and choose the type of counseling you feel most comfortable using.
10. Plan for personal and family time when developing your own business.

Assessing Your Own Situation

1. If you can't decide what kind of a business you want to start, ask yourself, "Why do I want to start a business?" "What part of me am I trying to fulfill?"
2. When you want information about a type of business, ask yourself, "Have I contacted similar companies to get information?" "Do I know the names of trade journals in that industry?"
3. When you're seeking ideas for a business, ask, "Am I open to unusual ideas?" and "Can I see myself enjoying my new role?"
4. If the timing is right, the concept is right, your funding is in place, and you still can't get moving toward your goal, ask, "What am I afraid of?" "Can I identify those fears?" and "What can I do to work around and through them?"
5. Are you plagued with an overwhelming sense of responsibility? Ask, "What can I do to prepare for possible failure before I get it going?"
6. If you don't feel secure in your decision to start a business, ask yourself, "Have I done enough research to validate my concept?" "Can I explain the idea clearly to someone else?"
7. When you aren't sure you're on the right track, ask, "Where can I find sound advice?"
8. Ask, "Am I willing to think big and start small?" and "Have I identified and prioritized my values?"

Affirmation

Commandment 2:
Take responsibility for your career.

"I will identify my values and create a successful and rewarding business."

ADVENTURE 6

HOW DO I REGAIN CONTROL WHEN I'M GOING THROUGH A DIVORCE, WORK AT HOME WITH TWO SMALL KIDS, AND JUST STARTED CHEMOTHERAPY?

Have you or a close friend ever grappled with challenges at work and at home when a severe health problem blindsided you? This may seem like an extreme case, but you will most likely find yourself dealing with all these problems (work, life, and health) at the same time, albeit in milder forms than you'll encounter aboard **The Good Ship Titanic.**

The Good Ship Titanic

After you pull into your driveway and set the brake on your maroon Honda Civic, you walk to the street and pull down the beak of the mallard head mailbox door to collect your mail. Inside you find a piece of junk mail addressed to "Occupant" soliciting business for a local Atlanta funeral home. You laugh at the sick irony of its arrival on the very day you've been diagnosed with cancer.

Once inside your rented home, you flop down on your slip-covered couch and call your mother to tell her the diagnosis. You both cry at the injustice of it all, though your combined tears do little to salve or dilute your overall anxiety over the difficulties you face. In two hours you must pick up the kids at day care. You try to compose yourself. Then you reach for the phone and dial your good friend in Washington, DC.

"Hello, Diana? It's Carol." You don't wait for her to respond. "Are you sitting down?"

You hear a tentative, "Hi, Carol. What's up?"

"Well, this is the year I'm finally going to lose my baby fat." You've fought an extra twenty pounds since the birth of Lisa, your second child, four years ago.

"Oh, really?" Diana replies, obviously confused.

"Yes," you laugh, trying to sound cheerful. "I've found a new weight loss program guaranteed to get results. Chemotherapy and radiation."

"My God, Carol. What's happening?"

"Right now, the doctors don't know exactly. I went to my doctor two months ago with chest pains and he said I had bronchitis, though he ordered no tests. He sent me home with some antibiotics. I called him again ten days ago explaining that the pain had become so severe that I can't stand even the pressure of my cat's paw on my chest. He finally ordered a chest x-ray and discovered what looks like a five-pound mass in my media stynum, my chest cavity. It's pushing against one lung and my heart. I went to an oncologist today who verified I have cancer of some sort. He took a biopsy with the biggest needle you've ever seen. If that doesn't explain it, he will make an incision to take a bigger biopsy. He's hoping it's only lymphoma."

"Instead of what?" Diana gasps.

"Instead of carcinoma and instead of it spreading to other organs."

"My God."

"It's going to be okay, Di. I didn't call to worry you, but I knew you'd want to know."

Your friendship with Diana formed fifteen years ago over Christmas cookie recipes. You'd tried by phone to set up a business meeting with her, but it had taken months of canceled appointments before you finally met. Diana worked as a meeting planner and you for a speakers' bureau in Atlanta. During one phone conversation to set up yet another lunch date, Diana said, "It's July, but it's going to be Christmas cookie time before we meet at this rate, Carol."

You remember laughing, "Do you make Christmas cookies, too?" When Diana answered, "Tons," you knew you'd like her. A few days later, you waited at the Hyatt for your lunch appointment. You sat back in your chair and laughed out loud when Diana walked into the restaurant. She looked just as she'd described, a slightly older version of yourself: tall, blond hair worn in a ponytail, Nordic. You both were wearing the same color outfit. Over the years you've "been there" emotionally for each other through Diana's divorce, and then your own from Bill. You've shared cookie recipes, home-based business schemes, computer knowledge, child rearing advice, eyelash curlers, and marketing ideas. She's like a sister.

Diana breaks your reverie when you hear her asking if there's anything she can do. "Di, it seems that everyone wants to do something for me. You wouldn't believe all of the unsolicited advice, or worse yet, the horror stories of people who have had cancer. I think I can handle things myself. Of course, I know I can't count on Bill's support. He's using this 'opportunity' to try to get custody of the kids. So I get to fight that battle as well. My Mom has enough on her hands with Dad's second brain tumor operation last week but, nevertheless, she wants to schedule my friends to come in at intervals to cook, clean, whatever. Since I don't know what schedules I'll be on myself, it's driving me crazy trying to keep everyone from running my life. I know they mean well."

"You know I'll fly down in a minute if you need me," Diana offers.

"I know. The biggest issue right now though is that I'm not sure just how I'm going to explain everything to the kids. I don't know much myself yet. To tell you the truth, Di, I'm feeling totally out of control."

"One step at a time, Carol. And here's another piece of unsolicited advice for you..."

"Oh, no," you groan, laughing.

"Just say 'yes' to all offers of help. You don't need to be fiercely independent right now, just gracefully dependent for a while until you get back your equilibrium."

After a few "I love you's" and "I'll be all right's" you hang up the phone. You love talking to Diana because with her you can express your deepest fears, discuss the greater scheme of life, and reveal secrets you'd never tell your mother. You realize the enormity of your situation, but refuse to think it's the end of the world, or of you, for that matter.

In an effort to regain control of your life, you create a list of options.

What Would You Do?

A. I will take it one day at a time until I get over the hump.

B. I can gracefully accept the help others insist I need.

C. I can join a support group to help me find out how to regain control of my life.

D. I can reduce my work hours with clients until I get back on my feet.

Turn to the option that most appeals to you. To learn the most from this adventure, read how the other options turned out, too. Then study the last three sections of this adventure: "Exploring the Issue," "Expanding Your Thinking," and "Assessing Your Situation."

A. I will take it one day at a time until I get over the hump.

You call your kids' pediatrician, Suzanne Swanson, who has also become a personal friend, to let her know about the biopsy.

"Carol, when do you go back to the oncologist?" she asks.

"Sentencing is Tuesday morning at ten o'clock."

"I'll reschedule a few of my appointments, I'm going with you," Suzanne insists.

Suzanne turns out to be a real savior. She translates the mumbo jumbo medicalese your primary care doctor dispenses. She's the one who tells you to check immediately with your HMO to see if you can get permission to see Dr. James, an oncologist who's not on their preferred list of doctors. What a fiasco that was.

When you called the HMO last Monday after your chest x-ray, the receptionist had asked you why you needed to see a different doctor. You answered, "Because he's the oncologist who my primary care doctor recommended."

"We'll get back to you in a couple weeks," the receptionist responded blandly.

"No, you don't understand, I need to see the oncologist on Friday and I need your approval first." You felt your ire rising but tried to control yourself.

"Is this an emergency?" the receptionist asked in her nasal monotone.

"I have a five-pound, malignant mass pushing against my heart. Yes, yes, I would say that I consider this an emergency. Look, I need that approval by Thursday. Okay?" You felt like grabbing her by the throat through the phone line. "Insipid, thoughtless insurance people," you muttered as you slammed the phone down. Nevertheless, Suzanne had advised you well. Your special dispensation came in time for your appointment.

On Tuesday, Suzanne meets you at Dr. James' office. He explains that you have non-Hodgkin's lymphoma.

Suzanne grabs your hand and says quickly, "Carol, this is not a death sentence."

You look Dr. James in the eye and ask, "If I were your wife or your daughter, would you tell me I'll beat this thing?"

"Absolutely," he smiles as he moves around his desk to give you a hug. Your tears well to overflowing.

Outside of the office, before Suzanne rushes back to her own practice, you say, "Thank you, that was a fabulous gift you gave me in there."

"No problem, Carol. Need a lift home?"

"Nope, I'm stopping by the costume store to buy clown wigs for the kids and me. We may as well have fun when mommy loses her hair."

"I've been truly impressed by how you've explained things to Lisa and Neil."

"Thanks, Suzanne. Thanks for everything."

That evening you call Diana with the good news, "It's only lymphoma. I start chemo on Friday."

"Great. So, Rapunzel, when do you start losing your long, flaxen hair?"

"Oh, I had it cut really short a week ago so the effect won't be as dramatic. I think what's left starts falling out after the second or third session. You know, Di, I've been explaining to the kids what could happen in sort of a storybook way. I draw pictures, they color them. I've been drawing bald mommies and mommies with silly wigs, so I brought home curly orange, blue, and green striped clown wigs for all of us this afternoon. We had a ball. Sometimes the kids draw their own pictures. Neil drew me an unhappy face at school. His teacher helped him spell out 'It's okay to cry.'"

"Oh, Carol, that's so sad, but sweet. You're doing a great job with the kids. I mean, it has to be hard for a four- and six-year-old to comprehend and not get too frightened."

"The concept is hard, but they can see the four-inch biopsy scar on my chest. They know mommy has an 'owee.' They can relate to that. I told them when mommy is all better, we're going to Disneyland. When Neil asked when that would be, I told him when my hair grows back."

"Have you thought of turning your storybook drawings into a coloring book? Other kids and their parents could use that."

You laugh. Throughout your relationship with Diana, some fun, crazy business scheme has always emerged. However, this idea definitely merits consideration, for many reasons.

Ten months later you're in what the doctor calls remission, though you say you've beaten the disease. The response to the small ad for your coloring book that you place in the back of *Mother's Day* magazine has absolutely floored you. Hundreds of orders come in monthly for *Mommy's Bad Hair Day*, the coloring book you designed on your computer. You're currently working on a series of them and *Mother's Day* is running a feature story on you next month.

You're happy, despite the hassles of the interminable divorce. You keep your focus on the children, living one day at a time. Your regular business has kept you afloat and now the success of the coloring book adds a new dimension to your life. Your hair has grown in curly, but luckily not orange, blue, and green striped. And you're all heading to Disneyland next weekend.

BENEFITS OF A:

- You maintain a sense of humor.
- You call for support when you need it.
- You confer with people who can explain the medical terminology and procedures you don't understand.
- You notify your HMO and make certain your insurance covers the oncologist.
- You think of the kids first, buy wigs, and draw pictures to explain what's happening to you.
- You follow up on Diana's suggestion to create a coloring book about cancer.
- You beat your cancer, appreciate your life, enjoy your coloring book business, and laugh at your curly hair.

DOWNSIDES OF A:

- You count on Suzanne to explain the medical procedures and terminology rather than discussing them with your own doctor.

- You do no reading or research to educate yourself about your disease.
- You fail to avail yourself of other sources of help, such as support groups and other women who have battled cancer successfully.

B. I can gracefully accept the help others insist I need.

You decide to "just say yes" to anyone's offer of assistance. After your first chemo session, you're glad you let your good friend Phoebe drive you, then take the kids for the weekend. No one had told you ahead of time that you would become a toxic mom for at least forty-eight hours after the needle pours your "chemo cocktail" into your veins. You quickly discover that you really do need help with the children after each session because you can't let any of your body fluids touch them. Not even a kiss, you're that toxic. No one is allowed to enter your bathroom, touch your toothbrush, or wash your clothes. You remember Karen Silkwood, the woman contaminated with radiation at the nuclear power plant where she worked, whose whistle-blower story was immortalized in the 1980s movie bearing her name and starring Cher. In the movie everything Karen touched became contaminated, too. She frightened herself, just as you frighten yourself.

You've learned that you can't count on Bill to honor his weekends taking the kids, so you accept your sister's offer to come and stay with you for an unspecified period of time. Your never-married-without-children older sister arrived on Monday and has commandeered your home in the name of sisterly assistance. Because of her allergies, she requires your bedroom with the filtered air conditioner to sleep safely sheltered from your dander-laden cats. You're relegated to the lumpy sofa bed in the living room, though your sister does loan you her eye shades to block out the early morning rays that blast through the opaque skylight. "A thoughtful gesture," you try to convince yourself.

Amazingly, within a matter of minutes after settling into her routine and replacing all of yours, your sister has transformed herself into Dr. Spock and Adele Davis rolled into one. Her heretofore unbeknownst wisdom concerning child rearing and nutrition rears its authoritative head and informs you how poorly your children behave and how pathetically their nutritional needs are met. "A truly brilliant observation," you tell her, as she proceeds to correct your misdoings.

She acts as grand marshal, leading the parade of well-wishers who supply an endless stream of casseroles, cookies, and offers to watch the children. You conclude that there's no need to lock the front door, no real reason to fix the broken doorbell, because the throng enters at all hours without knocking anyway. "*Mi casa es su casa*," has taken on an entirely new meaning for you: "My house is no longer my house, it's all *yours*."

You've named the second Tuesday after each Friday chemo session, spaced six weeks apart, "Alcatraz Day," and plan your work accordingly. You don't dare schedule any activity farther than ten feet away from "your" bathroom door. Though you *should* feel freer to concentrate on your home-based graphic design and marketing business with the help of everyone's well-intentioned assistance, you can't concentrate. It's not the drugs or your sour stomach that distracts you, but your total lack of control, even in your own home.

Finally, when you've taken all the kindness you can tolerate, you throw everyone out, politely but firmly. You call Inez, your once-a-week cleaning lady, to come in for a few hours daily after school to watch the children as she has offered. You reclaim your home and your sanity. Not surprisingly, you discover that you and the kids can now relax, and you find it much easier to complete your work.

BENEFITS OF B:

- You learn you really do need assistance and accept all offers of help.
- Your sister moves in to help you take care of the house and the kids.
- You're blessed with many friends who supply food and child care.
- You hire Inez for the help you want, when you want it.

DOWNSIDES OF B:

- Everyone's good intentions get out of hand and take over your life, rendering you helpless and increasing your out-of-control feelings.
- Your sister's support turns into smothering criticism.
- Your home no longer feels like a safe haven.
- You can't get your work done.

C. I can join a support group to help me find out how to regain control of my life.

Several weeks go by as you undergo chemotherapy, and your old routine has almost emerged from the chaos, but you continue to feel anxious. Your current support group consists of your family, friends, and your kids' pediatrician who has personally talked you through the scary first days of your encounter with cancer. You appreciate them all, but wish to find people who are going through the same experience so you can really let your hair down, so to speak.

You check out the Internet for non-Hodgkin's lymphoma and find a super lymphoma chat room, nhl-request@jubjub.wizard.com. You gain a great deal of insight and background on-line, but you long for personal contact, group camaraderie, the breathing of actual people. Your oncologist, Dr. James, suggests you join a cancer support group available through Northside Hospital. It turns out that the group meets every Wednesday evening at seven-thirty.

The following Wednesday, you hire the babysitter from next door. Then you drive along the now familiar route to Peachtree-Dunwoody Road and turn into the visitor parking lot at Northside Hospital. You hesitate before you enter the blue carpeted meeting room, straighten your wig, then laugh at your own vanity. "In the land of the bald, the woman with a wig is queen," you mumble.

In the rather austere meeting room you observe five people sitting in an imperfect circle of molded plastic chairs, two others standing in the corner by the coffee urn talking quietly. A pleasant looking man, six feet tall and trim, in his mid-forties, looks at you still frozen in the doorway. He gets up and welcomes you with an extended hand.

"Hi, I'm Andre Cutinnet. You're new here."

"Yes, thanks, I mean, I'm Carol Carlson. Hello." You find the warmth of his hand as comforting as his smile. "Am I in the right place? The lymphoma support group?"

"Baldies Anonymous, at your service," Andre teases.

You like him instantly.

By the end of your first meeting you have gained seven new cancer-bonded friends. Besides the inestimable benefit of listening to and airing your own fears and frustrations, you learn some very practical information. A silver-haired woman in the group tells you that if your husband's policy provides your health insurance, you should hold off on divorce proceedings until you can qualify for your own insurance. "It might be difficult getting new coverage with a pre-existing condition," says the group matron. You plan to check it out with your attorney tomorrow, but suddenly tears spring to your eyes.

"It'll be okay, Carol," Andre reassures you, his chestnut eyes locked on yours.

You learn that Andre lost his wife to breast cancer four years ago and now he fights his own battle with Hodgkin's disease. He has a ten-year-old son, two dogs, and a hamster. Though you feel totally unattractive—bloated by prednizone, the steroid you're taking—you feel an attraction to this lovely man. When he asks if he can phone you tomorrow to check how you're doing, you say yes, sensing that somehow, through this support group in general, and through this caring man specifically, you will gain control of your life.

Prophetically, eighteen months later, both Andre's cancer and yours have gone into remission, and when your divorce from Bill finalizes, you become Mrs. Andre Cutinnet.

BENEFITS OF C:

- You seek support from Internet chat rooms and a group at the hospital.
- You find comfort in the support group and receive useful information about protecting your health insurance.
- You meet Andre and start a new life.

DOWNSIDES OF C:

- While it's wonderful to feel cared for and supported, you are vulnerable to Andre's attentions, and may bond with him for the wrong reasons.
- You focus your attention on Andre rather than participating fully in the support group.
- You put your family and friends on the sidelines.

D. I can reduce my work hours with clients until I get back on my feet.

After your first chemo session you call Diana to tell her about it. Somehow, discussing it lessens the shock of it all. Your conversation drifts to how you're coping.

"What about your business?" Diana asks.

"I'm afraid to let my clients know about my condition right away, until I get a handle on things. I have two new marketing accounts and just landed a contract to manage a national convention and exposition for the National Speakers' Bureau in Fort Worth next October. Business is booming. Great timing, huh?"

"Murphy's Law #1,002 I'll bet," Diana concurs. "Is there any way you can cut back?"

"I've put a message on my business answering machine saying that I'm only available Monday through Thursday, 10:00 to 3:30, and I let the machine screen my calls. I hope I can work that much with the holidays approaching. The kids will be home more. But I've got to keep my clients happy to pay the rent."

"Yeah, and you've got to find time to bake your Christmas cookies," Diana laughs.

"Oh, I've already got a jump-start on that, I made dough last month and stuck it in the freezer!"

"Of course, why didn't I think of that? What about your client load, can you jettison any of them without losing sleep?"

"Well, my P.I.A. list is getting rather large..."

"P.I.A. list?"

"Yeah, Pain In the You-Know-What list," you laugh. "On the plus side, I'm working on a publicity program for a shopping center to sell to its board next month. I've worked with them before; they're a good group. If I win that, then I'll cut the P.I.A.'s. I'll let you know how it goes."

After your second chemo session your hair starts falling out in clumps, worse than a shedding dog, and scarier. Your children, Neil and Lisa, look horrified until you commission them to help pull out the rest "so it doesn't make a mess all over the floor." The kids found it great fun, especially when they helped you select a short blond wig from the three you'd purchased.

That's the wig you wear into the shopping center board meeting to present your publicity program the following week. Everyone present, save one curmudgeon, readily supports your plan. The curmudgeon asks you to repeat several points, which you do, then he blankly asks, "Why should I agree to this?"

You smile, whip off your wig and announce, "Bccause you can't say no to a bald woman!"

And he didn't.

You relish telling Diana that story, and how you plan to delegate the implementation of the campaign, since most of the work lay in the planning. "And Di, I can't tell you how delighted I felt when I called the top two P.I.A.'s on my list, both notorious complainers and rotten bill payers, to tell them that I would be out of commission for a while due to a health emergency. The amazing thing is I thought I'd be feeling really terrible about now, but I seem to have more energy than I've had in years."

"Well, you've been carrying around that five-pound mass for about the last four years. You probably had a hard time breathing."

"I thought I was just out of shape," you admit.

"Take it easy, Carol. Conserve your energy."

"Oh, I am. I've got my housekeeper, Inez, coming in a couple hours every afternoon so I can get some extra work done, take a nap, or watch silly movies with the kids. She's great."

"I'm really glad things seem to be working out, Carol."

"Well, I'll tell you, I truly believe in keeping a sense of humor. Have you seen Chevy Chase's *Las Vegas Vacation*?

"A long time ago."

"Well, rent the video again. It's hilarious, a real endorphin popper."

"So that's your secret to staying so positive. You're great."

"I feel a whole lot more in control of things now. Just knowing what the medical procedures entail and how they affect me is a huge help. Having Inez come in daily is wonderful. Also, working with clients who know what I'm going through makes it easier, because they appreciate my efforts. I asked one client when he actually needed the layout for his brochure, and he told me in one week. I looked him in the eye and asked if that was absolutely necessary. He reassessed on the spot, gave me three weeks and a wink."

Diana cracks up. "Hey, I haven't had that much attention from the opposite sex in years."

Her response makes you laugh until your sides hurt.

BENEFITS OF D:

- You discuss your medical experiences with friends.
- You don't discuss your illness with your clients until you can assure them that you can accomplish your work while undergoing treatment.
- You cut back your work hours and let your answering machine screen your calls.
- You cut back your client list by ridding yourself of the most annoying ones.
- You delegate the implementation of the shopping center publicity campaign.
- You get your housekeeper to come in daily.
- You maintain your sense of humor by watching funny movies with your kids.
- You feel more in control.

DOWNSIDES OF D:

- You use a rather shocking tactic to win the shopping center account.
- You take on the expense of a daily housekeeper.
- You try to keep too many business projects going instead of recuperating between chemo sessions.
- You ignore looking into other support groups, both formal and informal, who might offer assistance and information.

Exploring the Issue

Life does not dish out one problem at a time like a game of tennis, serving one ball we can hit back and forth until the end of the game. No, life likes to serve several problems at us all at once. Trying to regain a sense of equilibrium, let alone control, during those times seems like a Herculean task. Yet, none of us can escape to life's turmoil. If you find yourself grappling with multiple problems at some point in your life, you can gain guidance and inspiration by studying how others made it though similar crises. But you'll also want to believe in your heart that you will make it though with clarity and dignity.

The story in this adventure may seem like an extreme situation, but unfortunately it's not uncommon for people to become ill during or shortly after high-stress periods of their lives. This character didn't ask for, or expect, the new crisis which altered her life so quickly and dramatically, nor would any of us. But it does happen.

When I first developed the idea for this book and wrote down the questions for the chapter titles, my agent, Mike Snell, told me I hadn't hit some of the really gut-wrenching issues women face. When my revised list hit his desk, he called me.

"Pam, you've really given the woman in Adventure 6 a triple whammy."

"I know," I said, "I couldn't dream up something like that. It's what my close friend Julie is currently going through."

The most bizarre, difficult, and seemingly absurd stories in this book spring from real life situations. I change the names, places, and most of the details of the characters to protect privacy, but purely fictional situations simply don't compare to the real-life, sometimes unreal, sagas women face every day. A woman who contacted me via e-mail because she had read about *The Eleven Commandments* on the Internet, shared her situation and wanted my advice. She's almost forty, wants to start her own business, but since her husband has been disabled for six years and can't work, and since she's pregnant with child number eight, she feels she has to remain in her corporate job, though at under $50,000 a year salary, she finds it tough to make ends meet. Who could possibly make up a story like that? Not me. That's when I know life has no scruples when it comes to throwing problems at people.

When I asked Julie how she would advise women in similar situations, who may have a life-threatening illness, and who feel they've lost control, she offered the following helpful points:

1. Get a second opinion. Julie researched the number one research facility in the country for her kind of cancer, and made an appointment.
2. Set your own boundaries. Don't try to act or do as you think others expect. Honor your needs, not what others say you need. Ask others to honor those needs, but understand that it's hard for caring people to remain bystanders.
3. Know your limitations. Don't try to maintain your pre-illness pace. You have nothing to prove to anyone by trying to be superhuman. If you respect yourself and your abilities, others will, too.

4. Take one day at a time. Chemotherapy affects everyone differently, and it can affect you differently each time. Julie describes her "side effect of the day," from tingling fingers to exhaustion to nausea.

5. Don't be afraid to "pester" your doctor. At first Julie didn't want to bother her doctor with questions about all her ailments because she attributed everything to chemotherapy. She learned it's important to ask the medical staff questions and alert them to any difficulties, which may stem not from the chemo, but from something more serious. She refers to one nurse as "Goddess Vickie" who knew all the answers, and wanted Julie to know them too.

6. Befriend the medical staff. Julie brought in wine for the nurses on her first chemotherapy session. It's important to recognize that they are there to help you. They appreciate being acknowledged for doing their job. On Julie's sixth and final chemo session she brought champagne for the staff and thanked them. Later Julie discovered she needed two more sessions and six weeks of radiation.

7. Do something nice for yourself at least once a day. That could mean sitting with a cup of coffee and reading the paper for fifteen minutes, or taking a bubble bath. Take a walk, eat some caramel corn, buy yourself a box of chocolate truffles and allow yourself one a day. Buy flannel pajamas. Do something, large or small, for yourself every day.

8. Keep your sense of humor. Julie went to the Disney store and bought Goofy, Mickey Mouse, and Winnie-the-Pooh baseball caps for herself. A friend sent her two "Princess Caroline" turbans, and signed the card, "Love from Monaco."

9. Recognize that this is your journey. Keep a scrapbook or write in a journal. Look at it as a meaningful chapter in your life. Live it, appreciate the lessons and the kindnesses.

10. Keep lists. List what you need the week you go to chemotherapy: someone to come with me, someone to watch the children, flavored water in the refrigerator because plain water makes me sick, soda crackers, and cat food for the kittens. Keep a list of doctors, their phone numbers and addresses handy. List your medications. Make a new budget listing what you may need to spend related to your treatment, clothes, medications, treats.

11. Recognize that happiness is a personal choice. It's your choice to be happy in illness, in work, in life. Don't expect that others or any things will make you happy.

12. Give yourself and others the gift of laughter. Julie rented funny movies. She brought them into her chemo sessions and donated them when she was finished there. Funny things happened to Julie throughout her fight with cancer. She attended her children's school bowling night fundraiser and won the door prize, a free hair cut and color from a local beauty salon. Everyone at the bowling alley laughed because Julie allowed them to see the humor and not feel embarrassed for her.

13. Believe in prayers. Even if you don't have a strong spiritual background, trust that the prayers from others are pulling for you. Draw strength from that. If you are spiritual, trust your prayers.

14. Recognize your illness as a gift. Julie said she had no idea that she had so many friends. She felt like Jimmy Stewart in *It's a Wonderful Life*. Although she stopped working so hard, she still makes just as much money. She spends more time with her children and appreciates every day. She no longer sees her illness as an inconvenience. To her, this experience and what she learned from it are "pretty neat stuff."

We can't run away from problems, and we make a mistake if we try to ignore them, but we can adopt a positive, take-charge attitude to keep us from feeling smashed by them. Along with trying to keep a positive attitude, gather information. Knowledge combats fears. The most devastating thing you can do is give in to despair, thinking, "There's nothing I can do" "I can't change things" "I don't have any choices." Try writing down your own story with four different options. Think them through. Fantasize different outcomes. Believe you'll overcome your problems and treat them like opportunities to develop valuable tools to use and share.

Expanding Your Thinking

If, like the "you" in this adventure , you find you're living a real-life soap opera with multiple problems, perhaps you should follow all four options, since they each provide helpful insights: take it one day at a time, accept help, join a support group, and cut back your work hours. However, first let's look at the directions that don't work so well.

In this adventure you make very few dumb moves. Any of us can let well-meaning people overrun us when we aren't feeling well. We're susceptible to kindness when we're frightened. Letting your sister rule the roost, and falling in love with Andre, while not always probable, may help more than hurt your long-term well-being.

However, in your own life you may wish to avoid the following:

DON'T:

1. Think you're the only one in the world with multiple problems.
2. Avoid facing problems.
3. Think ignorance is bliss.

4. Feel you have zero control or choices.
5. Let others make decisions for you.
6. Make sweeping changes.
7. Disbelieve that time heals all wounds.
8. Listen to others' horror stories of people with similar problems to yours.
9. Wish this part of your life away, without finding the good or at least a lesson in it.
10. Try to go it alone.

The wise moves you make in this adventure abound. In Option A, you call for support from your children's pediatrician Suzanne, who explains the medical terminology you don't understand. She accompanies you to your appointment. You take her advice to call your HMO to get permission to see a doctor not on their preferred list. Probably your best efforts revolve around your children, helping them understand and not be afraid of your illness. You cut off your hair, buy wigs, and work with the inevitable rather than fighting it or mourning the eventual loss of your hair. You try to make it a game. You play with it, have fun with it. From your creative illustrations you diffuse your children's fears, then develop a coloring book that benefits others, too.

You learn to accept help in Option B, even though it gets out of hand. Once you figure out your own plan, hiring Inez, you regain control of your time and reclaim your home.

In Option C, you seek out several support groups, other than family and friends. The Internet chat room reveals helpful information, but the support group at the hospital gives you a new family of cancer-courageous friends. This leads to your finding a new mate.

The positive actions you take in Option D include not rushing to divulge your situation to clients until you know how you're going to handle the work. You cut back your work hours, use your message machine to screen calls, and eliminate P.I.A.'s from your client list. You keep yourself positive by relying on your sense of humor, watching funny movies, and not taking your situation too seriously.

DO:

1. Seek personal and professional support when you have a problem.
2. Locate many resources to educate yourself about your illness, problem, or dilemma.
3. Protect your children by explaining your situation simply and clearly in a way that matches their level of understanding and keeps them from feeling frightened.
4. Find a way to share what you're learning, keep notes, a diary, or draw a coloring book.
5. Learn to say "yes" when people want to comfort or assist you, but be aware of your boundaries.
6. Show appreciation for the efforts of friends and family who mean well.
7. Use discretion when informing clients of your difficulties.
8. Cut back on work hours.
9. Hire a housekeeper.
10. Watch funny movies, read Irma Bombeck, see the humor in your humanness.

Assessing Your Own Situation

How do you help someone or yourself during truly difficult times? Try asking these questions:

1. If you seek control, ask, "Am I letting others make my important decisions for me?" "Have I defined my own boundaries and limitations?"
2. Be clear about your own needs. Ask, "What is it I think I need most?" "If I don't know what I need right now, can I brainstorm new answers?"
3. If you feel overwhelmed, ask yourself, "Am I trying to go this alone?" "Where can I get help and support?" "Am I focusing on one day at a time?"
4. If you feel angry, ask yourself, "Who else with difficulties can I help?"
5. If you feel fearful, ask yourself, "Have I researched all the information I can find?" "Do I understand what is going on?" "Who can explain this to me?"
6. When you must keep up a good front for others, ask yourself, "Doesn't it feel good to act positive?" "How can I truly find something positive in this situation to share with others?"
7. When you want to cry, ask yourself, "How long do I want to grieve about this?" "Is there someone who will understand, cry with me, then help me move on?"
8. Ask, "Do I have the faith I need to pull me through tough times?" "Who inspires me?"

Affirmation

Commandment 4:
When the odds are against you, defy the odds.

"I see my future as full and bright. I'll overcome this inconvenience with the anticipation that I can help others. I see my problem as a gift."

Part II

Work Adventures

Career Choices and Moves

ADVENTURE 7

WHAT CAN I DO WHEN I GET STUCK ON THE CORPORATE LADDER?

Have you or has someone you know been scaling the corporate ladder toward the top only to find the rungs becoming too narrow, or too slippery? Has it dawned on you that you might be climbing the wrong ladder altogether? Perhaps you've believed that your brains, dedication, and determination would get you to the top when it turns out that office politics play a big role, too. If you find yourself teetering on a corporate ladder, thank your lucky stars you're not ***Rungless in Columbus.***

Rungless in Columbus

Your three wood powers the ball off the ninth tee 150 yards straight down the fairway. Your ball drops just beyond the sand trap concealed behind a grassy mound and rolls into a perfect position for an unencumbered shot to the green.

"Great, Anna Marie. Another amazing drive. You're in terrific form. You've certainly mastered this game," enthuses your friend, Maureen Hoolihan, CEO of Midwest Bottling Company based in Columbus, Ohio.

"Yeah, if only I had mastered the corporate game too. I want to become CEO so badly I can taste it, but it looks like I stand a better chance making a hole in one on a par four. No one at the company seems to take my desire seriously because I'm on the marketing side of the business."

You're forty-eight years old, widowed ten years ago, and you support your two children, ages thirteen and fifteen, in private schools. Long before you joined the marketing department of Styles, Styles, Styles, Inc. (SSS) in Columbus eight years ago, you had graduated from the University of Montana with a double major in English and Philosophy then went to work for J. William Thomas Advertising in New York City, where you met and married Charles. You coped with the fact that the doctors discovered his prostrate cancer much too late to save him, you fought to hold your own in the ephemeral advertising industry, and you tried to develop the skills you needed as a single mother. When a headhunter called you about the VP of Marketing position at SSS, you jumped at the chance to join a company that offered more opportunity for advancement. Your entire life has revolved around your work and your kids, often in that order.

The lure of SSS certainly wasn't the location, Columbus, rather it was that the women's retail apparel business provides more advancement opportunities for women than almost any other industry in the nation. Most women in upper management in retail have worked their way up as merchandisers, beginning in excellent buyers' training programs such as the one offered by Abraham and Strauss. You believed, however, that you could prove yourself through your successes in a different area of the company, in advertising and marketing. Climbing an alternate ladder to reach the CEO position turned out to be tougher than you'd imagined.

As far as you know, no CEO of Styles, Styles, Styles has ever reached the top from the marketing side of the business. J. Gordon Gordon, head of this family-owned business, believes that "those who make it to the top should start at the bottom." Every CEO had worked her way up through merchandising. The company structure at SSS places the CEO in a make-it or break-it position. She approves literally every item the chain carries, often based on her lightning quick decisions. The CEO grooms herself for her entrepreneurial, shoot-from-the-hip role with years of buying experience both at store and corporate levels. Ultimately, she decides what the marketing team sells. That's why trying to reach CEO from marketing is like trying to move from waitress at a world class restaurant to the job of head chef. The skills don't mesh.

On the ninth green Maureen lines up her twenty-foot putt. "You've picked an industry that makes it tough to climb all the way to the top from your position as head of marketing, Anna Marie. You know, other industries find marketing experience a plus in a CEO candidate. Have you thought of looking around?" Maureen taps her ball into the cup with a resonant "ping." Her putter sounds like fine crystal flutes clinking together in a champagne toast, a sound that makes you smile. But you answer seriously, "I've been so focused on SSS that I haven't really thought of alternatives. I don't want to look around unless I'm serious about changing jobs. Moving the kids at their age would be a nightmare."

"If you don't look around, how do you know what might work better?" Maureen counters. "Headhunters call me regularly about positions. When I tell them I'm not interested, they always ask if I know a likely candidate. Why don't I drop your name a time or two?"

"I don't know, Maureen. I don't want to be a second thought. And I just feel there must be a way I can maneuver my way to the top of SSS."

"Have you thought exactly how you could accomplish that?"

"I know I have to make myself more visible as a problem solver, someone who goes above and beyond the job requirements. I thought if I could pull off a dynamite marketing campaign, they'd rethink the path to CEO and let me in."

"Well, you can't go wrong with that approach, but, frankly, I can't see you 'kissing-up' to J. Gordon Gordon, which you'd have to do to demand the attention you'd need."

"Granted, that's not one of my strong points and I'm not embarrassed to admit it."

"So, what else could you do?"

"Well, I could backtrack. You know, switch from marketing to merchandising. I'd have to get training and experience, but I know the company would offer me the opportunity to do it, even encourage me. It'll take a few extra years and a drop in salary, though."

"Is that a sure way to the top?"

"I'm not positive it's a 'sure' way, but it fits into the corporate structure better. I wouldn't be trying to recreate how the company functions."

"There's another way to become CEO, Anna Marie. Become CEO of your own business."

"I've thought of that, but I'd have to break the noncompete agreement they forced all of us to sign a year ago. Could get messy."

"Well, good luck, Anna Marie. See you next Saturday. Thanks for the game."

When you get home, you write down the alternatives you discussed with Maureen:

What Would You Do?

A. I can develop a knock-em-dead marketing campaign to prove that I'm CEO material.

B. I can backtrack for a few years to get on the right ladder.

C. I can start my own business.

D. I could tell Maureen to go ahead and drop my name to headhunters and see what's out there.

Turn to the option that most appeals to you. To learn the most from this adventure, read how the other options turned out, too. Then study the last three sections of this adventure: "Exploring the Issue," "Expanding Your Thinking," and "Assessing Your Situation."

A. I can develop a knock-em-dead marketing campaign to prove that I'm CEO material.

You decide that you simply can't accept the "it's not done that way" attitude toward promotion at SSS. You wouldn't have made it this far in your career if you ever let that sort of prejudice hinder you. After all, you were one of the youngest account execs at J. William Thomas, even though everyone told you that couldn't happen. Your rise to stardom came about because you gladly worked as the "gopher" for the account exec working on the image update of Acorn Manor, a once well-respected Manhattan hotel suffering a decline in business. You dug up more information for him than he had requested, and partly because you did something no one else in the firm had done, you visited the hotel. You noticed that even with the new coat of paint, freshly oiled paneling, and refurbished sofas, it smelled decrepit. It made Acorn Manor unwelcoming.

You contacted your sister, Charlotte, who works for U.S. Scents in New Jersey. On her recommendation, you presented the concept of using hidden, automatic atomizers to spritz a blend of bergamot, cedar, and rosewood throughout the main lobby and the hallways. After installing the "aroma therapy," the stately hotel smelled tranquil and inviting. You suggested a publicity blitz for the grand re-opening including "party favors" of smart wooden gift boxes with three machine-tooled cedar acorns tucked inside. The campaign attracted a lot of media attention, and you won both recognition for your ingenuity and a big promotion. For years after the successful campaign, those little wood acorns bedecked desks and side tables in businesses around the country.

You think you can pull off a similar coup for SSS. You design a marketing campaign using aromas to attract more attention to the lingerie departments. You know that many of the companies that make materials used in lingerie buy fragrances from U.S. Scents. Though you don't know what comprises those proprietary scents, you discuss with Charlotte what fragrances she thinks might appeal to women customers ages thirty to fifty-five, the mainstay of your market.

Charlotte comes up with an Eternal Spring Bouquet scent, heavily accented with vanilla. Your marketing campaign, Eternal Spring, also features seasonal flower shows in the lingerie department of every store. The local garden clubs and florists that participate in the program increase community interest. The Eternal Spring Bouquet scent draws women to the lingerie departments but they seem more interested in buying bouquets than brassieres. Local media loves the campaign and SSS lingerie departments become the background setting for many articles and photos, but none of this dramatically boosts sales nationally. You thought you'd come out smelling like a rose, but, unfortunately, the campaign has left you stuck on the ladder with potting soil under your nails.

J. Gordon Gordon says, "I told you so. That campaign was a milk toast idea, nothing but frills. No substance, no sales." He's got a point. You never piloted your campaign in different markets to test results, which annoyed J. Gordon. You feel terribly discouraged that your efforts haven't budged you one rung up the ladder, until a headhunter calls you directly. He has been searching for a CEO to head a sizable perfume business. When he saw your picture in the paper and connected you with SSS's Eternal Spring campaign, he felt you might be just the person for the job. You would have to relocate to New York City immediately. If you accept, however, your kids will feel completely uprooted. Becoming a CEO has preoccupied you so much ever since Charles died, but now, with your children in high school, you don't know if you should put your goal to become CEO ahead of your children's welfare. You don't know what to do.

BENEFITS OF A:

- You don't let an "It's not done this way" attitude hinder you.
- You try to create a successful marketing campaign based on a past success.
- You include local florists and garden clubs to increase community interest in your marketing campaign.
- You know the age of your best customers and design a campaign to attract them.
- You attract the attention of a headhunter who thinks you could head a perfume company in New York City.
- You consider how a move might affect your children.

DOWNSIDES OF A:

- You think you can work around company policy.
- You focus on proving yourself as a marketing whiz knowing that CEO's don't rise up the ladder through marketing.

- You don't conduct pilot campaigns to test the results of your ideas.
- You seem more concerned with show than increasing the bottom line.
- You're disappointed when your marketing coup attracts only local attention.
- You don't prove to the company that you're CEO material.

B. I can backtrack for a few years to get on the right ladder.

As you slip on your cross-training shoes for your early morning workout at the gym, you realize exactly what you're missing in your career: cross-training. You know other women who have left the marketing department, and, unfortunately, their impressive salaries, for a new ladder in another department. You always thought those people acted foolishly. In your eyes, they didn't sidestep, they backtracked. Who knows if doing that will ever pay off? But now you realize that if you want to move toward the CEO position, you had better backtrack yourself. You realize that you've been wearing blinders, falsely assuming that if you display your brilliance in one area, the company must recognize your brilliance in other areas. To your dismay, they couldn't, and you resented them for it. You don't know why you hadn't seen the benefits of cross-training before now and can't wait to get started.

Fortunately, SSS has always encouraged creative career development. It values interested employees who wish to expand their knowledge within the company. Partly due to this, SSS enjoys a relatively low turnover rate. Currently, you're head of marketing, wildly successful in your own right, and should feel extremely satisfied, so your request for a transfer surprises your superiors. The higher ups are nonplused by your request to start over in a buyers' training program, because you'd never voiced an interest in becoming CEO. You'd only confided that dream in your kids and Maureen.

Nevertheless, two weeks later, the head of HR sits down with you to explain what your career change entails. She outlines the training you need, the length of time it typically requires, and the salary normally paid. You negotiate a generous pay plan, based on your extensive knowledge of the company, and a fast-track training program. You don't sense that SSS wants to groom you for CEO, but at least the company has given you a fair opportunity to prepare yourself and get on the right ladder.

During your first year in buyers' training, you briefly visit stores across the country. Since you had negotiated not to be assigned to stores outside of the Columbus area, you never travel away from home for more than a week at a time. Though this works best for your children's schedules, it holds you back from learning as much as you could in the high-traffic stores in Manhattan and Los Angeles. Still, you manage to grasp the trends and develop your buying sense. Your marketing background and knowledge of your customers greatly helps you judge what items will sell.

Though your rise to stardom seems to take forever, you remain patient. Every time it looks like you should have a shot at CEO, the job goes to someone else. And every time you tell yourself to wait, you become more savvy about playing the game and parrying with the players. For the longest time you feel that you are simply treading water, but you come to realize that patience is an underrated skill in corporate America. Sink or swim had always been your motto. However, because you can tread so well, you hang in there long enough, developing more contacts and personal rapport, until the right time arrives.

When J. Gordon Gordon offers you the job six years after you switched ladders, he praises your loyalty and dedication. "You deserve this job," he says, "because you practiced the Three P's: patience, perseverance and professionalism."

When you grasp your brass ring, you do it with a clear conscience because your children have now graduated from high school. Now you can travel endlessly for SSS without worrying about their welfare.

Today, you love being CEO and know that you never would have been as effective if you hadn't backtracked and worked your way up the right ladder.

BENEFITS OF B:

- You redefine career "backtracking" as "cross-training."
- You realize that your narrow thinking kept you from seeing the value of backtracking.
- Your company gives you the opportunity to train and develop skills in other areas of the company.
- You tell higher ups of your ultimate goal.
- You negotiate a decent salary and geographic territory during your training.
- You learn patience and the value of starting over in a new area of the company.
- You appreciate that you learn more and become more valuable each time you must wait longer to become CEO.
- You become CEO when your children no longer demand so much of your attention.

DOWNSIDES OF B:

- You hold yourself back for a long time thinking that people who sidestep their careers are foolish.
- You waste years thinking you didn't need to play by the corporate rules to get to the top.
- You mistakenly think that brilliance in one area will win you recognition and promotion to another area of the company.

- You surprise the higher ups with your request to enter the buyers' training because you never voiced your goals to anyone except to one friend and your children.
- You restrict your training by negotiating not to be assigned to stores outside of the Columbus area.
- You must tread water without knowing if you'll ever get to the top.
- It takes longer than you expect to make it to the top.

C. I can start my own business.

For weeks, you struggle with the thought of starting your own marketing consulting business. You know how to do it and where to find high-paying clients, but you don't know when you should do it. What's holding you back? The noncompete agreement you signed with SSS a year ago. J. Gordon Gordon, the neurotic owner of SSS, insisted that you, along with every other senior executive, sign a document which forbids you from joining a competing company or to consult in any way, shape or form to anyone in the retail business for three years. At the time, you thought the agreement ridiculous and unfair, but you'd acquiesced to J. Gordon's whims before. You had no choice but to sign if you wanted to keep your job and, along with it, the big salary and great perks.

You hadn't put much credence in the agreement because SSS isn't in the information technology industry where proprietary software or hardware information are at stake. SSS is a women's clothing retailer, for Pete's sake. But now that measly piece of paper hamstrings you. Could you be sued if you break away and started your own marketing consulting business? Suddenly, you feel stupid that you've limited your options.

You contact your brother-in-law, an attorney, who advises you not to feel intimidated by SSS's noncompete agreement. "Several states, California, Montana, and Georgia for instance, make noncompete agreements almost impossible to enforce."

"Great, but I'm in Ohio," you counter.

"I know, but the more restrictive the agreement, the more courts refuse to enforce them. Any state and any court could find your agreement too restrictive to your ability to earn a living."

"Oh. So what do I do?"

"I'll check to see if Ohio has what many states call the Blue Pencil Rule."

"What's that?"

"If the courts find an agreement unreasonable, they can cross out what they consider unfair, pencil it out. I'm not an expert in this area of law, Anna Marie, but I have a partner who would be glad to read over your agreement and advise you further."

"So, do you think I'll have to go to court? What if it takes three years to get through the courts?"

"Oh, I don't think it would take that long."

"Promise?"

"Can't."

"I know you can't. I'll send over a copy of the agreement tomorrow."

You wonder if the effort to fight the noncompete agreement will be worth the time and money. You hate legal hassles, and this one would bite the very hand that has fed you for so long. What if it turns ugly? And even if you do win, would the suit affect future clients' interest in doing business with you? You don't know the answer to these questions. You feel more confused about your choices than ever.

Two weeks later, a thought occurs to you in the middle of the night: Talk to J. Gordon personally. To your great relief, J. Gordon finds your desire to consult most interesting. He surprises you, however, when he says, "I'll tear up the agreement if you agree to consult to SSS exclusively for eighteen months."

You're thrilled at first, because you won't have to go without an interim income while you develop clients. But within six months, the thrill is gone. You're managing marketing projects for SSS and you get paid well enough, but you receive none of the health, dental, or retirement benefits you have enjoyed previously. Also, benefits aside, you discover, much to your dismay, that you've stalled your career because your exclusive contract prohibits your developing new business. Your exclusive arrangement with SSS that had looked like a good transition into launching your own consulting business, has, in fact, tethered it. But at least you're no longer tied to the noncompete agreement and assume the eighteen months will go by quickly enough. In the meantime, you draft a business development plan so that you can hit the ground running once you complete the SSS contract.

BENEFITS OF C:

- You know that you want to start your own marketing consulting business.
- You contact a lawyer about your noncompete agreement.
- You research what a law suit would take in time and money.
- You discuss your concerns directly with J. Gordon.
- You take J. Gordon's offer to consult exclusively for SSS for eighteen months.
- Your contract with J. Gordon releases you of the noncompete agreement.
- You prepare a business plan for launching your consulting business.

DOWNSIDES OF C:

- When you signed the noncompete agreement, you didn't take it seriously.
- You didn't question the agreement for fear of losing your job, perks, and healthy salary; now it restricts your future.
- You didn't seek legal advice before you signed the agreement.
- You will have to spend time and money to fight the legal restrictions of the noncompete agreement.
- You jump at the opportunity to consult exclusively for SSS without thinking through how you want to grow your business.
- You put you career development on hold for eighteen months.

D. I could tell Maureen to go ahead and drop my name to headhunters and see what's out there.

"Okay, Maureen. Give my name to your headhunters," you say as you dig your way out of a sand trap in four angry strokes during your Saturday morning golf game. "Just make sure they know I can't go to work for a competing company because of the noncompete agreement I signed."

"If that display of flying sand resembles your outlook, I would say you feel pretty stuck where you are," Maureen teases you. "I heard at my YPO (Young Presidents Organization) meeting last week that Sisters Cookies here in Columbus has put out feelers for someone to turn around the company. Sales crumbled a year ago, burning investors. Top management made matters worse by cutting back in the wrong areas. 'Can't make a good cookie with poor ingredients,' my grandmother used to say."

"Too bad the sisters didn't listen," you quip.

"That's the crux of the problem. The Carrow sisters don't see eye to eye, and Sisters Cookies has suffered for it. Olivia just quit, demanding to be bought out for an exorbitant amount, and sister Ester doesn't have a clue how to run the company. She's the baker in the family. When Olivia, the one who ran the company, stopped purchasing quality ingredients to save money, the sisters got into a huge cat fight."

"Turning that around sounds like a lot to bite off," you mutter.

"Ah, but Anna Marie, you'd be a great Cookie Monster. I can see you with your marketing and financial savvy turning that company into a mouth-watering winner."

"Yeah, I can see the marketing campaign now," you say, gazing off into the distance and waving your sand wedge expansively. "Instead of a warm, friendly grandmother in a lace-collared calico dress smiling at you from the package, there will be two feuding sisters with their arms crossed glaring at each other!" You both laugh at the ridiculous image.

"You should talk to them, Anna Marie."

"I think I will," you say, surprising yourself.

To your further surprise, you not only find the company's problems fascinating, but during the third interview with the board of directors, you accept the position they offer you: CEO.

"Maureen, I got it!" you squeal over the phone later that day.

"Perfect! When do you don your Cookie Monster suit?"

"I've told SSS I would stay for two weeks, then I'm taking my kids on a three-week trip to Europe. EuroDisney is number one on the list. The crowds should be huge in August, but kids never outgrow Mickey Mouse, and we'll have a ball."

"Fantastic. Congratulations, Ms. CEO."

"I feel so lucky."

"Hey, Anna Marie. Nothing's wrong with a little luck. And besides, don't you know that luck is just preparation colliding with opportunity? You wouldn't have landed this position if you hadn't been preparing yourself for years. Give yourself a little credit, and enjoy the 'luck.' Will I still see you for our regular Saturday golf games?"

"You bet."

The following week you receive a note in the mail from Maureen with a simple quote: "'When you want something, all the universe conspires to help you achieve it,' from *The Alchemist* by Paulo Coelho." You feel blessed to have such a caring friend.

Two years later, about the time your oldest child graduates from high school, Sisters Cookies surpasses all financial expectations. The truly crazy thing about it is that the ad campaign featuring two sisters fighting over cookies has caught the consumers' attention. What you had joked about on the golf course years earlier has turned into one of the most successful ad campaigns in the food industry. Your children report that kids at school mimic the commercials and act like teasing sisters to steal cookies from one another. The only thing better than having consumers sing an ad jingle is when they reenact the commercials themselves and believe the slogan: "Nothing's better than your Sisters Cookie!"

BENEFITS OF D:

- You accept the possibility of changing industries to reach your career goal of CEO.
- You listen to the suggestion of your friend Maureen.
- You become CEO.
- You take time off when switching companies to vacation with your children.
- You maintain your weekly golf game to stay in contact with your friend and business equal.
- Your ad campaign catches consumers' attention.

- You successfully turn around the company.
- You have prepared yourself with skills so that when you're offered the CEO position at Sisters Cookies it looks like luck.

DOWNSIDES OF D:

- You rely on a chance comment from your friend to find a new place to work.
- You do no research on your own to find another company to run.
- You fail to consider the difficulties of running a troubled company compared to a healthy one.
- Your ad campaign works, though many negative ads do not.

Exploring the Issue

If you still believe that merely doing an incredibly good job will automatically get you noticed and promoted, you may want to think again. Companies rarely base promotions on merit alone. Successful women will tell you that climbing the rungs on any industry ladder requires more than doing a good job, it requires knowing how to play the game wisely.

While not everyone aspires to become a CEO, the example in this adventure shows how women can inadvertently create self-inflicted obstacles on their climb up the corporate ladder. In this character's case, she thought she could buck the system and still get to the top when, in fact, she knowingly approached the pinnacle from the wrong ladder. Today, strong women get deeply involved in their own career development plans. They find creative ways to improve their odds. They talk to the right people and review their progress every six months. If they feel stuck on the corporate ladder, or "plateaued," they think: A. How do I get back on track? and B. What is the best use of my time while I'm plateaued? Most likely, they use their plateau time to learn new skills, develop more contacts, or to take a vacation, pull back, see the big picture, and enhance their mental health.

However, many other hidden issues hold women back. Those range from the inflection of their speech pattern to their "schmooze" ability, otherwise known as their aptitude for playing company politics.

Let's look at these issues. First of all, voice inflection matters. Speech patterns often affect whether higher ups see people as promotable. Women devalue themselves when they speak tentatively, making every statement sound like a question. Self-sabotaging phrases like, "This may be a dumb idea, but..." don't give anyone credibility. Confident women sound decisive and self-assured by listing the points they want to make and offering strategies rather than tentative suggestions. However, much more than voice inflections, other factors come into play.

A brilliant corporate ladder-climber told me that in assessing the ladder issue women should focus on two key components: the person and the job position in the industry. First, why are you, the "person," attracted to a certain job? Is it to reach your career goals, achieve high profile and status, earn more compensation, or obtain accessibility to perks? What kind of personality do you display? Are you a controller, a facilitator, an analyzer, or an advocator?

What kind of personality fits different job positions? For example, picture three jobs: an investment banker, an advertising account executive, and a savings bank manager. An investment banker builds her own base of business as an entrepreneur within the company framework. Teamwork could actually conflict with her business development. The "right" personality for this job probably would be an advocator or an analyzer. An advertising account executive, however, uses an entrepreneurial approach to develop select accounts, but works with a team. A socially outgoing personality, a facilitator, might succeed best in this position. A person in a managerial position at a large savings bank works in a lower risk environment, she's not entrepreneurial at all, and feels comfortable in a hierarchical setting.

The investment banker climbs up the ladder on the basis of the productivity of her clients' investments. The advertising account exec's promotion depends on the success of her ad campaigns and, accordingly, her ability to attract new clients. The bank manager must depend on the normal hierarchical route for advancement. She counts on the person above her to carry her ideas to higher ups, and she waits to get noticed.

In these examples, personality types and each industry ladder differ. While access to entry level positions in each of these industries no longer poses a problem for women, subtle obstacles can get in the way of their reaching the top. In the more entrepreneurial positions in corporations, if you don't have access to important clients, you can't build a base to get ahead. For example, a woman in investment banking may be assigned accounts with debts and an uncertain future. The corporate mentality says that women handle "challenged" companies like this better than their equally paid male counterparts. By contrast, the account list of a male investment banker may include the shining star of the computer industry. He enjoys the growing company's need for frequent financing and may introduce some creative deals because the company has better credit. What happens at the end of the year? Bonuses are based on a profit-based formula including what the firm, division, industry group, and the individual investment banker brought in. Who do you think will get the higher bonus? Who do you think will be sought after as a future partner based on revenue generated? Certainly not the woman with her accounts gasping for their last breath. If she goes to her superiors and demands a raise, she stands on flimsy legs. The advertising account executive has more clout to demand a raise if she's built a successful client base, because she can threaten to leave and take her accounts with her. Investment bankers usually can't take theirs as easily.

In the hierarchical positions, such as the savings bank manager, her boss may actually become an obstacle to promotion. He or she may be less talented, more opportunistic, and threatened by her. She must trust that her boss won't claim credit for what she's done or recommended.

If you feel stuck on a corporate ladder, you need to determine why. If there's something you can correct yourself, do it. If you need more education, get it. If you feel you have to fight city hall, or the old boys' club, every rung of the way, choose your battles carefully. Decide if it's worth it. Some corporate women jump off the ladder because they get tired of the politics. Sometimes they disagree with policies, or philosophies, or with whom the company does business. Women can get tired of the corporate focus on the bottom line despite human casualties, feeling there's more they want to focus on in their lives.

Those of you who decide to jump off, anticipate success in your new business based on the skills you've worked so hard to attain in the corporate world. Whether you decide to use or expand your current skills (consulting or working in the same industry), or not (starting a fudge factory or following some other fancy), look at your leap of faith as a positive move, the springboard to an exciting new alternative way of life and work. Give yourself credit for going the corporate route, learning valuable experiences, facing difficult challenges, connecting with interesting people, and then give yourself credit for your courage to jump. Thus you'll be ready to start over confidently.

For those of you who choose to continue the corporate climb, learn the rungs. Thinking that hard work and loyalty will win you a promotion in a man's world, which still prevails in the workplace, simply doesn't work. Successfully scaling the ladder of your choice depends on knowing your value to the company and how your efforts contribute to the bottom line. Think like an entrepreneur. Take responsibility for building your own "sand box." Keep an ear to the ground, know what else is going on in and around your industry. Determine your worth on the open job market. Couple this information with knowing how to play company politics and how to present yourself as a confident, decisive, visible candidate for promotion, and you'll more fully control your advancement in any company.

Expanding Your Thinking

In this adventure, "you" set your sights on becoming a CEO shortly after your husband died. You're bright and talented, but find that isn't enough for advancement. When you try different ways to reach the top of the ladder, some work out well, some do not. What doesn't work?

In Option A, you try to prove yourself as CEO material through a clever marketing campaign, even though you know the way to the top in your company is through merchandising. You disdain "it can't be done that way" attitudes, but that doesn't help you because you don't prepare yourself in the essential areas needed to advance in your company. When your Eternal Spring campaign doesn't attract the national attention you'd hoped for, you realize you'll never make CEO of SSS.

In Option B, you again hold yourself back by thinking you could reach the top through marketing, when you know otherwise. You expect your talents in one area to win a promotion in another, but you haven't taken steps to prove yourself in other areas. You slow your advancement by neglecting to express your CEO aspirations to higher ups. When you do backtrack in your career path, you restrict your training by refusing to leave the Columbus area. Plus, backtracking doesn't guarantee that you will make it to the top even through merchandising.

In Option C, you wonder if you should fight the noncompete agreement you signed. You feel it restricts your future earnings, but don't know if you should spend the time, money, and mental anguish dealing with a legal hassle. When you decide to talk to

J. Gordon directly, you aren't prepared to analyze his offer to consult for SSS exclusively because you have not thought through how you would develop your consulting business. It turns out that you feel you've put your career on hold.

In Option D, you make little personal effort to find another company to run, relying instead on your friend Maureen to push you. When you do change companies, your ad campaign works well, but often negative ads fail.

Having gone through all the options in this adventure, you have learned a little about what you want to avoid if you're stuck on a corporate ladder.

DON'T:

1. Plan to move ahead in any company by working around company policy.
2. Climb the wrong ladder, then blame the company when you're stuck.
3. Set yourself up for disappointment by waiting to be noticed and promoted.
4. Overlook opportunities for advancement in other corporate divisions or in other industries.
5. Override the possibility of backtracking your way to the top.
6. Neglect to state your career aspirations clearly to those who count in your company.
7. Expect a smooth climb up the corporate ladder in any industry.
8. Sign noncompete agreements if at all possible.
9. Rely on others to guide your way to the top.
10. Assume your best chance for advancement comes from staying with one company.

What works well for you in this adventure? In Option A, you draw great self-confidence from past successes and don't let comments like "It's not done that way" deter your goal. You call on your past experiences to develop an innovative marketing campaign. Though your campaign does little to increase revenues at your company, you spark the interest of a headhunter looking to fill a CEO position in New York. You consider whether such a move would be beneficial to your children at this time.

In Option B, you experience an "Ah-ha" moment when you slip on your cross-training shoes, seeing the potential of cross-training yourself in your company, and thereby placing yourself in a more advantageous position to move toward CEO. You take advantage of your company's career development policy to switch divisions and receive fast-track training in merchandising. Though it takes longer than you anticipate, you appreciate the extra time it takes to reach CEO because you continue to develop more skills and rapport with others in the company and feel you have more to offer. Becoming CEO comes at a good time as well, when the last of your children leaves for college.

In Option C, your own marketing business idea looks impossible because of the noncompete agreement you had signed, but you try to find a way around it. You contact a lawyer to advise you, but realize the direct approach with J. Gordon would work best. When J. Gordon tears up the noncompete agreement in exchange for your consulting to SSS exclusively for eighteen months, you gracefully get out of the sticky situation and avoid negative legal proceedings.

In Option D, you accept the fact that to reach your career goal of CEO you must expand your thinking and see yourself in a different industry. You hear about a company in need of new direction, find their problems fascinating, and win the position of CEO. Your innovative, if irreverent, ad campaign attracts needed attention to the business and helps you pull the company out of its slump. You enjoy being at the top.

What positive points do you want to remember from this adventure?

DO:

1. Set your sights high.
2. Know your strengths and demonstrate how they benefit your company.
3. Ignore naysayers, but learn how to play the corporate game in your industry.
4. Learn the best path up the corporate ladder in your company and anticipate the obstacles.
5. Cross-train yourself by accumulating new skills.
6. Take advantage of every opportunity to receive training in your company.
7. Keep your mind open to switching divisions or companies or industries to enjoy career success.
8. Negotiate your own career development plan including promotions, perks, and salary increases.
9. Know your value in the open market.
10. Explore your own motives and what reaching your goal requires of you and your family.

Assessing Your Own Situation

If you're stuck on a corporate ladder, or otherwise stalled in your career, ask yourself several key questions.

1. If you feel stuck on the corporate ladder, ask, "Can I take specific actions to promote myself?" "Is this problem specific to me or an industry-wide problem?" "Is there any room at the top in this company?"

2. Have you let the *right* people, high-level and politically connected people who can make things happen, know your intentions and goals? Ask, "Have I asked directly for a raise?" "Have I applied for positions available, or simply hoped that I would be recognized for my talents?"

3. Do you know your worth? Ask, "Have I looked around for other jobs in the industry?" "Do I network with others in the industry to know what's going on?" "Do I know what I can do to increase the bottom line?"

4. Are you in the right position to get promoted? Ask, "Do I hold a position where I can affect the bottom line directly?" "Are there other areas in this company where I can find more advancement?"

5. Have you done everything you can to make yourself promotable? "Have I kept my skills up to date?" "Do I take advantage of continuing education programs offered by the company?"

6. Do you really want to move up? Ask, "Do I really want the extra responsibility tied to the advancement?" "If I take this promotion, will I make more money but enjoy less freedom?"

7. Do you know what you need to accomplish in order to gain a promotion? Ask, "Have I discussed with my superior exactly what I can do to get promoted?" "Have I determined the parameters to get the advancement?"

8. Do you reset your priorities as needed? Ask, "Am I flexible with my priorities?" "Do I set them by project, by opportunity, by the week or month or year?"

9. Do you involve your family and friends in your career plans? "Do I explain my priorities to my family and friends?" "Do they think that if I make enough money, it will improve our quality of life?" "Do I believe that?"

10. Are you in the right career? It may sound a little late, but it's never too late to find what you really enjoy doing. Why straddle a ladder you don't really like? Ask, "Is my personality right for what's expected of me in this job?" "Do I feel like I have to sell my soul to get ahead?" "Do I disagree with company policy or who we do business with or where we get our products made?"

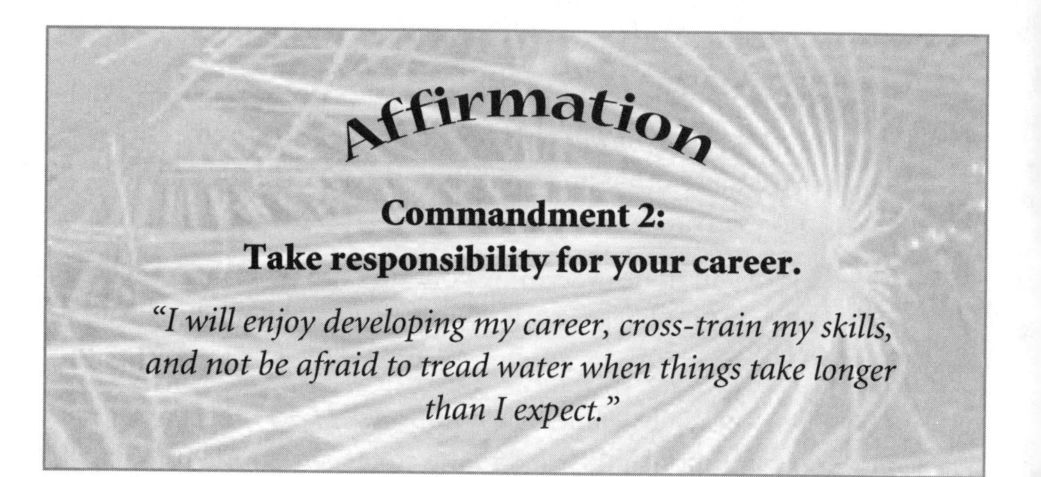

ADVENTURE 8

How do I make sure gender and age issues don't hold me back?

Can you recall a situation in which you felt the oppression of discrimination? Sometimes subtle, sometimes blatant, discrimination comes in many forms: gender, age, appearance, economic or ethnic background, to name a few. You may have suffered effects of discrimination yourself, or you may have tried to help a friend or family member who has been victimized by prejudice. To discover an antidote to that sort of poison, put yourself in the shoes of the woman **Sandbagged by a Whippersnapper.**

Sandbagged by a Whippersnapper

Until a few weeks ago, you had begun to think that "5" was your lucky number. You had just turned fifty, you were approaching your fifth anniversary at work, and your daughter was expecting your first grandchild on June 5. Then, just as you were thinking that you had hit your stride, that you would win a major promotion at work, and that you would be holding your first grandchild in your arms, a bolt of lightning strikes.

When the Gardener Tool Company downsized six months ago, you couldn't believe you'd kept your job in Human Resources. Soon, however, you understood why: the company had laid off many veteran workers, reassigning their work to junior, lower-paid people, like you, who soon found their workload "upsized."

Doing the jobs that two people used to do hasn't really bothered you, though, because you love the work and get great satisfaction from it. You regularly work ten- to twelve-hour days, and you've managed to reorganize and streamline the company's record-keeping systems in addition to your normal duties, typing and filing all the department's forms and correspondence. Proud of your accomplishments, you didn't feel nervous about the performance review your boss, Ben Stiller, unexpectedly sprung on you, despite the fact that Ben has done nothing but dump more work on your desk and treat you like an indentured slave.

Imagine your astonishment when you read Ben's summary of your last six months' performance: "Although you have accomplished many of your goals, you have taken far too long on most projects, which is compounded by the fact that you work twelve hours a day to accomplish what you should be able to do in eight hours. This inefficiency makes it impossible for the company to give you a salary increase at this time. The next six-week probation period will determine the future of your employment here."

You couldn't believe it. You've spent five years at Gardener, never complaining, even when Ben treated you aloofly or rudely, and never balking at the steadily increasing workload. In fact, you had fully expected this performance review to praise your dedication and hard work and to reward you with that long-deserved promotion to Human Resources Manager.

Now, you're feeling old and abused and sorry for yourself. "Why couldn't I see this coming?" you wonder to yourself. "Ben Stiller is a chauvinist pig. He'd never promote a woman. As far as he's concerned, I'm just an old housekeeper, cook, and chief bottle washer around here. He's never appreciated anything I've done."

You choke back your anger as best you can, continuing to work long hours, but coming into the office early, before Ben arrives. You'll show him, you think. Then a second bolt of lightning strikes when Ben gathers the five-person HR department in his office and introduces the new head of the department, Stephen Brown, a handsome twenty-three-year-old who has just graduated with an MBA from Stanford. Tall, masculine, and well-dressed, this kid is actually younger than your daughter, Caroline!

Blindsided by this turn of events, you curl up on your sofa late that night with a cup of Chamomile tea and review your situation. You're a single mom who's slowly paying off your only daughter's wedding, held last June at Wente Winery in Livermore, California. You live in a small, functional condominium in Hayward, complete with a sizable mortgage. You make ends meet, but just barely. "No frills living" you call it. There's no room for error or extravagance. To put it bluntly, you simply can't afford to lose this job. You were expecting a salary increase and even a promotion when you hit your five-year anniversary at Gardener Tool Company. Now, this surprise and Ben's negative performance review derails you.

You feel like the granny of the office, and you're certainly the oldest person still working there. Your age didn't seem to matter to the company five years ago. When you accepted the job, it looked promising, if hard, and you firmly believed it would offer you a chance to build a secure future. Ben, the young wet-behind-the-ears manager who hired you, had encouraged you to take on more and more work, which fooled you into assuming he respected your maturity. Now, you can see that he only used you for a doormat.

You had agreed to start at a lower salary than you wanted because Ben had implied that your pay would increase rapidly. That didn't happen. While straightening out the personnel files as part of your new job, you had even discovered that your predecessor who performed only half the duties required of you, had earned twenty-five percent more than you. And *he* was there only two years!

"It's unfair," you complain to your daughter, Caroline, over the weekend, hating yourself for feeling old, isolated, and unappreciated. "I'm on salary. I don't get paid for overtime. And they wouldn't dream of offering comp time. I've put in the extra hours to get the double job done. I've put my nose to the grindstone to help this company. I deserve a raise and a promotion, but instead I'm getting pushed out."

Then it hits you. During the downsizing at Gardener, the company had offered bonuses to encourage people to take early retirement at age fifty-two. You stayed on.

"Why had they retained me during the downsizing?" you ask Caroline rhetorically. "Because I'm a year too young to take advantage of the early retirement offer. Now, they're trying to squeeze me out before I reach fifty-two so they won't have to pay."

Each day that follows you gingerly walk through the mine field that was once your comfortable office, wondering what you should do about this untenable situation. You can't imagine completing your workload in an eight-hour day as Ben insists you do. You feel stressed and resentful, and quite a few sleepless nights haven't helped your mood a bit.

Caroline wants you to quit your job. "You don't have to put up with being treated that way," she insists. You agree, but you don't know where you would find another decent paying job at your age. However, the tension at work escalates each day, along with your own sense of helplessness. You must do something.

On Caroline's advice, your write down your options. You try to chuckle at the absurdity of your situation, but realize that, along with your self-confidence, you've lost your sense of humor. You write the following on a sheet of company stationery:

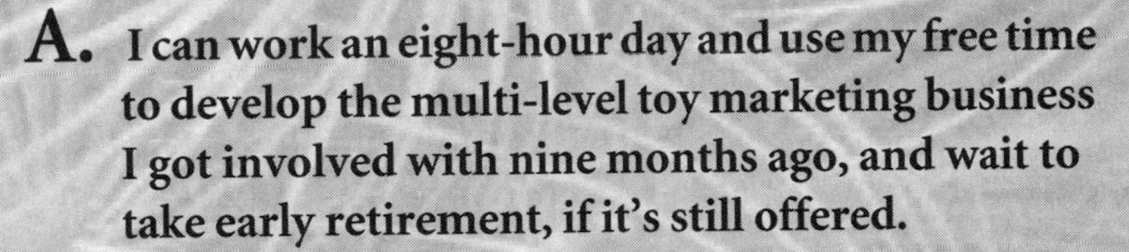

A. **I can work an eight-hour day and use my free time to develop the multi-level toy marketing business I got involved with nine months ago, and wait to take early retirement, if it's still offered.**

B. **I can start gathering information about women's rights in the workplace and fight this injustice.**

C. **I can take Caroline's advice, quit my job, and start over again.**

D. **I can keep a stiff upper lip and ride out the storm as long as I can.**

Turn to the option that most appeals to you. To learn the most from this adventure, read how the other options turned out, too. Then study the last three sections of this adventure: "Exploring the Issue," "Expanding Your Thinking," and "Assessing Your Situation."

A. I can work an eight-hour day and use my free time to develop the multi-level toy marketing business I got involved with nine months ago, and wait to take early retirement, if it's still offered.

You smile as you remember the excitement you felt during the toy party at your neighbor Connie's home nine months ago, just about the same time Gardener Tools started downsizing. You recall the lively conversation among the twelve women gathered around Connie's rosewood dining room table for tea and sugar cookies. Everything looked straight out of Martha Stewart's kitchen. When you had all settled in the living room, Connie introduced Betsy Burns from the Tantalizing Toy Company. Betsy had already set up her display of colorful educational toys on a card table draped with a hand-crocheted cloth that Connie's aunt had given her for Christmas. You felt the energy in the room revitalize you like a welcome shower at the end of a long dusty drive.

Betsy played master of ceremonies, explaining the joys and benefits of each toy, advising the appropriate age group and price for each tantalizing item. At the end of the evening, to a ruffle of "ooo's and ahhh's," Connie bowed her head when Betsy presented to her a silver money clip with the words "Tantalizingly Successful" monogrammed on it. After the crowd dispersed in a cloud of complimentary good-byes, Connie pocketed 5 percent of the $1,500 sales generated by the party.

As you helped your friend clean up the kitchen, Betsy asked you if you would be interested in becoming a party hostess yourself. You responded enthusiastically, envisioning yourself throwing an even more exciting party while helping young mothers, and soon-to-be grandmothers like yourself, find appropriate and safe toys. It seemed like a festive way to meet people, have fun, and earn extra dollars.

It had worked nicely for a while. After your first successful party, when you earned your own money clip and $120, Betsy invited you to make presentations at other hostess's parties. Within the first two months, you had given two presentations, pocketed 15 percent of sales for a total of $600. It happened so fast, you barely had time to read the manuals about properly presenting the toys, but with Betsy's coaching, you pulled it off gracefully. Unfortunately, phoning women who might play hostess and setting up and making presentations required much more time than you expected. Reluctantly, you put your newfound, in-home sales business on the back burner because of the time demands at work.

With Ben Stiller's edict to cut back your hours, however, you renew your interest in your multi-level marketing (MLM) business. You spend nights and weekends calling friends and friends of friends to find hostesses. Though the toy parties have not begun occurring every week, you're gathering momentum. You've attracted two women into your own sales team who need the same attention, training, and encouragement Betsy gave you.

This evening and weekend "moonlighting" begins to pay off when you manage to organize six parties a week, two run by you, four run by your two-woman sales team. Your take-home checks (15 percent for your own presentations and 5 percent for your team's presentations) now total as high as $550 per week, or $2,200 per month, but usually much less.

After six months, the pressure at work persists but the income from Tantalizing Toys looks promising. These realizations dawn on you: you still can't afford to quit your day job, you need to create a larger sales team to generate more income from toy sales, and you feel happier than you have in months. The stress at the office seems more palatable because it no longer absorbs all your time and attention. You've developed a new, more efficient way to handle most of the office workload in the time allowed, which you hadn't dreamed possible. However, getting the toy business up and running smoothly and consistently, despite its many challenges, has improved your situation, though not dramatically nor with any great degree of security.

BENEFITS OF A:

- You focus on something positive rather than rehashing negative and debilitating thoughts all day and night.
- Your energy level increases as you find yourself looking forward to doing something that stretches you and makes you grow.
- Tantalizing Toys provides a social life as well as a modest income.
- You sharpen your organizational skills and learn new sales skills.
- You feel happier than you have in months.

DOWNSIDES OF A:

- You do not know how far you can develop your toy business, which you fear will soon reach a saturation point in your community.
- Your job limits your moonlighting efforts.
- The money you earn from Tantalizing Toys comes in sporadically, sometimes as much as $2,200, sometimes as little as $300 per month.
- You doubt your ability to make enough money at toy sales to enable you to leave your job.

B. I can start gathering information about women's rights in the workplace and fight this injustice.

While you were rummaging around your kitchen desk drawer for a pencil to write down your options, you found a yellowed newspaper article by Julia Angwin in the *San Francisco Chronicle* about

Ida Castro, acting director of the Women's Bureau of the U.S. Department of Labor. You'd clipped it out for Caroline more than two years ago, but had forgotten to give it to her. As you reread the article you remember why you cut it out in the first place. Coming across it now feels like more than a coincidence.

Angwin notes, for instance, that on average women today earn about 72 cents for every dollar white males earn. Simply being female costs you 28 cents an hour. You can personally attest to that. But you hadn't thought about the impact of lower earnings throughout your working life on your Social Security pension benefits. Since your contributions to Social Security are based on wages, the less you contribute, the less you'll receive in retirement. "It's exponential," you realize. "Maybe it's too late to make a huge difference in my life, but not in Caroline's."

Angwin's story focuses on the Women's Bureau, established in 1920 to improve the working conditions of wage-earning women. It conducted a study of women workers that provided the basis for the law that enacted the forty-hour work week, it supervised the research for the Glass Ceiling Report, and it implemented the Family and Medical Leave Act of 1992. More important to you right now, the Bureau offers ongoing assistance to working women.

You debate whether to call their toll-free number, (800) 347-3741, or to visit their Internet site. Deciding in the end to use this opportunity to practice your Internet skills, you connect to www.dol.gov/dol/wb/public/ programs/fpc.htm. The information you find there astonishes you. You download an article, "Worth More Than We Earn: Fair Pay for Working Women," which recounts the Bureau's 1994 national survey, *Working Women Count!* In it more than a quarter of a million women responded that their number one concern was "improving pay scales."

You also download a series of "Don't Work In The Dark" publications on wage discrimination, age discrimination, and sexual harassment. The wage discrimination publication offers sound advice on what to do in your situation with Ben:

1. Write down what happened and keep a record of comments. Keep your notes in a safe place, not in the office.
2. Get emotional support from friends and family.
3. Keep doing a good job and keep a record of your work.
4. Find out how other women have been treated at your workplace.
5. Talk to your employer and explain your complaints in writing. Determine whether you can work out the problem informally or file a complaint with an agency. Check your employee handbook for procedures. Don't let your time to file a complaint run out before you've made your decision.
6. If you belong to a union, talk to your union steward or representative.
7. You have a right to file a charge, but the law limits the time frame for filing: as short as 180 days for filing with the U.S. Equal Employment Opportunity Commission (EEOC) at (800) 669-EEOC.

You're delighted with the information you've received from the Women's Bureau Clearinghouse, which includes a phone number for information on women workers' support groups in your area: (800) 827-5335. You call the number and find a support group near Hayward.

Four months later, you feel confident that you have assembled a strong case against your company, but you don't want to lose your job. Encouraged by your support group and armed with the knowledge you've gathered through your research, however, you present a well-thought out and well-written complaint to Ben. You can tell he's dumbfounded at your boldness and thoroughness, an understandable reaction since you've allowed him to verbally "beat you down" over the years. Not only do he and the company's President and CEO apologize to you, they offer you both the promotion and the salary increase you requested in your complaint, insisting on only one condition: that you drop the case.

BENEFITS OF B:

- You supported yourself with knowledge of your rights.
- You no longer plagued yourself with negative feelings about Ben because you found something more constructive to think about.
- You changed your victim mentality into that of a go-getter.
- You joined a support group and found women who understood and encouraged you.
- You took responsibility to take back control of your career.
- You got the raise, the promotion, and the security you wanted from your job.
- You share the information with Caroline to protect her from a similar predicament.

DOWNSIDES OF B:

- You still work for a company and a boss who won't quickly, if ever, change their fundamental age and gender prejudices.
- You must take time away from other tasks to build up your relationship with the now wary and fearful Ben Stiller.
- You wonder if your dogged determination to stay at Gardener Tool has prevented you from searching out and finding better career options.
- Working long hours once again, you have no time to experiment with entrepreneurial pursuits.

C. I can take Caroline's advice, quit my job, and start over again.

"Yes, you're right, Caroline," you say during the umpteenth telephone conversation with your daughter about your miserable situation at work. "On Monday I'm going to tell Ben I'm leaving."

When you hang up the phone, a burst of unexpected energy courses through your veins. Is it an adrenaline rush, or just plain fear? Whichever, you take some comfort from the fact that you have finally decided to *do* something. You're tired of complaining about work, Caroline's sick of hearing about it, and you're ready to move on.

You have enough money in savings to pay your rent for two, maybe three, months, long enough to survive while searching for another position. You're acutely aware that your age may work against you, however. Should you dare ask for a recommendation from Ben? You doubt it. You figure that if things get really tight, you could move in with Caroline for a while. You've neglected mentioning that to Caroline, however, because she's got her hands full with her new baby.

Having rehearsed your resignation over the weekend, you're shocked on Monday morning when your plan backfires. You approach Ben in the hallway to tell him you need to talk to him, but he brushes you off. Too busy. By noon, you feel like a robot, just functioning on autopilot. At three o'clock you walk into Ben's office while he's on the phone and stand four feet in front of his messy desk until he puts his hand over the mouthpiece and asks gruffly, "What the hell do you want?"

Despite rehearsing, you can barely choke out the words, "I'm giving you two weeks notice. I'm leaving."

Ben just smiles. "Do us both a favor. Clean out your office and leave right now."

You stand there horrified. What have you done?

On the way home you try to gather your thoughts. You feel angry, embarrassed, humiliated, and in shock. When you unlock the front door of your condo, your hands shake so badly you drop the keys. When you finally get inside, you walk straight to the medicine cabinet and grab the bottle of Valium. You take the elevator down to the basement to find the *San Francisco Sunday Examiner and Chronicle* in the newspaper recycle bin, opening the paper to the Career Search section on your elevator ride back up. You pour yourself a glass of Sutter Home white zinfandel and flop on the couch with a red pen and the paper. "No turning back now," you tell yourself. "I'm not telling Caroline what happened until I land a new job."

BENEFITS OF C:

- You decide not to put up with mistreatment at work.
- You react to Ben's response by immediately looking for another job.
- You have moved from inaction to action.

DOWNSIDES OF C:

- You don't start your job search soon enough, *before* you announced your leaving.
- You jump out of the frying pan into the fire.
- You avoid confronting Ben with your grievances, a fact that will nag at you in the future.
- You burn your bridges.
- You form only a vague back-up plan: the unlikely possibility that you could move in with your daughter without disrupting both of your lives.
- You react in a harmful way to Ben's quick dismissal by mixing a tranquilizer and wine.

D. I can keep a stiff upper lip and ride out the storm as long as I can.

Over the weekend you go to your hairdresser and tell her you want a complete makeover. "I need a new hairdo, a new make-up routine, a whole new me," you announce.

Much to your surprise, Angie, your hairdresser of ten years, replies, "Thank God! I've been dreaming about this for years."

Four hours later you look in the mirror and see your old shoulder-length, lifeless, brown pageboy transformed to a highlighted, layered, chin-length swing cut. Your familiar heavy black eyeliner has been replaced with soft brown mascara, and your blush and lip color has been transformed from the bright pink matronly look you've sported for years to softer brown hues.

"Angie, I love it!" you say, delighted.

"You look like a million bucks. What's the big occasion?"

"No occasion. Just trying to get out of a rut."

On Monday morning you stroll into your office determined to not let Ben or anyone else get you down. You figure you'll stay in your job as long as you can by simply withdrawing from your co-workers as much as possible. After all, you still have two jobs to do.

You stop by the office kitchenette, grab a Styrofoam cup, fill it with brewed coffee, Creamora, and Equal, and slip down the hall to your bland, impersonal office, embellished only with a silver framed photo of Caroline in her wedding dress. Before you do anything else, you tack a couple of posters to your wall. One shows a kitten clinging to a branch over the caption: "Hang in there." The other displays a sunrise over the Rocky Mountains. Sure, it's the same old office, but if feels a little more like home now.

During the lunch hour you stay in your office and eat your usual white bread with sliced Colby cheese, French's mustard, mayo, and iceberg lettuce. You unwrap your chilled Diet Coke from the newspaper and foil you use to keep it cool. You're a creature of habit. Your rituals make you feel in control of some aspect of your life, and today, you feel particularly daring having changed your hair and make-up and office decor. No one has seemed to notice, but you could care less.

Weeks go by. Your work situation doesn't improve one iota, which makes you feel even more resentful and depressed. Where will you find the sustenance to continue? Suddenly, it dawns you: talk to Pastor Smith.

After church on Sunday, you ask your pastor at Calgary Presbyterian Church if you could make an appointment to talk with him. Beaming his usual smile, he warmly invites you to stay after the eleven o'clock service. You're no stranger to him because you've sat on many church committees over the dozen years you've been a member.

Thirty minutes later, you glide out of the pastor's office elated. "You're the answer to *my* prayers," Pastor Smith had told you. Amazingly, the church accountant had suddenly resigned the week before due to health problems and you had walked in at precisely the right time. You love the congregation and the pastor. The salary compares favorably to what you earned at Gardener, and you have at last gained the job security and the sense of belonging you've so desperately craved. You can't believe your good fortune.

BENEFITS OF D:

- You decide you can weather any storm.
- You treat yourself to a makeover, not to impress anyone, but to lift your own spirits.
- You find solace and some form of control of your life by practicing your daily rituals.
- You seek help from your minister to overcome your frustrations.
- You find that sharing your concerns with others stimulates them to help you.

DOWNSIDES OF D:

- Your ostrich-like decision to stay in your job no matter what avoids the real issue of discrimination and mistreatment.
- You think it's better to live with the awful "known" job than to risk the "unknown."
- You get more angry and depressed.
- By choosing to stay in your job, you remain a victim, relegating responsibility for your miserable existence to conditions beyond your control.

Exploring the Issue

Most women at some time have experienced gender discrimination, and as we get older we begin to experience discrimination because of age. Whether you have felt discriminated against because of your appearance, your age, your economic or ethnic background, or whatever, and whether it's unfair or not, you can learn to deal with these situations more skillfully.

When women earn less than men for the same job, they get hit with a double whammy: lower take-home pay and lower Social Security pension payments at retirement. Today, according to the U.S. Department of Labor, more than 25 million women between the ages of forty and sixty-five work for a living. Every year that number increases as the Baby Boomers mature. The chances that you or someone you know will face age, wage, or gender discrimination have risen dramatically. What's the best defense against work discrimination of any kind at any age? Knowledge.

Women's associations for every trade, the Women's Bureau of the U.S. Department of Labor, and advocacy groups like the Women's Legal Defense Fund conduct surveys, provide advice, and offer seminars. They want you to reach out to them. They want to help you.

While progress toward wage equity has occurred in the last decade, it primarily has affected the public sector, partly because government employees' wages and job descriptions are public information. In the private sector changes are coming about slowly, but steadily. Be aware that twenty states have passed laws requiring fair pay and pay equity for state employees: California, Connecticut, Florida, Hawaii, Illinois, Iowa, Maine, Massachusetts, Michigan, Minnesota, New Jersey, New Mexico, New York, Oregon, Pennsylvania, Rhode Island, South Dakota, Vermont, Washington, and Wisconsin. You may not wish to become a Carry Nation and strap on battle gear for reform, but you should arm yourself with enough knowledge to win your own skirmishes in the workplace, should the need arise.

A nurse I met at a conference said her grandmother had advised her early on to demand equal pay. "Get paid for what you do, the same as a man," she had instructed. The nursing profession had long been considered a "woman's job" and, surprise, subjected to lower pay. The woman I spoke with works as a head nurse in a Bay Area hospital and strives diligently to enforce pay equity programs. She feels the fight has only just begun and hopes her daughter will carry on the fight in whatever field she chooses.

Knowledge, too, helps you determine if you're actually suffering from discrimination. If you think you may be, first evaluate yourself. Ask yourself if there's something in your life that's distracting you from doing the best you can at work. Have you let things slip? Have you lost interest? What part do *you* play in the equation?

Next, talk to your boss to learn his (or her) expectations. Confront him if you feel he hasn't treated you fairly, consistently, and respectfully. At a women's conference in San Jose, California, a bright young woman in her thirties who wants to become a manager and even a CEO in the future stood at the microphone to ask my panel of three successful women for advice. She stated that her boss consistently avoids her when she tries to talk to him or sends him memos about applying for the management training programs that her company offers. She explained how she thinks her boss feels about her, though she's never really talked to him about any of these issues "because he never makes time for me." She said she's so upset about the discrimination, she's contemplating quitting her job and finding another company where she may enjoy a better future. She asked the panel, "How can I get my boss's attention and make him realize I'm serious about moving up in my career?"

Panel member Betsy Bernard, former CEO and president of Pacific Bell Communications and currently USWest's Executive Vice President of Retail Markets, suggested to this eager young woman that she renew her efforts to speak with her boss. Betsy explained that as CEO of a huge corporation she often heard rumors about what she said, what she thought, what she was going to do, but *no one asked* her point blank. People *assumed* she would say, think, or do things, but never verified it with her. Betsy allowed that this woman's boss may or may not be trying to ignore her or keep her from moving up in the company, but if she were to quit, she would never know. Betsy pointed out, too, that rather than blaming the boss for not communicating, it was this woman's responsibility to create a time and setting to fulfill her needs.

If you're in this sort of situation, you must communicate what you want. Try setting up an appointment with your boss away from the office, perhaps over lunch, so you can get his undivided attention. Don't assume the worst. Find out the facts. Research. Talk. Communicate. Don't let anything hold you back in your career, especially yourself.

Expanding Your Thinking

The "you" in this adventure felt her age and gender kept her stuck in a job with inequitable pay, working for an insensitive boss. While your age clearly plays a role in this story, it can come into play for people at any age. As your office situation deteriorates, so does your self-confidence and pride. And that can happen to a twenty-five-year-old as well as a fifty-five-year-old woman.

You can weigh many options, but not all of them lead to beneficial solutions. Why? Ineffective, incomplete, poorly thought out decisions prevent you from seeing the big picture and your role in it. In Option A, you have no idea how far you can develop your business. You have no regular salary to count on, and doubt that you can earn enough from the toy business to enable you to leave your regular job. In this option, you got swept up in the festive atmosphere of the in-home parties, but you didn't fully understand the business commitment it requires.

In Option B, you doubt that your company will ever change its age and gender prejudices. You feel you may have wasted your time there, instead of pursuing other job opportunities, but you stay anyway.

Quitting your job in Option C will undoubtedly escalate into a major disaster if you continue to handle your depression by drinking wine and taking Valium. Disastrous results will occur, too, if you try to move in with Caroline. Certainly you think of your daughter as your safe haven in a storm, but you never mentioned to her that you're considering living with her if you run out of money. Rather than creating a plan of action to leave your job with someplace to go, you make matters worse. You hope to rectify your job situation by looking in the Career Search, but you're operating from a position of zero strength.

In Option D, you choose to do nothing to change your work situation, but rather to "ride out the storm." But the storm never ends. In this scenario you practice the passive approach, "If I try not to think about it, maybe it will go away." For a while you find comfort in your personal rituals, but eventually you realize you're still stuck in a job you hate. You keep your victim mentality and feel that things are beyond your control. Your cosmetic change isn't enough. You need to change your work conditions, and that takes changing your thinking so that you can see yourself somewhere else, earning decent money even at your age.

Stay aware of the following points:

DON'T:

1. Assume change for the better will happen without your making an effort.
2. Let self-doubt keep you stuck in a job.
3. Ignore the value of professional advice.
4. Think you can do it all by yourself.
5. Jump out of the frying pan into the fire.
6. Act or react in anger.
7. Burn your bridges.
8. Hold on to the "victim mentality."
9. Believe you must suffer through your "lot in life."
10. Think that any decision comes without consequences.

You do many positive things in this adventure. In Option A, you get involved in the MLM, Tantalizing Toys, which requires commitment, though maybe more than you realized. It takes effort, time, persistence, follow through, and organization. You develop a sales support staff.

In Option B, you research the information and tools you need to make a decision about your work situation with Ben. Rather than quitting, you prepare your case and present yourself as a professional woman who knows her job, and her rights.

You stand up for yourself in Option C. You do not put up with mistreatment and decide to quit your job.

In Option D, you recognize the need to make a change. You change your outward appearance and your office environment.

Doing so doesn't accomplish much, but it's a step in the right direction, if only to verify you *can* effect change. Finally, you seek advice from your pastor. His surprise job offer is pure luck. Or is it? You didn't know the church needs an accountant, but by reaching out to someone who might help you, you open yourself up to new ideas and opportunities.

Let's look at what "you" learned in this adventure that the real you can apply to your own life today.

DO:

1. Tap resources for information about work laws and discrimination to know your rights.
2. If you feel you may have a grievance, keep detailed notes.
3. If you think your job is in jeopardy, maintain records of your own work accomplishments and tasks.
4. Keep such records in a safe place away from the workplace.
5. Take responsibility for your situation and the future of your career.
6. Make certain you believe you can make changes productively.
7. Communicate with your boss regularly.
8. Seek professional advice to help direct you.
9. Look for another job while still employed, if possible.
10. If you're planning to change jobs, create a realistic fall-back plan.

Assessing Your Own Situation

What can you do to avoid the harmful effects of discrimination or feelings of victimization at work? What can you do if you feel stuck in a job?

1. Ask yourself, "Am I right for this job, and do I really want to be here?" "If I don't like my job, does it show?"
2. If you feel you are suffering from discrimination, ask yourself, "Do I know my rights?" "Have I read the employees' manual?" "Have I determined my company's position on age and gender issues?"
3. If you work for an insensitive or harassing boss, ask yourself, "Am I resentful of my boss because he doesn't appreciate me?" "Have I communicated what I want?" "Do I understand what he expects of me?"
4. If you think you want to "weather the storm" in your office, be sure you know what it takes to survive the long haul. "If I choose to stay, what will that mean in one year, in two years?" "How will staying effect my mental state?" "Will I be easy to live with, or will I take out my frustrations on friends and family?"
5. Understand the cycles in your industry. "Am I frustrated at work right now because it's the busy season and everyone is uptight?" "Can I handle this stress if I know it's only temporary?" "Do I want to be in a business with huge seasonal swings?"
6. Assess whether you've narrowed your thinking, and paralyzed yourself. "Have I lost the confidence that I can land a different job?" "Do I fear change more than this unpleasant atmosphere?" "If I choose not to confront my boss, or change jobs, can I do anything to make my work happier?"
7. Consider the worst case scenario if you stayed or if you left. "If I didn't have this job tomorrow, would I die?" "If I didn't have to come in to this office again, would I feel relieved?"

8. If gender, wage, or age issues disrupt your work, have you checked if they affect any of your co-workers? "If I feel this way, am I the only one?" "Would someone else benefit from the workers' rights information I'm researching?" "Could I help even one other woman avoid the hassles I've faced?"

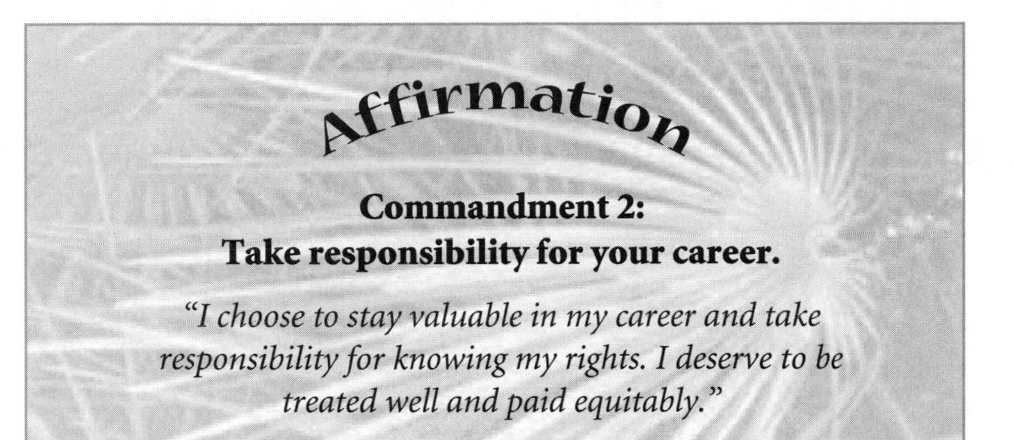

ADVENTURE 9

HOW DO I DEAL WITH RIVALRY AMONG WOMEN IN MY OFFICE?

Men may think of business as a "dog eat dog" affair, but dogfights look like child's play compared to rivalries among women. Have you ever felt the hairs on the back of your neck bristle when rivalry among women at work turns into a "cat scratch cat" affair? Perhaps you're dealing with a co-worker or a boss whose claws are always unsheathed. Maybe you threaten someone in your office with your own competitive zeal. To cope with the catfights that can cause so much disruption in the workplace, think through what you would do if you found yourself ***Stalked by the Tiger Woman.***

Stalked by the Tiger Woman

You describe your upbringing in "a blue collar middle class neighborhood" in Paramus, New Jersey this way: "My parents both owned their own businesses, my mother ran a hair salon and my father a bakery. I come from life-hardened people who lived through World War II in Berlin and then immigrated to America. I learned the value of hard work and obeying the household rules. I was a good girl who always did what I was told without complaint."

You put yourself through college by working as a waitress in a hotel restaurant, eventually earning a degree in Journalism. After college, you married a Navy man whose career moved you all around the world on assignment. You spent countless years in nameless locations involved with officers' wives' clubs, often as a protocol advisor. Through your experience in the wives' clubs, you learned many valuable lessons, from how to organize and motivate people to the most effective ways to guide gossiping groups into cooperative teams that implement and complete projects. When your husband, Tony, transfers to his last and permanent station in Coronado, California, you land a position in the telemarketing department for TELUSA, a long distance communications provider. Within two years you move up to middle management, heading up your own sales team.

While you never worked in an office setting prior to TELUSA, you believe that all your life experiences will enable you to succeed beautifully in your new job. After all, you possess a strong work ethic, know how to motivate people, and can operate comfortably within a strict chain of command. That's why when Patricia Donnelley, your immediate superior, tells you to crack the whip over your telemarketing team, you find yourself in a moral dilemma: whether to defy your boss's orders and manage your people in an inclusive, empowering way or to go against your grain with a more controlling style.

You arrive home after work on Friday emotionally wiped out. "Tony, this really ticks me off. I just don't get it."

"What's wrong, Meredith?"

"My boss, Patricia. She's wrong. She thinks that sales will increase if I come down hard on my group. She gave me an edict to 'Kick butt.' Not 'Let's see how we can increase revenues,' or 'What do you think will work?'"

"Why do you think she acts that way?" Tony asks simply.

"How should I know? She may be getting pressured from the top, but, you know, everyone calls her the Tiger Woman."

"Whoa, hold on a minute. You're making this personal. Think objectively for a moment."

"What do you mean?"

"You need to find out what revenue the company expects your team to bring in. Has it changed? By whose authority? Why? Have they set a deadline? Pretend you're an investigative reporter. Find out the who, what, why, when, and where of the situation." Good old Tony, always favoring the head over the heart. But maybe he's right.

When you try to apply a little logic to the predicament, however, you keep coming back to Patricia's personality. You've never felt comfortable around her. She's nothing like what you imagined in a corporate boss. She looks for things to criticize, finds nothing to compliment, and shares her goals in the form of tirades. You thought a woman in the corporate world would rely on her feminine preferences for communication and respect, not on following and issuing orders like a man. You know you do a good job, and you haven't experienced this kind of treatment before at TELUSA. Strangely, you've seen Patricia cheerfully encourage others in the office. But when she relates to you, she never looks you straight in the eye, and she seems ready to pounce on your every move. More and more, you feel like a mouse in the Tiger's lair.

You ask Tony, "Could Patricia possibly be setting me up for failure?"

"I don't know. If you fail, she fails. So maybe her approach comes from somewhere else? How secure does she feel in her position? Have you been nipping at her heels? Is the ladder getting narrower toward the top?" Logical Tony throws out question after question, trying to get all the facts straight before an enemy engagement.

"Okay, what do you suggest?"

"You need a battle plan. Study the enemy and the terrain, gather your weapons, then choose a course of action you think will create a win/win situation. Can you think up four ways you might win this skirmish?"

When Tony smiles at you, you don't smile back. You're too busy mentally strapping on your bulletproof vest.

Over the weekend you develop these four plans:

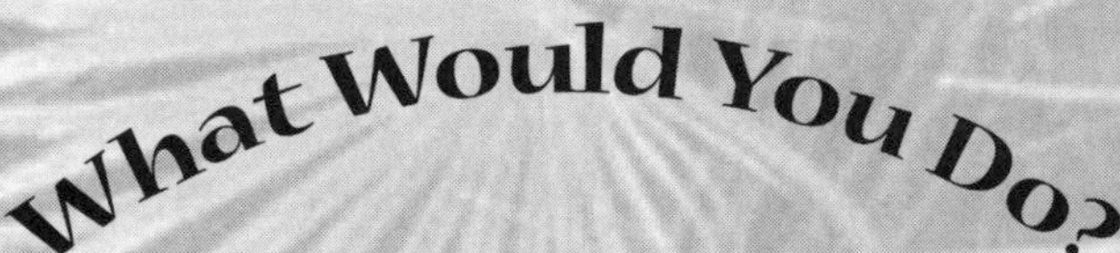

A. I won't try to tell Patricia she's wrong, I'll just show her I can get results without "kicking butt."

B. I can research company policy and procedures to verify what's expected of my team, then I will confront Patricia if necessary.

C. I can try to make Patricia an ally.

D. I can ignore Patricia, do my job, and hope she'll ease off.

Turn to the option that most appeals to you. To learn the most from this adventure, read how the other options turned out, too. Then study the last three sections of this adventure: "Exploring the Issue," "Expanding Your Thinking," and "Assessing Your Situation."

A. I won't try to tell Patricia she's wrong, I'll just show her I can get results without "kicking butt."

At work Monday morning you call a team meeting to announce your new sales strategy: "Every Monday for the next six weeks will be 'Silver Bullet Day.' The person who closes the most sales that day gets a bonus." You emphasize the point by throwing fifty one dollar bills into the air and watching as they flutter onto the polished teak conference table, the gray carpeting, and into your team's outstretched hands.

"I'm in!" shouts the buff, bike-to-work jock and super sales go-getter, as he gathers up bills and stacks them neatly on the table.

"That's the spirit. Why are we here? To close sales. For the next six weeks we're blitzing. I'll pay the bonus on Monday, but I want you to make every day a Monday. On the wall over here, you'll see an orange day-glow bar chart just waiting to be filled in. I've written incremental dollar amounts along the left side. And across the bottom I've made thirty marks denoting five days a week for six weeks. At the end of each day your individual sales figures will go on this graph. In six weeks I expect it to look like Mt. Everest."

You look around to make sure everyone gets it, then you continue. "At the end of every 'Silver Bullet' day the top-selling team member that day will get a real silver bullet, a $50 bill, and the privilege to provide pizza for the entire team the following Monday for lunch. Any questions?"

"Do you have any specific target market in mind?" asks Eileen, the bright brunette fresh out of Cal Poly.

"What works best for you, Eileen?"

"I like targeting small businesses."

"Fine, you choose. Anyone else?" As you look around the room, you see that everyone seems eager to get back on the phones. "Okay, take no prisoners!"

Your team's sales beat expectations for all six weeks of the contest. When two team members tied for sales the third Monday, you presented both with the awards. Everyone seemed happy and revved up, everyone except Patricia, who grew more annoyed at you than ever. You just can't figure her out. You achieved the results she demanded without coming down hard on your team. She should have congratulated you, but she's still got her claws out. You keep looking over your shoulder to make certain she won't find an opportunity to rake them down your back.

BENEFITS OF A:

- You create a plan to increase team sales through an incentive game.
- You motivate your team with a theatrical presentation of your plan.
- You let your team decide which target group to attack during for the six-week blitz.
- Your plan works and revenues exceed goals.
- You display strong, positive managerial skills.

DOWNSIDES OF A:

- You disregard a direct request from your manager.
- You alienate Patricia even more.
- You choose to "Show Patricia" a better way, but in reality make her look ineffective.
- You feel more uncomfortable in the office around Patricia.
- Your boss does not appreciate your managerial skills.
- You don't try to build rapport with Patricia.

B. I can research company policy and procedures to verify what's expected of my team, then I will confront Patricia if necessary.

You step into the Human Resources (HR) department to learn more about company philosophy. You fully expect to discover that Patricia's "kick butt" mentality runs counter to the way the company wants managers to operate. What you do find surprises you, however. Dottie, the HR manager, has quit to start her own consulting business and April, the office manager, has been juggling both jobs for two weeks.

"Help yourself to the policy manual over there, Meredith," April says with a wry smile, nodding to a splayed binder on a shelf half hidden under a jumble of file folders and displaced papers with "to file" stickers attached.

"Wow, what happened? Dottie nuke the place before she left?"

"It seems that none of the updates to the manual have been added for, oh, I don't know, months. When I looked for something the other day I caught my jacket sleeve on the corner of the binder, flipped it off the shelf and sent pages, dividers, everything, flying across the room. It looked like a jumbo jet had blasted its engines through here. I stacked the stuff back on the shelf, and it's been there ever since."

You like April. She handles frustration with such an endearing sense of humor. "You need help. Has anyone applied for the job?" you ask.

"We haven't had time to start a job search, Meredith," April groans.

"Who do I talk to? I could do this job," you say out loud, thinking to yourself, "I'd certainly enjoy this mess more than working under the Tiger Woman."

When you ask Patricia's boss, the general manager, Monty Steele, about the opening, he welcomes you to step in to assist in the personnel department until the company can hire someone else. You would earn less than you would as a sales manager, at least to start. It's an "iffy" move, you could find yourself replaced by an HR professional in a matter of months, and there's no going back to sales manager, but you decide to take the chance. You'll do anything to avoid engaging in a cat fight with Patricia.

The new assignment turns out well. Three months into it, you find that HR work suits you much better than sales management. Not only have you escaped Patricia's rancor, but you really enjoy dealing with rules and regulations. You value the need for written policies and procedures, which remind you of military regulations. You like that. You can still motivate and guide people without cracking a whip to increase performance. And you're so happy you created a sensible way to get out from under Patricia's domination.

April, relieved that she no longer must perform both her own and Dottie's jobs, constantly tells you what a great job you're doing, and says that she thinks upper management feels the same way. Her suspicion proves true when you win the full-time position and a substantial raise.

BENEFITS OF B:

- You research company policy to learn if it supports your standing up to Patricia.
- You see an opportunity to move out of sales management into HR.
- You believe you'd enjoy the work of an HR manager.
- Your personality and background match the position's requirements.
- You take a risk by assuming a temporary HR position, even though you would forever give up your sales manager position in the company.
- You prove yourself effective and win a permanent HR position.

- You feel comfortable in personnel because it taps the best of your abilities.
- You receive a raise for your good work.

DOWNSIDES OF B:

- You seek the HR job to escape from Patricia.
- You find a way out of your situation with Patricia by default.
- You risk losing a good paying job for a temporary position.
- You take the temporary position in a department with which you have no previous experience.
- You never tried to communicate your frustration with Patricia, so you'll never know if you could have worked things out.

C. I can try to make Patricia an ally.

You sense that your difficulty with Patricia stems from her insecurity working for her own boss, Monty Steele, a former San Diego State University fullback. He approaches sales the same as he moved the football down the field: with unrelenting pressure. "Kick butt" could be his middle name. As Patricia's superior, he acts like a tough-minded coach whenever she misses her sales goals, which in his eyes amounts to fumbling the ball inside the ten yard line. He regularly rebukes her efforts and continually demands that she give it the old "110 percent." He has created a company atmosphere that smells like a losing team's locker room at the end of a game, and he has turned Patricia into the cheerleader from hell.

Somehow you need to convince her that you can create a plan that brings in sales and makes her look like a Heisman Trophy winner to Monty Steele. You explain to her your idea for a six-week sales blitz and a weekly "Silver Bullet" award to the person with the best sales record each Monday during that six weeks.

"Can't you just see this?" you urge. "With the $50 weekly bonuses, the award of a real silver bullet, and Monday pizza lunches, we'll get the team rolling."

"I wonder if it could work," Patricia purrs. "You know, Meredith, I never really felt comfortable with Monty's pressure tactics." In a way, you feel sorry for Patricia. Who in her right mind would ever try to stand up to Monty? If she accepts your idea, however, she won't need to confront him. She'll prove to him that she can carry the ball to victory.

"I sure would feel uncomfortable reporting to him," you confide. "So let's just win the game our way. Here, look at this contest chart. I've got this sheet of orange day-glow poster board. I'll draw it up, and you can explain it in tomorrow morning's sales meeting. Okay?" You can see her wavering, but she finally comes around.

"Okay But if this doesn't work, it's your butt he'll kick, not mine."

The meeting goes exactly as you planned, and so does the entire sales blitz. Patricia takes full credit, also as you planned. When she receives public recognition from Monty Steele, she takes you more and more into her confidence. She's changed from Tiger Woman into Pussycat, albeit one you wouldn't want to spend your free time with. Your personalities still don't mesh. You can't refuse, however, when she insists that the two of you meet after work to go shopping for new shoes. Since you've made her look good, she thinks of you as her new best friend (one she needs to assure her future success). You don't know which you dislike more, old Tiger Woman or the new Clinging Kitten.

BENEFITS OF C:

- You develop a win/win situation with Patricia.
- You convince Patricia to support and lead your incentive plan to increase sales.
- You try to make her look good to her boss.

- Your plan works, both to increase sales and make Patricia look good.
- You turn Patricia into your ally.

DOWNSIDES OF C:

- Your plan to get Patricia off your tail backfires.
- Patricia now won't leave you alone because she sees you as her key to success.
- You're stuck with an entirely different, but just as sticky situation.

D. I can ignore Patricia, do my job, and hope she'll ease off.

Monday morning you show up at work as if nothing has happened, ignoring Patricia's insistence that you "kick butt." You've resolved to do your job your way. After all, she has given you no specific direction concerning what she expects you to do—no guidance, no leadership—so you decide to go about "business as usual" for as long as you can. Who can figure out such a woman anyway? Nevertheless, you feel tense and wary, as though Patricia could pounce on you at any moment.

You sense that Patricia, a master meddler, watches your every move, reporting your every little misdeed to her boss, Monty Steele. You can almost hear her shrill voice blaming you for her own lack of leadership, laziness, and ineptitude. Your resentment toward her blossoms into full-fledged disgust.

Eileen, a mediocre salesperson on your team, comes to your office door. "Meredith, can I talk to you a minute? I have a real problem."

"Come in. What's the matter?"

Eileen leans toward you as she sits on the edge of the navy blue upholstered chair across from you, looking every bit like a little girl bursting with a juicy secret. She looks around and almost hisses, "Dawn ticks me off because she's always talking about me behind my back."

"What do you mean? About what?"

"I'm not sure exactly, but every time I walk by her desk I hear her whisper something to Rod next to her. It gives me the creeps. I hate whisperers."

"Have you asked her about it?"

"No, I was hoping you'd say something to her, or to everyone about the whispering around here."

"She's new here, you know. Give her a chance. Try asking her to join you for lunch. In the meantime, remember it's irrelevant what others think about you, except me, as long as you're meeting your sales quota. How are you doing this week, by the way?"

"Okay, I guess. Dawn really distracts me, though."

"I'll see what I can do," you sigh.

You don't understand the younger women in your office any more than you do Patricia. They seem to lack focus and self-discipline. You've started doubting your abilities to motivate and manage them. Navy wives posed no problem, they understood the chain of command. These young people seem distracted by every little commotion and want their hands held all the time. Maybe Patricia knows what she's doing, maybe these people respond to getting their butts kicked. "Such a gross term," you think. You equate that form of management with people who use four letter words only because they lack command of the English language.

Sitting behind your Steel Case desk, you think that your self-imposed neutrality sucks every bit of enjoyment from your job. You feel powerless both to confront Patricia and to keep peace in the office. You laugh at your own hypocrisy: you refuse to stand up to Patricia, but you encourage Eileen to fight her own battles with Dawn. You seriously consider quitting before you get fired.

BENEFITS OF D:

- You try a non-confrontational approach.
- You remain true to your convictions.
- You see you own weakness when you advise Eileen to communicate with Dawn even though you can't with Patricia.

DOWNSIDES OF D:

- Your plan to ignore Patricia's requests makes you feel uncomfortable and powerless.
- You adopt the ostrich approach, hoping that an ugly situation will disappear, but it doesn't.
- Your new plan of "staying out of the way" robs you of any enjoyment you formerly felt in your job.
- You thought you could manage anyone but discovered you know only how to manage Navy wives.
- You assume Patricia complains about you to her boss, but you never confront her or communicate your concerns.
- You give bad advice to Eileen that it doesn't matter what others in the office think of her.
- You realize your own hypocrisy and consider quitting your job.

Exploring the Issue

Healthy competition in an office challenges players to perform at peak levels, keeps their sense of adventure alive, and makes reaching the common goal more exciting. A woman exercises healthy rivalry when she respects the best in others. That said, most of us think rivalry in an office engenders backbiting, jealousy, and malicious gossip. What causes this sort of rivalry?

You need not personally experience unhealthy rivalry in an office to understand how distracting and uncomfortable it can be. At first glance, rivalry may seem to stem from someone feeling insecure, but it's usually more complicated than that. Knowing the reasons, spotting the causes, and identifying how to correct or avoid them can arm you with powerful tools to keep in your briefcase.

Perceived injustices breed insecurity and cause negative rivalry. An office "fairness" balance is fragile, and sustaining it requires the wisdom of Solomon. Office equilibrium falls apart when even one person sloughs off her responsibilities, or regularly shows up late, or circulates office gossip and gets away with it. In an office where management identifies clear goals, communicates clearly and often with employees, acknowledges and appreciates individual efforts, and requires that everyone must set standards, negative rivalry automatically diminishes.

Does one person in your office appear to receive preferential treatment? Does it appear that bigger clients or new business get funneled to her and not to others? Does one of two people with equal seniority and responsibilities receive higher pay than the other?

From a managerial point of view, how can you deal with negative rivalry in your office? The short version: identify, clarify, communicate, appreciate, and if necessary, replace. For example, let's look at how rivalry wreaked havoc in a mortgage company branch office, and how one manager, whom I'll call Shannon, handled the situation. As in any office, the situation sometimes gets pretty far out of hand before a manager gets wind of dissension among the troops, and Shannon didn't know it existed until she was practically blown away when three brokers wanted to quit. At the time, the housing market was exploding, and sales practically threw themselves in the brokers' laps, so what could have been going wrong?

Shannon called every broker individually into her office. After each had presented their comments, an interesting and unfortunate tapestry of misinformation, half-truths, and misdirected jealousies unfolded. The source of the communications mess pointed to the receptionist. Shannon understood that a receptionist typically has her finger on the heartbeat of a company and knows what's going on better than almost anyone else because she's privy to every incoming call, to what deliveries go to whom, and to the comings and goings of employees. But a receptionist doesn't necessarily understand how it all fits together.

Shannon believed that if she had communicated to Bobbi, the receptionist of three years, how valued and appreciated she was, then perhaps she wouldn't have needed to establish her importance in the office by parceling out bits and pieces of misinformation and half-truths. Bobbi, the Queen of Gossip, gave her "official" answers to everyone who wanted to know why so-and-so's name was on a brochure rather than their own, or why somebody else got the package of mortgages from a new development, and so on. Bobbi violated the number one rule: do your own job and refer office questions to the manager. When Shannon called Bobbi into her officc to tell her how her comments had dispirited individual brokers, how those comments pitted one broker against the other, and how her comments contributed to the unrest and unhappiness in the office, Bobbi cried. "I didn't mean to upset people. I didn't know I did that."

Shannon reiterated to Bobbi her specific boundaries and duties, and the importance of her handling situations with discretion. She gave Bobbi more projects to complete "because you obviously do not have enough to keep your mind occupied." About three weeks after the incident, Bobbi resigned, giving two weeks notice. Shannon chose not to hire someone during those two weeks because she didn't want Bobbi training the new receptionist. Shannon wanted to do that herself.

Once Shannon identified the source of the problem, she clarified the situation to everyone in the office and communicated why she expected them to come to her, not the receptionist, with questions. Shannon also told me she realized she needed to show more attention and appreciation to the brokers in the office in order to make sure they felt secure in their positions.

If you think people in your office see you as brighter, prettier, quicker than others in the office, you're ripe for resentment. Why? Your peers or even your immediate superiors may fear that you're raising the bar so high that they can't hurdle it. You threaten the office equilibrium, and possibly their careers. Sometimes you can become the "bad apple" simply because you're the best worker. Unfair? You bet. But don't throw in the towel. Instead, assess how you present yourself to others in the office. What role do you play in this drama? If you feel you've conducted yourself properly in a non-threatening way, and that you've identified the source and tried to dispel any misunderstandings, but see the unpleasant rivalry continuing, you have a real problem. When that happens, people usually do one of three things: one, lower their personal standards and expectations to fit the mold; two, "stay out of the way" and create a situation of zero power and growth for themselves, which stifles any enjoyment from the job; three, change companies to one that values their assets.

To avoid negative rivalry, never assume to know what someone else said, did, meant, or thought. And, certainly, don't tell others what you think someone else said, did, meant, or thought. Ask. Your best defense against rivalry? Communication.

Expanding Your Thinking

In this adventure "you" stumble into rivalry. Despite your years dealing with groups of women, the problem baffles you. In your past experience, you managed women of similar ages and backgrounds, the women in the officers' wives' clubs. In your Navy years, you motivated and led women similar to yourself, who honored the chain of command. You didn't understand that the dynamics of managing people with different ages and backgrounds can differ. In business, though people should follow their boss's demands, employees can choose to trust their manager or someone outside the office. When this happens, the manager doesn't know where she stands because someone else can override her authority. She can grow insecure, resentful, and even malicious.

You experience this firsthand when your boss, Patricia, issues an order to "kick butt" that you don't agree with. You were greatly influenced by Tony, your husband, and by your own successful experiences leading officers' wives. Tony's advice to you is only partially correct because the who, what, when, where, how, and why of journalism doesn't fit an office situation in which the dynamics change daily. You feel you have to strap on battle gear to enter your office. You doubt Patricia's methods and motives, which leads to your moral dilemma: to obey or not to obey. When making that decision, you did some things that didn't work out well.

In Option A, you feel ill at ease when you ignore the direct request of your boss. Your idea to increase sales does not jibe with your boss's, and when it works, you take away her power and alienate her.

In Option B, you use a different job in the company as an escape from your problem with your boss. You never try to communicate with your boss to work things out. You accept a temporary job, in hopes of turning it into a permanent position, but there are no guarantees.

In the wrong office environment a strong personality becomes a threat. In Option C, you pose a threat, hoping to keep the situation at bay until you can help others around you feel more secure. But you can't always accomplish that. You form a game plan that makes Patricia look good in her boss's eyes, but you don't expect that Patricia now associates her success with you and wants to exploit your relationship beyond the workplace. You create a different kind of monster and a new dilemma.

In Option D, you try to ignore the entire situation, counting on it to magically disappear. You mistakenly believe that a non-confrontational attitude will save you from Patricia's pressure. It doesn't work. You feel uneasy and continue to distrust Patricia.

You cannot enjoy your work, because you feel you constantly must look over your shoulder. Worse, you become a hypocrite.

What sorts of ineffective thinking should you avoid in your own life?

DON'T:

1. Try to make the best out of a bad situation indefinitely.
2. Avoid confronting your rival.
3. Lower your quality of work or self-expectations because someone else does not appreciate them.
4. Play hurtful "behind people's back" games.
5. Enter into office gossip.
6. Subordinate your principles and values.
7. Hope that an ugly situation will get better without your efforts to change it.
8. Assume that you know what others are thinking without asking them.
9. Isolate yourself in a job you dislike.
10. Waste your life in a company where you aren't appreciated and feel uncomfortable.

You entered the business world as a strong, confident, mature woman with valuable experience from your years as a military wife. In the right circumstances, a company would appreciate your strengths and allow you to blossom. In this adventure, when that doesn't happen, you must learn how to handle the problem gracefully.

In Option A, Patricia's "kick butt" speech mimics her boss, Monty Steele, who has made her feel inept and insecure. Her insecurity makes her pass the pressure on to you. You decide to show her a positive way you can achieve the goal to increase revenues.

Your "Silver Bullet" sales incentive program works. However, by creating your action plan, whether it proved productive or not, you make Patricia more insecure. She fears being replaced by you, and continues playing Tiger Woman.

In Option B, you find the right fit in HR. You like procedures and regulations, black and white rules with gray areas. The personnel position you land suits you perfectly, because in it you can be nice and friendly, yet knowledgeable and firm. You draw on your organizational skills and enjoy a position where you can encourage and direct people.

Your decision in Option C to create an action plan for which Patricia can take credit and prove her effectiveness to her boss produces good results. You want Patricia to look good in her boss's eyes, to feel more secure in her position, and to become your ally.

In Option D, you choose to stay neutral and out of Patricia's way. You see your own weakness dealing with Patricia and feel like a hypocrite when you advise one of the younger women on your team to stand up to her nemesis.

What positive points can you glean from this adventure to use in your life?

DO:

1. Face your dilemma, and your nemesis, head on.
2. Use your own values as a compass.
3. Identify the source of your problem and your role in it.
4. Clarify any misunderstandings as they occur.
5. Check out company policy with personnel.
6. Create a plan to form a win/win situation with your rival.
7. Smother your rival with kindness, or at least understanding.
8. Keep the quality of your own work high.

9. Acknowledge your own strengths.
10. Look for openings in other departments within your company before you quit.

Assessing Your Own Situation

If you suspect rivalry in your job, try asking yourself broad questions.

1. Ask yourself, "Do I like the culture of this company?" "Does this company culture bring out the best in me?" "Can I be myself here, or do I hold back?"
2. If you feel uncomfortable, ask, "What or who bothers me?" "Can I approach that person/situation to clarify issues?" "Can I expect change?"
3. When someone in your office treats you unfairly, ask, "Is there something in my behavior I can change to alleviate the problem?" "Do I understand this person's motives, pressures?" "Can I find a way to make this person my ally?"
4. If your boss annoys you, ask, "Does she annoy everyone, or just me?" "Is there a pattern in her behavior, or am I the brunt of her harassment?" "Have I tried to communicate my concerns with her?"
5. Have you talked to the personnel department? Ask, "Do I understand company policy?" "Are there openings in another department?" "What are my options in this company?"
6. How does rivalry affect you personally? Ask, "Am I on the defensive all of the time?" "Am I constantly distracted from work because of this annoying person?" "Has my quality of work suffered?" "Do I take my work problems out on my family?"

7. Where do you want to go? "Is sticking this out part of my vision for myself, or do I just feel I don't I have a choice?" "Is what I'm doing consistent with what I'm striving to achieve in my life/career?"

8. Have you pulled back to put things in perspective? Ask, "Have I tried to calm down or meditate, or do I constantly repeat frustrating conversations in my mind?" "Can I forgive my rival for making my life difficult and find a way to help her out of her insecurities?" "Is it time to look for another job?"

Affirmation

Commandment 3:
Change your thinking, change your life.

"I will enjoy what I do in an environment of mutual trust and respect."

ADVENTURE 10

HOW DO I MANAGE FORMER PEERS WHEN I GET THAT BIG PROMOTION?

Has a promotion ever altered your relationships in your office? Perhaps you've experienced both sides of it, either as the one promoted or as one of those passed over in favor of a peer. If not, imagine how office dynamics might change if your peers today were to report to you tomorrow. You could easily find yourself Puzzled by Peer Pressure.

Puzzled by Peer Pressure

You've always loved solving jigsaw puzzles, playing solitaire, and working with numbers. You enjoy seeing how puzzle pieces, playing cards, and combinations of numbers fall into patterns that create both desired and unexpected outcomes. That explains your proclivity for accounting, the subject in which you earned a degree at Michigan State University.

After graduation, you felt comfortable and confident crunching your beloved numbers for Tool Express, a small machine tool manufacturing company in West Bloomfield, just outside Detroit. However, after five years of disruptive competition from overseas competitors, resulting in cutbacks in production at the major U.S. automobile manufacturers, the founder of Tool Express, your boss and sole owner of the business, Harold Bernstein, decides to close the company's doors forever. "I'm ready to retire, anyway," Harold tells clients and employees, though you could see through his false cheerfulness.

Harold, fatherly to a fault, has always provided the best he could for his employees, so when he closes shop, he awards everyone a bonus of two month's pay. Struggling not to drown in your depression, you walk away from the single story shop on a typical gray winter day. The weather matched your mood. You felt the loss like you would a death in your family. After all, Tool Express *was* your family.

Your roommate, Maria Ramirez, tries to cheer you up, encouraging you to look around, go to a placement center, read the classifieds. But for six weeks you can do nothing but grieve. "You don't understand," you tell Maria when she scolds you for being so gloomy. "Working for Harold has been much more than a job. I felt safe there, as if the company wrapped me up in a comfortable cocoon."

At the end of two months, however, Maria gives you a tip she's picked up from an insurance broker friend about an opening for an accountant at a large insurance firm. She encourages you to interview for the position at the Chambers National Insurance Company in Detroit, saying, "It's supposed to be a great place for women to work." You land the job easily, despite the fact that you feel uneasy about working for a large firm that you assume can't possibly provide the family-like atmosphere of your old company. Much to your surprise, though, it doesn't take long before you form close working relationships with co-workers in your department. As you gain a reputation as an efficient and dependable team member, you once again begin to feel like part of a happy family.

Now, three years later when your manager marries and moves to Memphis, you can't believe your good fortune when the company offers you her position. For the first time in your life, you face the daunting task of leading a group of people—your accounting group, your pals, your family. It all makes you feel a little sheepish. "One day I'm a sister, the next day I'm a mom," you confide to Maria. "I know the business, I love numbers, but I fear managing these people I love."

"You'll be terrific at it, " insists Maria.

"Oh, trust and approachability are not my problem, but discipline and accountability are," you counter.

"Nonsense, Yolanda. No one has a problem with you as their boss."

"They may not, but I do," you lament.

"Buy some management books, read up, take classes, go to seminars, but whatever you do, don't 'wing' it. Know what you're doing and why. Look at managing people like a jigsaw puzzle, see how the 'pieces' interrelate to complete the picture. Make it fun."

Maria always makes everything sound so simple. You envy her attitude toward life, her consistent ability to make things fun. "I suppose you're right, Maria," you concede.

"Of course I am. Now take advantage of your great opportunity. Remember, it's not about you, it's about getting the job done."

She's right, of course, but you can't help imagining your former peers growing jealous of your new power, unconsciously sabotaging your performance, or simply growing distant from you. How, you wonder, can you make sure that doesn't happen?

You decide to follow Maria's advice, adding a few other ideas of your own. You write them down.

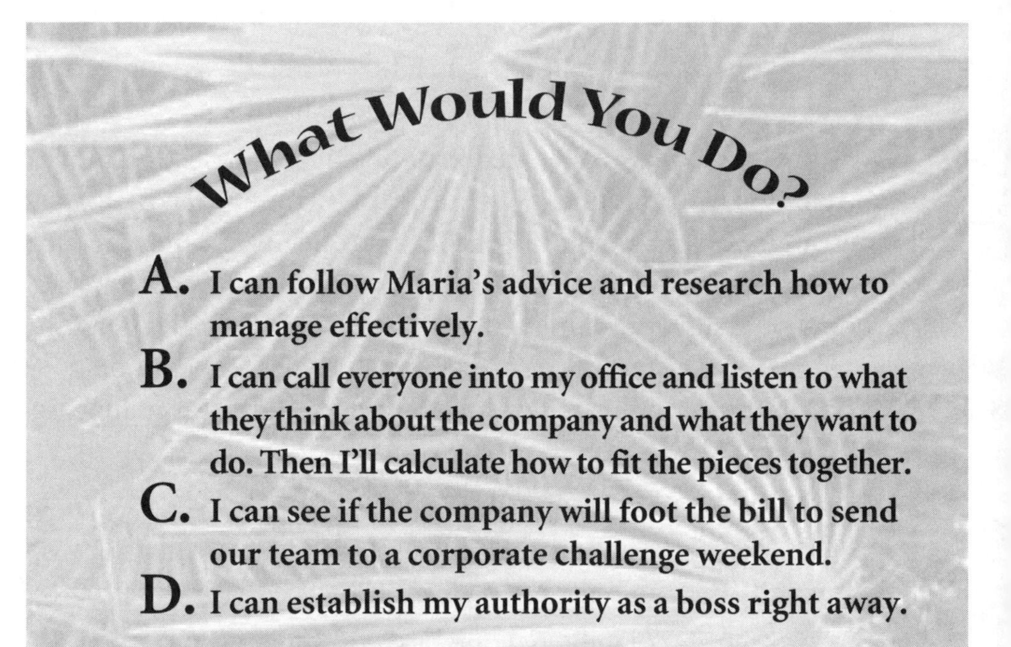

What Would You Do?

A. **I can follow Maria's advice and research how to manage effectively.**

B. **I can call everyone into my office and listen to what they think about the company and what they want to do. Then I'll calculate how to fit the pieces together.**

C. **I can see if the company will foot the bill to send our team to a corporate challenge weekend.**

D. **I can establish my authority as a boss right away.**

Turn to the option that most appeals to you. To learn the most from this adventure, read how the other options turned out, too. Then study the last three sections of this adventure: "Exploring the Issue," "Expanding Your Thinking," and "Assessing Your Situation."

A. I can follow Maria's advice and research how to manage effectively.

On your first day as boss, you nervously approach the door of your new office. Inside, you find a note on your desk from Lydia Rothberg, the head of Human Resources. It reads: "Congratulations,

Yolanda. Welcome to the management team at Chambers National Insurance Company. Please join me for lunch on Wednesday. Best, Lydia Rothberg."

You feel thrilled at the thoughtfulness of the note, which Lydia must have known would arrive at exactly the moment you needed it most. You're not worried at all about the work itself; you're an ace at accounting and have mastered the nuances of the insurance business. You're worried about the people side of managing, especially overseeing the work of former peers.

You've been reading management books, and you particularly like *The One Minute Manager*, but everything sounds so oversimplified in print. Real life seems much more complicated than the gurus suggest. Nevertheless, you're happy to have a resource library at your fingertips. You assume that every time someone comes to you with a question, you'll say, "I'll get back to you on that," then you can madly research the situation at night in one of your tomes on effective management.

At the luncheon on Wednesday in an intimate Italian restaurant kitty-corner from the office, you're surprised but pleased that Lydia brings along three other women managers from the company: Maureen Nickelson, Brenda Bogner, and Adrianne McNalley. They all share their stories of their first week as managers, and their experiences—both good and bad—comfort you a lot. What a gift! They suffered every fear that has plagued you, they handled or mishandled all of them, and they survived to tell the tale. The key, they all insist, is to rely on a support group. You had never imagined that such a group of helpful women existed in your company. They each literally extend their hands to help you sail safely through your new responsibilities.

"Welcome to The Old Girl Network, Yolanda, Chambers National's mentoring program," explains Lydia. "We've all used it, both to learn skills and solve problems. TOGN gets together every Wednesday for lunch, but attendance isn't mandatory, nor does it restrict itself to one day a week. Think of it as a lifeboat. It's always there when you need it. You'll meet many different women here.

Some you might relate to more closely than others, so feel free to develop whatever mentoring relationships that work for you. We come from all departments of Chambers National. It's a great way to keep your finger on the heartbeat of the company, to learn and grow and solve problems. Before long, you'll be an Old Girl, too."

"I feel better already," you admit, feeling greatly relieved that you can so easily join this new family of peers.

"I'll put your name down for the next management training session Chambers offers, Yolanda. But take advantage of these lunches, they teach you more about the nuts and bolts of managing than ten MBA classes."

"I certainly will. Thanks, Lydia."

"Oh, by the way, I've written down the names of professional associations you should consider joining. There's a strong chapter of the American Business Women's Association (ABWA) here in Detroit. It's a good group. It offers seminars, training in management and leadership, and mentoring. Also, the American Society of Women Accountants (ASWA) recently chartered a chapter here. It offers professional and technical training and promotes networking and mentoring among managers from different companies. Another useful association is the Business and Professional Women USA (BPW/USA)."

You look down at the paper Lydia hands you. It lists:

ABWA, 9100 Ward Parkway, Kansas City, Missouri 64114-0728, (816) 361-6621.

ASWA, moving to Chicago, check end of June for new address and phone. Call Gretchen Blumingberg (800) 326-2163.

BPW/USA, 2012 Massachusetts Avenue NW, Washington, DC 20036, (202) 293-1100.

"Thank you, again, everyone. Really nice meeting all of you," you say as you gather your coat and purse. You head back to the office feeling excited about your new challenge, and a bit overwhelmed by all the resources available. You want your former peers to trust and respect you as their manager, and you fully expect that all this support will enable you to develop into an effective leader.

BENEFITS OF A:

- You listen to Maria's good advice and don't try to "wing" it as a manager.
- You assemble your own reference library of management books.
- You go to lunch with the head of human resources and other women managers who share their experiences.
- You find out about weekly luncheon meetings of The Old Girl Network and plan to attend.
- You get a list of associations that could help increase your leadership skills and put you in touch with other potential mentors.

DOWNSIDES OF A:

- You don't sit down with your former peers to find out if any of your fears are justified.
- You think that you can hold off answering questions until you go home and consult a management book for guidance.
- You do not actively seek help from other women who have "been there" before you.

B. I can call everyone into my office and listen to what they think about the company and what they want to do. Then I'll calculate how to fit the pieces together.

On your first day as manager you hold a meeting with your eight-person team. You explain that you want to be fair and equitable, and that you want to know what's on everyone's mind about the direction of their jobs, the company, and their futures. "I'm passing around this calendar. Put a day and time down next to your name for a one-on-one conference with me. I'll post the schedule tomorrow for the hour-long individual meetings. Thank you very much," you say, pleased with your open, direct first-day manner.

During the next two weeks you meet with all of the members of your team. You're surprised and disappointed at their lack of candor during their conferences. It's as though they can't or won't any longer share their true feelings with you, as though you already know too much about their personal opinions and worries. Some even seem to resent your "prying" into their thoughts. But when it comes to their opinions about the direction of the company and their particular jobs, they talk nonstop.

At home that night you tell Maria, "I didn't learn as much as I expected during the individual meetings. But I think I know enough about each person to see how they could fit into a neat pattern to make the department run smoothly."

"Great, I told you you'd enjoy this managing stuff."

The next week you hold a group meeting when you present your plan. Everyone seems to like the idea that you want to run the team by consensus. You encourage team members to be creative and take risks to create positive results. You even devise an award for this: "Superturtle." You explain, "A turtle can't make progress without sticking his neck out." You set up weekly meetings during which the team can set short-term goals and agree on ways to measure results. Everyone seems excited, for a few weeks. Then everything starts to unravel. It turns out that people do not strive for the

"Superturtle award" for fear that they might get their extended necks cut off. When the team fails to achieve its goals, individual members argue to change the goals! No one, least of all you, can rally the group into a cohesive unit. Anarchy breaks out. No one agrees. Everyone argues. You have created a tribe with too many chiefs and not enough Indians, and everyone's on the war path.

Morale and production hit an all time low. Afraid to alienate your old co-workers, you formed a team of mini-managers instead of taking the leadership position. You can see it now, but it's too late. You don't know where to turn. You're too embarrassed to ask for help now. You feel like a fool.

BENEFITS OF B:

- You hold individual meetings.
- You develop a team strategy in your mind.
- You focus on developing each person.
- You meet to set goals and discuss how to measure results.

DOWNSIDES OF B:

- You see your role as a master manipulator, rather than a leader.
- You expect former co-workers to confide in you.
- You involve the team in setting corporate goals, but when the going gets rough, they opt to change the goals.
- You never establish your leadership role.
- You let the team flounder because you don't want to take command.
- You don't seek help.
- You feel like a fool.

C. I can see if the company will foot the bill to send our team to a corporate challenge weekend.

Two years ago your friend, Danielle Delaney, participated in the Professional Development Program given by the nonprofit expeditionary learning center, Outward Bound. At first you dismissed Outward Bound programs as adventures for kids—daredevil kids who yearn for hair-raising, terrifying physical challenges—but Danielle dispelled that myth.

"They offer programs to develop managers and corporate teams, too. They're really cool. Sure, you do some challenging athletic stuff, but it's always safe. My company, Doane Associates, sent the division managers from all of our offices around the country to Outward Bound. By the end of that three-day course, I felt more confident in my abilities to communicate, motivate, and trust. I learned that I'm capable of a whole lot more than I thought. It made a huge difference in the way I see myself as a leader."

Recalling that conversation, you wonder if such a program could help you overcome your "New Manager Jitters." Wouldn't it be great if Chambers National would send your entire department to a retreat? With that in mind, you approach the head of HR to see if the company has ever sprung for such a program.

"No, Yolanda, not to that extent," Lydia Rothberg, head of HR, replies. "But I don't see why the company wouldn't support something like that on an individual basis. Why don't you look into it for me. I think it's an excellent idea for new managers."

Your request for approval from Chambers National to attend a corpoarte challenge weekend is approved. You depart from Detroit Thursday night, and on Friday morning you catch the ferry at Black Falcon Dock in downtown Boston out to an island in the harbor. Luckily, your toasty Patagonia fleece jacket permits you to stand in the boat's bow during the chilly early morning cruise without freezing to death. It takes only twenty minutes to the reach the 157-acre island. Once the rest of your group of twenty-two men and women managers from a variety of companies across the country arrives on the island, the Outward Bound facilitators lead you in exercises designed as ice breakers, mind puzzlers, and trust builders all rolled into one. "Thinking on your feet" takes on an entirely different dimension than you knew possible. The rest of the first day includes a series of problem solving activities that challenge you to devise innovative solutions as a team.

The second day you play out a communication skills activity, similar to hide-and-seek, but with your dinner and tent depending on the right choice. Your group sets out in two different sailboats. You can't remember the last time you sailed and worry that you'll get seasick. The game involves not only navigating the beamy boat successfully, but, with a mere handful of clues and a radio, communicating with the other boat to solve the mystery and sail to the right island where the team can set up camp that night. Wrong island, no dinner. What an incentive!

The third day challenges you the most. Afraid of heights, you don't look forward to climbing the sixty-foot alpine tower, which looks like a monstrous jumble of telephone poles, rope ladders, and cement hand/toe holds all strapped together with rope cables. It resembles a tinker toy construction made by giants. Your safety net becomes your trust in the person belaying the safety rope attached to your harness. At first you think maybe you'll escape from having to perform this feat because you can't find a crash helmet that fits, but, of course, some helpful person finds one for you. Monika Kolowski belays your rope, helping you climb halfway up to where cables lashed together two poles. As you balance on your right tippy toe on the fist-sized cement toe hold, you stretch as far as you can searching with the fingers of your right hand to find something you can use to pull yourself up. Meanwhile, you hold on for dear life by wrapping your left arm around a pole. Your knees shake so badly you don't think you can go up or down. The adrenaline rush takes your breath away.

You cling there for what seems like hours as Monika and the rest of your team cheers you on. As the cold wind whips around you, you realize you face two choices: either let Monika lower you to the ground or simply find a way up. You risk unwrapping your left arm from the pole to reach out for a rope ladder with your left hand. It works. You pull yourself up and brace yourself between a higher pole and the rope ladder. Once you slip a toe on top of the cables that lash the poles together, a relatively easy ascent presents itself. In only a couple more minutes you actually stand triumphantly on the platform atop the sixty-foot tower. Raising your arms and pumping your fists, you whoop out a victory cheer. You've just done something you deemed impossible.

Ready to return to *terra firma*, you communicate your intention through hand signals to Monika. You perch on the edge of the platform and push yourself out as if on a swing, fully trusting that Monika and her backup Gina holding the end of the safety rope will control your decent. Slowly and carefully Monika and Gina let out the support rope and you glide down to earth. Your knees buckle underneath you as you touch ground, and you flop down in a heap of ropes and harnesses on the grass. Team members rush over to congratulate you.

Whew! By changing perspectives, by pushing yourself beyond your imagined limits, and by trusting a well-trained team member, you have learned something valuable about teamwork and communication. You have learned, too, that being a leader isn't about a position in a company, but about having the right attitude.

You leave the island resolved to apply the right leadership attitude to your job as manager. While you look forward to the follow-up reviews from Outward Bound, you can't wait to get back to the office and test what you've learned. You've even got a new motto: "No limits, no fear."

BENEFITS OF C:

- You research an alternative method to learn leadership skills.
- You convince your company to sponsor your Professional Development Program.
- You stretch beyond your self-imposed limits through trust and communication.
- You increase your self-confidence.
- You look forward to sharing your newfound team building skills with your group at Chambers National.
- You look forward to the follow-up from Outward Bound.
- You feel confident that you will manage your former peers well.

DOWNSIDES OF C:

- You do not immerse yourself in your immediate management situation.
- You do not ask about other professional development programs that the company might offer.
- You go alone to learn new skills that might or might not apply to your own team.
- You rely on only one resource for gaining the skills you need.

D. I can establish my authority as a boss right away.

Having witnessed how loosely your predecessor managed the group, you consider adopting that style yourself because it allows for individual flexibility, but, on the other hand, you suspect that a more strictly disciplined and finely tuned team might produce more streamlined and measurable results. Under tighter leadership, you envision each team member developing a deeper sense of accountability. A strong leader can monitor the performance of the team and keep everything running like a well-oiled machine. You love machine tool analogies, because they remind you of Harold Bernstein and your first job.

You're excited and nervous about holding your first team meeting as manager to establish yourself as their new leader. You've prepared for it diligently over the weekend by reading *The Leadership Secrets of Attila the Hun*, and you have truly enjoyed outlining a program, the blueprint of the new structure, complete with strict assignments for each member. In your mind you see each "warrior" performing defined tasks that will enable the team to win every short-term battle and the long-term war. You believe you know each of their strengths and weaknesses because you've worked so closely with them, and you want to place them in a situation where each can stretch and grow.

You've prepared a dossier for each person in which you've detailed their responsibilities and how you will hold them accountable. You've divided the group into two-person mini-teams and have included in their dossiers designated calendar dates when each member will assume the role of mini-team leader. Whoever serves as leader for that two-week period will prepare a one-page written report, itemizing what the team has accomplished to fulfill its assigned responsibilities. You've even drawn a chart that will graphically display the results of the collective biweekly reports. You believe that your intricate plan will motivate the group and boost morale because now everyone will know exactly what to do and whether or not they've gotten it done.

During the first meeting you hand out the dossiers and explain your program. Your team looks through them glumly. Why, you wonder, don't they appreciate your display of authority and your desire to break out of the status quo? You continue explaining your plan, "I have selected Conrad Purdue as my number two person in the department. He'll take over when I'm out sick or tied up. This way, you can get an immediate answer to any question that comes up. May I have a round of applause for Conrad? Conrad, stand up." You know Conrad is a go-getter who loves to show off his intelligence. This appointment acknowledges his value to the department and keeps him beholden to you.

"In each of your folders you will find a copy of the list that I've posted by the coffee maker in the snack room. Every week one of you will be in charge of making coffee in the morning and keeping the room tidy. And speaking of neat and tidy, I've been appalled at messiness in our department. At five minutes to five everyday, I expect you to straighten your desktops for the following day. We're going to have the most organized department in the company, as well we should since we deal with numbers." You expect nods of agreement, but everyone just sits there blankly staring at their dossiers. You assume, however, that they'll see the soundness of your reasoning once they get into the program.

Before you call the meeting to a close, you add one more item. "Since I may need to discuss a situation with any of you at any time, I'll need to know your whereabouts at all times. I bought this blackboard with magnetic color-coded buttons. When you need to use the little girls' room or little boys' room, just slide your button to the space marked accordingly. The board is located just outside my office. Thank you."

Three weeks later you hold your second meeting. You want to clear up some problems that surfaced in the first set of biweekly reports you've received. While much of each report looks good, you concentrate on areas that demand improvement. In doing so, you publicly criticize the author of each report, so that others can learn from their mistakes. You feel that you're establishing a firm hand of authority over your department.

After six months, no one has caught on to the "soundness" of your program. Three people have asked to be transferred away from your department, one complaining that you run the department like a military unit. Worse, performance has eroded from previous levels, and you receive a rather scathing review from your own boss that gives you six months to turn things around.

BENEFITS OF D:

- You create a plan to develop a well-oiled team.
- You want everyone in your department to accept accountability for their jobs.
- You diligently prepare for your first meeting as manager.
- You want to set an atmosphere where people can stretch and grow.
- You give your team clear, outlined expectations.
- You design a method for the office to look orderly and clean.

DOWNSIDES OF D:

- You discount the effective style of your predecessor because you wish to establish your own leadership style.
- You change office proedures overnight, disrupting not only the status quo, but everyone's sense of equilibrium.
- You treat your team like children, assigning them lists of duties.
- You play one person against the other with your mini-team format.
- You "move everyone down a rung" when you assign one team member as your number two man.
- Your program is unnecessarily complicated, insulting your team's intelligence and wasting their time.
- You act like "Big Sister" watching their every move.
- You publicly criticize people, which humiliates them and fosters distrust in you as a manager.
- Performance sags, turnover rises, and you put your own job in jeopardy.

Exploring the Issue

Traditional management structures of authority, like the command and control leadership style, no longer work so well in today's workplace. Today, the best leaders build trust, encourage risk-taking, and develop and support a spirit of camaraderie.

It may seem that some people are born leaders, but the most successful leaders will tell you that they emulate the best role models. They remember who encouraged them to do their best. They educate themselves to lead wisely and believe others can learn to do the same. The true test comes, however, when they find themselves managing former peers.

If you listed the attributes of effective leaders, you would find they are results oriented, good listeners, effective communicators, and givers, as well as inspiring, persistent, committed, and able to turn challenges into opportunities. But most leaders are self-made, not born, and they consciously cultivate the necessary attributes. They develop their own leadership qualities and styles.

Effectively assuming the new role of manager of former peers takes a lot of thought and preparation. In this adventure , the roommate's suggestion not to "wing" it is good advice. Pave your own way by learning as much as possible. Associations, courses, books, and seminars provide excellent leadership training. Much of effective leadership calls on courtesy and common sense. "How would you want to be treated?" "Do you treat people as adults?" "Do you look people in the eye when they, or you, speak?" "Do you explain the relevancy of what you ask others to do?" "Do you create an environment of mutual respect?"

The roommate's other suggestion, to "look at managing people like a jigsaw puzzle" is awful advice. The role of a leader does not include becoming a manipulator, the master moving the chess pieces across the board. While a leader needs to know the strengths and weaknesses of her team, she does so in order to help everyone work efficiently together, not to control them.

Carolyn Elman, Executive Director of the American Business Women's Association (ABWA), who conducts leadership workshops at ABWA conferences, says that she encourages women in every field first and foremost to keep their skills current, to prepare for the big promotion before it happens. She believes that education provides the key and that people learn differently, some preferring a more formal style including reading and seminars, others relying on on-the-job training. Carolyn recommends a low risk way to get on-the-job leadership training, such as participating in a professional organization. "If you get involved in how a local chapter works, it's like a small business. You learn leadership skills running an organization that directly apply to business. Since we tend to replicate what works well for a manager, working in an association exposes women to a greater number of role models than she would have in the normal workplace."

Here are some other tips Carolyn offers that may help you as a new manager:

1. Understand your own strengths. Are you results oriented, a good listener, an effective communicator, persistent, committed? Do you like to encourage others? Are you comfortable taking responsibility? "Female strengths" referred to in books such as Sally Helgeson's *Female Advantage*, emphasize women's ability to encourage participation, build relationships and collaborative teams, and to solve problems together.

2. Ponder which style of leadership makes you feel most comfortable. The directive style where you set the goals and the deadlines is more authoritative and manipulative. The downsides of this style are that your people will not necessarily become as committed as you. When you must meet a deadline, you may be the only person in the office who stays late. Carolyn believes women achieve more success with a collaborative style where they set the parameters but the team sets

their own strategies to reach the goals and meet the deadlines. The team, too, sets its own style within the confines of corporate policy. For instance, they may choose to take advantage of flex time. Another style, the *laissez-faire* approach, illustrated in Option B, doesn't exhibit much leadership at all.

3. Analyze your team. Are they experienced? Do they know what to do by when? Who needs to learn what? Spend time getting to know their strengths. If you've worked with the team previously as a co-worker, you'll know who gets projects done on time, who comes in late, and who may have difficulty blending with the rest of the team.

4. Know the risks. How much time does your team have to complete a project? Will you be under the gun? Is the goal of the project clear and attainable?

5. Develop a sense of teamwork. Set boundaries and direct goals, but encourage group involvement to decide how to achieve them. Give them confidence to do the work by providing adequate training and a supportive environment. Show them the relevancy of their work to the overall success and goals of the company.

6. Monitor your team inconspicuously. Keep your finger on the pulse of your team at all times. You are the point person and you want people to come to you with problems early, before they get out of hand. You may want to conduct short, fifteen-minute, stand-up meetings twice a week to assess the activity of the team and detect any possible problems.

7. Create a new network of management peers within the company. Especially look to the Human Resources department. It's their job to help you succeed. Take advantage of their knowledge and consult them about any questions concerning policy.

8. Make certain you keep your boss updated. Number one rule: Never surprise your boss, especially publicly. Ask your boss how she likes to be kept informed—by notes, memos, e-mail, recaps of meetings, or a visit to her office.
9. Keep aware of your balancing act. If you formerly lunched every day with your peers, you may not want to continue that practice on a daily basis. Your presence may make them feel restricted. They may not feel they can speak as freely about the rumblings of the office. Your increased workload will also demand more of the free time you once enjoyed.
10. Remain accessible and approachable. Keep a low profile. Don't flaunt your new position by requesting a fancy title or the corner office with a view.

Successful managers around the country have told me that it's extremely important to be yourself. Experiment with your own management style, become comfortable with your position and express your self-confidence naturally. Never take yourself too seriously, and always remember to smile.

Expanding Your Thinking

Since "you" never thought of yourself in a leadership role, you feel truly scared about managing your peers. Though you know accounting blindfolded, you struggle to become a good manager.

The real you may not want to emulate what the character "you" does in this adventure. In Option A, you assume you can hold off answering questions until after you go home and read about them. This squelches on-the-spot decision making. You feel overwhelmed by all the information your HR director gives you.

In Option B, you ask your group how they feel about management issues and set yourself up for failure. You create too many chiefs and not enough Indians, letting your team think that if they can set goals, they can change them, too. You see your managerial role as that of a master manipulator, rather than as a leader, and you try to pre-program and grade your team's efforts. Your program flops royally and your team resents you. Ultimately, you feel like a fool.

In Option C, you get a great deal out of your experiences from your corporate challenge weekend, but you still must translate what you experienced and learned to your team.

You make many poor decisions in Option D. In your eagerness to put your own stamp on your managerial position, you discount what worked before. You try to instigate sweeping changes, treat your ex-co-workers as children, and redefine what they do. You hope that they will "get into" the program and will eagerly work for the gold star you will put on their report cards, but they don't. Several ask for transfers because you act so domineering. You show no respect for them and publicly humiliate them by criticizing them in front of their peers. Ultimately, you put your own job in jeopardy.

What can you learn "not to do" in this adventure? Plenty.

DON'T:

1. Let your new position overwhelm you.
2. Treat your team like "dummies" or "complete idiots."
3. Think that the title "manager" translates into "manipulator."
4. Discount the effectiveness of predecessors.
5. Think you need to divide in order to conquer.
6. Devise complicated, unnecessary programs to prove you're in charge.
7. Expect former peers to confide in you once you get promoted.
8. Encourage your team to think they can set company policy.

9. Try to be one of the gang and let your team flounder without a leader.
10. Think you can "wing it" as a manager.

Despite all the stupid things you do, you do take some positive steps. In Option A, you listen to Maria's advice and try to learn how to become a good manager. You read books and join your company's Old Girl Network, which provides mentoring and information sharing. Your HR manager also gives you a list of associations you might join.

Things don't go particularly well in Option B. While Maria's advice to gain knowledge was right on, her concept of managing people as if they were puzzle pieces was way off course. Still, you do hold individual meetings to show interest in each person.

In Option C, you talk your company into sending you on an unusual professional development program, which you love. You stretch yourself physically and mentally, find new self-confidence, and learn leadership skills.

In Option D, you try hard to appear organized and leader-like. You take your love of solving puzzles and card games to the extreme by drafting an elaborate set of rules and procedures for your team. You think that if you communicate what you want clearly that your group will understand what they need to do and want to do it. You're partially right in that concept, but the execution falls short.

What positive points should you remember from this adventure?

DO:

1. Learn all you can about managing people and about effective leadership.
2. Build your own reference library of management books.

3. Form a strong relationship with your company's HR department.
4. Ask other women managers what they faced when they were first promoted to a management position.
5. Research and join associations that can advance your management skills and network you with other managers.
6. Hold individual meetings with your team to learn about their goals and aspirations within the company.
7. Know the company philosophy toward team management and goal setting.
8. Research different methods to learn management skills.
9. Treat team members as adults.
10. Create a work atmosphere of mutual respect and trust.

Assessing Your Own Situation

What questions should you ask yourself, or a good friend, if either of you found yourselves in a position similar to the character in this adventure? Try these:

1. If you're worried about managing former peers, ask yourself, "Do I respect them?" "Can I put aside my personal fears for the betterment of the team?" "How would I expect one of them to behave if they were promoted instead of me?"
2. If you've never managed before, ask, "What do I respect about managers for whom I've worked?" "Whose management style would I emulate?" "What management techniques make me want to perform to my highest capabilities?"
3. When you manage, do you follow the golden rule? Ask, "Do I treat my team as I wish to be treated?"

4. How about your body language? Ask yourself, "Do I show people that I care about them?" "Do I look people in the eye, or do I look over their shoulder?" "Do I offer a sincere handshake?"

5. When you instruct your team, do you really guide them? Ask, "Do I make myself understood?" "Do I explain the relevancy of what I ask them to do?" "Do I listen when they ask questions or do I become impatient?"

6. Are you judgmental? Ask, "Do I encourage people to challenge me?" "Do I express little tolerance for questions?"

7. Are you fair? Ask yourself, "Do I give people a second chance?" "Do I offer them responsibilities that will further their goals?" "Do I play favorites?"

8. What is your management style? Ask yourself, "Do I see myself as a camp counselor or a cheerleader?" "Do I see myself as the office mother or confessor?" "Do I know where I want the team to go and convey that in an encouraging way?"

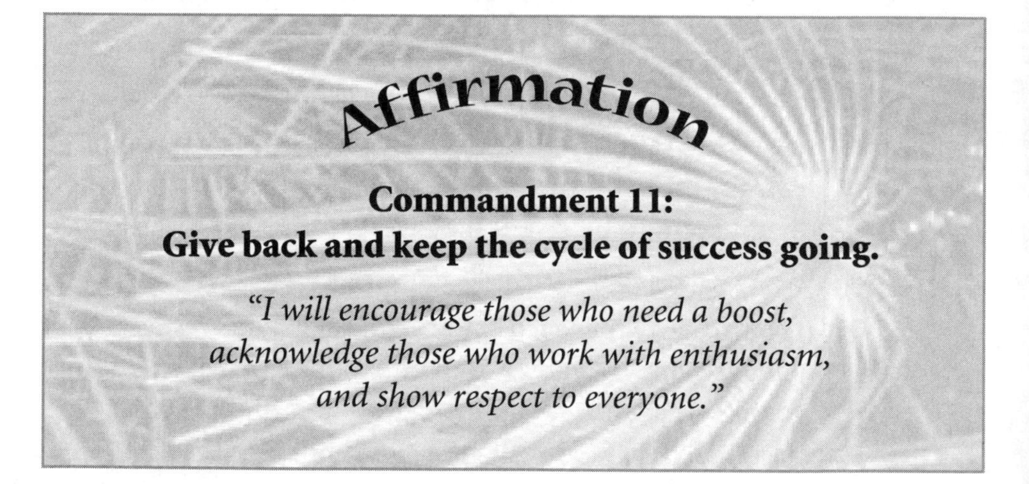

ADVENTURE 11

CAN A SINGLE MOM LIKE ME, WHO CAN'T WORK A LOT OF EXTRA HOURS, STILL PROVE SHE'S A VALUABLE EMPLOYEE?

Just because you put the welfare of your children ahead of your job, does that mean your career must suffer? Have you ever felt that raising children would stall your career? Do childless women move more smoothly up the ladder? To discover some of the answers to these questions, try slipping into ***Cinderella's Slipper****.*

Cinderella's Slipper

"I can't believe Tim packed up his car and drove off leaving you and Ryan," your best friend Hope consoles you. "That rat."

"Oh, it's probably for the best," you say. "We've been fighting so much, I think I can make a better life for Ryan without all that tension."

"You're a great mom," Hope agrees.

"Ryan's the most important person in my life. And after him, there's my job. Tim promises to pay child support. With that and my salary, we'll get along fine. Maybe now I can concentrate more on getting promoted."

Hope salutes you. "Thatta girl. This is the beginning of a great new chapter of your life."

Later, sipping a cup of jasmine tea after Ryan has gone to bed, you resolve not to wallow in sorrow and self-pity or to succumb to the numbing effects of denial. You mull over the past few years and think hard about how you can make Hope's prophecy come true.

You moved to Somerville, a suburb north of Boston, a little more than two years ago with Tim and Ryan, then three years old. Tim traveled around the country working his wizardry to salvage computer systems faced with the "Year 2000" glitch. His work kept him away from home the greater part of every week. He didn't seem to mind. You did, and told him so. The grueling fights about it finally resulted to his saying, "Adios."

You work as a graphic artist with account management responsibilities at The Art Factory, a small design company in Boston, a good job for a second income, but not enough by itself to keep up car payments, the mortgage and taxes on your condominium, the phone and utilities, and Ryan's medical costs not covered by insurance. Ryan's chronic asthma plays havoc with both your schedule and your pocketbook. If Tim honors his commitment to pay child support, you might eke by, but you need that promotion and the raise that comes with it.

On your commute to work on the "T," the nickname for the local commuter rail system that connects Somerville with Boston and beyond, you practice your "I need a raise" speech. You keep changing your mind about how to approach the subject, knowing you won't succeed by merely begging for a "sympathy raise." Instead, you plan to base your argument on your two-year track record, though lately your profit center's resources have suffered a blow from the closure of a local restaurant chain. You have sharpened other talents, though, especially your understanding of the Computer Aided Design (CAD) program on The Art Factory's computer. You prepare ideas to demonstrate how you'll convince your boss to promote you to head of CAD for the whole company. You believe your loyalty and talent deserve both recognition and more pay.

Denise Lancaster started the company six years ago. During that time the staff grew from one to four full-time employees and an intern. Denise lives with her husband, two cats, and one dog in Brookline. You've never been invited to her home, but you assume it looks as perfect and orderly as her sleek silver and blue, well-lighted office near Faneuil Hall. The fact that a woman owned the company drew you to The Art Factory in the first place, because you assumed a woman would understand another woman's problems. You were also impressed by the stylish yet functional office space, which sets The Art Factory apart from the usual chaotic warehouse offices occupied by other graphics businesses. From the beginning the job felt like a fit and then, although you haven't developed a particularly close relationship with Denise, you believe she appreciates your accomplishments, even though her own round-the-clock work habits set an impossible standard. The two other single women in your office manage to keep pace, but you simply can't, not with Ryan and all your recent personal problems. Ryan still comes first, but without Tim around, you think you might now match Denise's own commitment to the company.

"Yes," you mentally note as you reach Faneuil Hall station. "This new chapter of my life will start today."

When you walk into the conference room for your ten o'clock appointment with Denise, however, you feel your throat constrict when you see her sitting there staring impatiently at her watch. Scolding yourself for thinking she closely resembles the stern stepmother straight out of the Cinderella fairy tale, you present your case clearly. When you conclude, Denise rests her arms on the burnished aluminum conference table and flattens the palms of her hands of the table's cool surface. You hold your breath.

"Anne, I can't afford to create a better paying position at this time," Denise announces.

"What do you mean?" you ask, hurt and bewildered, fighting back tears.

"You do good work, Anne, I'm not faulting that, but you haven't excelled at this job. How could you possibly succeed at an even more demanding one?"

"But I explained..."

"You have to bring in more revenue to justify a raise. Do the math. Show me what you can do. Bring in more dollars. Then we can talk about your future here." She really does look like one cruel stepmother as she rises from her swivel chair and announces, "I've got a 10:30 appointment."

That's it. End of discussion. You watch her grab her briefcase and fling her royal blue wool coat over her shoulder and disappear around the corner.

"It's Ryan," you say almost out loud. "Darn it, I have a child whose health I have to worry about and she resents me for it. She's never had a child, and doesn't want one, so how could she possibly understand?" You sense you're barred from the bargaining table because of Ryan.

After you slink off to your office, you pull out a yellow legal size notepad and draw a mind-map with the goal "$$$" encircled in the center of the page and connect it to smaller circles encasing different strategies to reach that central goal. Inside these circles you write:

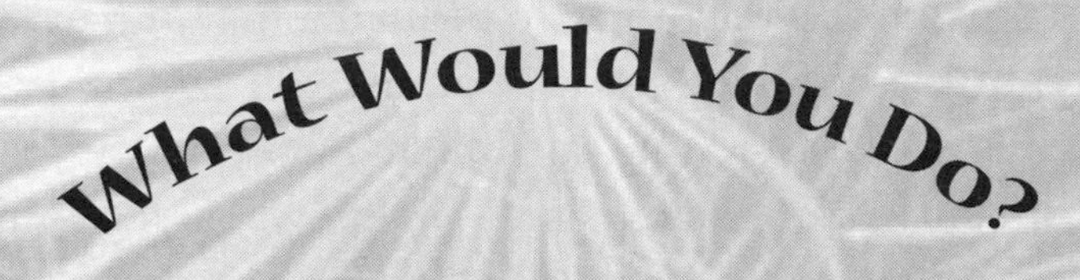

A. I can organize my thoughts and set up another meeting with Denise, away from the office, to explain my dilemma and work out a plan to demonstrate my worth.

B. I can take my existing client list and start my own graphic design business out of my home.

C. I can place an ad in the paper for a woman to share my living space in return for watching Ryan after school.

D. I can go to work for my new friend and bag Denise's restrictive job.

Turn to the option that most appeals to you. To learn the most from this adventure, read how the other options turned out, too. Then study the last three sections of this adventure: "Exploring the Issue," "Expanding Your Thinking," and "Assessing Your Situation."

A. I can organize my thoughts and set up another meeting with Denise, away from the office, to explain my dilemma and work out a plan to demonstrate my worth.

You fight back tears as you collect your thoughts and regain your fragmented composure with a strong cup of black coffee and two Advil. You pick up the phone to begin dialing for new clients, but your enthusiasm fizzles quickly because you can't muster the strength to make a dazzling sales pitch. How can you? You feel like a reprimanded school child, and you know you'll sound less convincing than one if you make the calls today. After leaving a few uninspired voice mail messages, you halt the blitz. "I need to know exactly what Denise expects of me," you conclude. "Only then can I surpass her expectations."

At the end of the day you stop by Denise's doorless corner office with the tall window concealed behind silver mini blinds. "Excuse me, Denise. I'd really like to chat with you more about my situation here. Can I take you to lunch tomorrow, someplace where we can relax and let our hair down?"

"I thought I made myself pretty clear this morning, Anne, but I do appreciate your offer," Denise flatly replies, peering over the cobalt blue rimmed granny glasses perched on her petite patrician nose.

You stand stone still, stricken by the brush off, but rally your nerve. "Well, actually, I need your advice."

"Okay, Anne," Denise sighs, "Tomorrow at 11:30. How about Legal Seafood?"

"No, actually I'd like some place a little quieter. I'll make reservations at Rebecca's. Sound good?"

"Fine, see you in the morning," Denise mumbles as she reaches for the phone.

The next day you meet Denise at Rebecca's, where you both order scrod from the special's board. Before the food arrives, you get right to the point, "Denise, can you tell me exactly what I must do to prove my worth and get ahead at The Art Factory?"

"Look, Anne, owning a business may look glamorous, but you have no idea about employment taxes, Social Security payments, health contributions—costs go through the roof for every employee. That's over and above business insurance and taxes. Every employee is an investment that either pays off, or it doesn't."

"Don't you feel I'm contributing?" you ask.

"Oh, work is fine, but your dedication..."

"You mean the days I leave early to care for Ryan?"

"Not just your leaving early, but your time on the phone concerning him, your lack of concentration. You've created a lot of animosity around the office over this. People feel you don't hold up your end of the work."

"I didn't know I was creating such ill-will. I never know when Ryan's asthma will flare up. So, how can I make up the 'down time?' Can I take projects home?"

"What if everyone wanted to leave early and take home projects?"

"I don't know."

"I do. It wouldn't work. So, concentrate on the bottom line, Anne. Expand your client list and put in the hours that everyone else does to justify her salary. Talent isn't good enough, not if you're not in the office carrying your weight. When you do that, then we might talk about a promotion and a raise, but not before then." Denise wipes what's left of her red lipstick on her cloth napkin.

You know the conversation, and possibly your job, just ended. You feel numb. You've reached an impasse. Your life and your career at The Art Factory will never mesh. You don't appreciate the pressures Denise feels owning the company, and she'll never comprehend your overwhelming concern for Ryan. Few words pass between the two of you as you finish lunch.

"There are other places to work," you tell yourself later, remembering an article in the *Boston Globe* about a couple of women who got fed up with a large Boston area computer company because it had refused to let them job share. Both women had babies at about the same time and found their eighty-hour weeks no longer tenable. When they had approached their customers to ask them if they'd mind if they shared the accounts, they found that their customers wholeheartedly supported the concept. Naturally, their employer was outraged that the women would sneak behind his back to create policy change. The article went on to describe how these women formed their own consulting group, hired women with children, worked in an above-garage office at one of their homes, conducted business from their cell phones while waiting to pick up their kids at kindergarten, and hired a babysitter to watch the children after school in the main part of the house.

That night after you tuck Ryan into bed, you write down your description of the perfect work setting. You also make a note to call the *Boston Globe* to get a reprint of that article so you can locate that firm. You also decide to call the chamber of commerce for a list of other women-owned businesses. You'll investigate them to see which ones are run by women with children. Perhaps you'll find a company that shares your family-first philosophy and that can appreciate your willingness to bring home work. You concede that it may not be easy, but you'll never know unless you try.

BENEFITS OF A:

- You confer with Denise over lunch to nail down her expectations.
- You choose a quiet restaurant conducive to conversation.
- You ask Denise to clarify exactly what she expects from you.
- You get right to the point at lunch.
- You offer a solution: to bring home projects.

- You recognize an irreconcilable difference in philosophies with Denise.
- You start to research a work setting that better matches your own philosophy and needs.

DOWNSIDES OF A:

- You don't stay focused on work or make the needed sales calls.
- You don't appreciate that Denise has every right to run her business according to her own standards.
- You feel disappointed and resentful that Denise doesn't understand your problems with Ryan.
- You can't convince Denise to grant you preferential treatment.
- You reach an impasse and may lose your job.

B. I can take my existing client list and start my own graphic design business out of my home.

You contact several current and prospective clients on your own time during your lunch hour away from the office, but instead of seeking business for The Art Factory, you represent yourself as a freelance graphic artist. When you get one strong nibble, you set up an appointment to meet with that potential client a week from Thursday after work. You feel a bit sneaky, but you convince yourself you'll only be calling on a potential client and you'll be visiting him on your own free time.

When you introduce yourself to Mr. Velasquez at his restaurant space south of town you hand him your "freelance" business card which you had printed at The Office Club.

"I'm looking for a catchy logo," explains Mr. Velasquez. "I fired the last graphic design firm. Too big. Too confused. Too slick.

I'm not looking for slick. I'm looking for 'down home, tastes good.' You get it?"

"I think so, Mr. Velasquez. I'll bring you some drawings next Monday. About the same time, okay?"

Over the weekend you work on the project on your white drafting easel tucked in your kitchen bay window where most people would place their breakfast table. Your drawings include not only the logo design, but also the menu, business cards, and stationery, and a direct mail piece for his new Mexican restaurant The Big Enchilada. As you develop the layout design, the thought of enchiladas makes your mouth water. Then, wham, it hits you! What if the mailer included a scratch-and-sniff enchilada plate on it? You sketch out a new design for the flyer and can't wait to present your idea to Mr. Velasquez on Monday evening.

On Monday at The Art Factory you're more distracted than usual. At five o'clock, you rush out the door with your art folder tucked under your arm. "My future," you think as you hug the accordion folder closer to your breast. At your meeting, Mr. Velasquez exclaims his approval of your presentation: logo, cards, menu, everything. He wants to know if he can get scratch-and-sniff business cards, too. To your delight, he becomes your first official freelance client.

The next morning you give a tight-lipped Denise your two weeks' notice. She asks you to leave on Friday instead. Choking back your resentment over what you perceive as her unjust treatment, you depart in a flurry of fresh hopes for your future, free of her stepmother harshness. You feel like Cinderella on the way to the ball.

Five months later that dreamy feeling has soured like milk in an open carton with a sell date seven weeks past due. You should have smelled trouble when Mr. Velasquez wouldn't pay a deposit or a retainer. You should have inquired about the graphic design firm he had hired before you and abruptly fired. Did they lose money, too? Stiffed by The Big Enchilada, you struggle to make ends meet with only two other small jobs on the books, all the while watching your meager savings dwindle. You desperately start searching the classifieds for job openings. At this point you're ready to take any job that provides a weekly paycheck. Cinderella's slipper, it turns out, didn't fit your foot at all.

BENEFITS OF B:

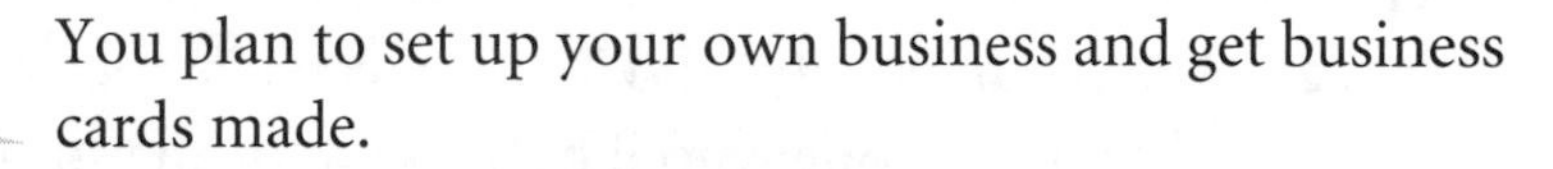

- You plan to set up your own business and get business cards made.
- You design more than the logo requested to win the account.
- You come up with a creative "taste-tempting" scratch-and-sniff concept.
- You feel hopeful about your foray into the world of business ownership.

DOWNSIDES OF B:

- You feel sneaky when you contact potential clients to set up your own client base.
- You jump too soon to start your own business, falsely assuming that one client can support you.
- You do no careful business preparation.
- You don't insist on a deposit or a retainer and lose money on the project.
- You find that the freedom you sought comes with a heavy price because you approached it unrealistically.

C. I can place an ad in the paper for a woman to share my living space in return for watching Ryan after school.

You prepare a simple, straightforward ad: "Single working mother with five-year-old son will share three bedroom condo in Somerville with female student in exchange for babysitting weekday afternoons, some light housework." You notify local college housing departments and place the notice on bulletin boards at Boston College, Boston University, and Tufts. Since it's nearly May, you hope you'll find someone who'll be around for the summer and stay on through the next school year. You know it's a long shot, but you prefer a co-ed rather than a grandmother.

Within a week you've heard from three young women and have set up appointments over the weekend. The first shows up late, doesn't apologize, lights a cigarette in your face without asking if you mind, and asks if her boyfriend can stay over on weekends. The second young woman, Janelle, comes in smiling, explains that she's on a scholarship that she'd won through the American Business Women's Association for tuition at BU. She's from the Boston area, Roxbury, but finds it difficult to live at home with seven younger siblings underfoot. This position would be perfect for her. Although you sense her sincerity and her eagerness to make something of her life, you still insist on checking her references. The third woman calls to say she isn't coming because she has accepted a better offer. You wonder what that could be, free rent in exchange for feeding a parrot once a day? On Monday you call Janelle's references, primarily professors and a pizza parlor owner. Everyone seems to love this charming young woman.

Once Janelle moves in, she and Ryan develop a special relationship of their own, complete with invisible buddies and magic recipes dreamed up by Janelle. A few weeks later, she asks you, "Would you mind if I did some of the cooking? I'm studying nutrition, and I think that a gluten free, dairy and egg free diet might reduce your son's asthma attacks. Some people believe asthma stems from common allergies, you know. Good idea?"

"Great idea, Janelle. Thanks." You couldn't believe your good fortune. "You're a real gem."

Over the summer, Ryan's health improves noticeably. He plays outside with neighbor children whom he hadn't been able to keep up with before. Janelle has added such a positive and courageous spirit in your home that you no longer spend office time worrying about Ryan. As you put more concentrated effort into your work, you find yourself feeling far more creative, your positive attitude generating more business. By the end of the summer, Denise calls you into her office and offers you a promotion and a substantial raise.

Later that day you stop by The Wall Flower, the neighborhood florist shop, and buy a dozen yellow roses for Janelle. "You've been sent by an angel to this household," you tell her. "I really appreciate all you do for both Ryan and me. I will be giving you a monthly stipend starting today, as well. We couldn't have survived without you."

BENEFITS OF C:

- You decide to find someone to share your condo in return for watching Ryan in the afternoons, which will save day-care expenses.
- You choose a college co-ed who wants to get ahead in life and has won a scholarship.
- You check her references.
- You agree to let Janelle try recipes used by allergy sufferers that she's learned about in her nutrition classes.
- Ryan's asthma attacks lessen.

- Released from your constant worry over Ryan, your work improves and you get the raise you wanted.
- You reward Janelle and offer her a monthly stipend besides her free room.

DOWNSIDES OF C:

- You interview very few people for the job.
- You take a chance by inviting someone to live-in without testing whether or not such a situation will work for you.
- You never consider that your current job may be wrong for you, no matter how much help you get at home.

D. I can go to work for my new friend and bag Denise's restrictive job.

You met Carter six months ago when you presented a bid at his office on behalf of The Art Factory to design the brochure for his new construction project in the Back Bay. You felt immediately attracted to him, though at the time you were not at all in the mood for any sort of romantic relationship. Still, this lonely widower has been a friend. His wife, he has confided, died two years ago in a car wreck when she was driving home with a girlfriend on a rainy night from a Billy Joel concert. Carter was working late that night and had never forgiven himself for not escorting her to the concert. Now, with Tim out of your life, you and Carter begin a more intimate relationship, which starts innocently enough over a glass of Kendall Jackson chardonnay during a "brochure planning" lunch. One evening he discloses that he had felt so vulnerable after his wife's death that he remarried on the rebound but planned to rid himself of his new wife as soon as possible. Stunned by Carter's revelation, you listen dumbfounded as he assures you that he loves only you. You choose to believe him.

The day of your ill-fated "I need a raise" meeting with Denise, you called Carter for comfort. "I can't stand working for that woman. She's wicked."

"Hey now, take it easy," Carter consoled you, adding, "You know, my personal secretary, Doreen, turned in her resignation two days ago. She's pregnant with triplets, a victim of *in vitro* fertilization, sick as a dog and flat on her back for the rest of her pregnancy. Why don't you come work for me? You'd be perfect." He purred that last word as if he were whispering from a pillow next to your ear. "I'll double your pay. You'll have a ball."

How could you refuse?

The following day, you stop in Denise's corner office. "Denise, I need to talk to you."

"Sit down, Anne."

"I'm resigning. I can give you two weeks."

"Where are you going? Just yesterday you wanted a raise."

"I'm going to work for Carter as his assistant," you say hesitantly. Denise and the entire office know about Carter because he had escorted you to the office Christmas dinner, though no one knew he was a married man accompanying his girlfriend to the company bash. You had only confided that to Hope, who felt outraged and had warned you about dating a married man, especially one who says he's leaving his wife for you.

"You may want to reconsider your decision, Anne. You're a truly talented graphic artist, why would you want to be an office assistant? Plus, it's really hard to work for someone with whom you have a romantic relationship. Matter of fact, it's stupid, and you're not a stupid woman."

"Well, I've made up my mind. You're not my stepmother!" you retort.

"Just be careful. Do you really want to stay here for two more weeks?"

"Not really."

"Fine. Well, good luck. I'll have your final check cut by the end of the day."

Five months later, you hate your job, but you hate Carter more. He hasn't left wife number two, he didn't take you on his company cruise to Cancun as promised, yet he still expects favors from you. Every day, just walking into his office reminds you what a fool you've been.

BENEFITS OF D:

- You confide your problems to a friend and seek advice.
- You receive an offer for a better paying job.
- You leave a company you feel doesn't suit you.

DOWNSIDES OF D:

- Your vulnerability, due to Tim's abandoning you and Ryan, makes you susceptible to Carter's advances.
- You don't heed advice that it's unwise to date a married man.
- You go to work for a loser who uses you.
- You give up a creative career for a dead-end job.
- You feel like a fool.

Exploring the Issue

Work/family issues, or, more correctly, "work/life" issues, affect every woman. Before we focus on the topic of this adventure—the difficulties of a single mom proving her worth in the workplace while staying a vigilant mother—let's talk for a minute about resentment in the workplace that can occur when one group feels the balance has tipped in favor of one or the other, whether that involves workload, benefits, pay, time away from the office, or work assignments, whether the women involved have children or not.

This adventure presents only two sides of this issue, the point-of-view of a single mother and that of the business owner. Yet, it's a far more complex issue that resists sweeping generalizations. For instance, does this issue relate to all workers with children in the same company? Is the business owner someone with or without children? Is it a large or small company? Do singles without children co-pay the same amount for health coverage as workers with families? Are singles without children assigned to travel more?

Consider, also, according to the U.S. Bureau of Labor Statistics, more than 60 percent of workers have no children, a statistic that includes those with grown children eighteen years and over who have left the home. After the year 2005, the most common makeup of households in this country will be singles or couples without children. In addition, the number of people ages twenty-five to forty-four who have never been married has doubled in the past twenty years. Thus, corporate efforts to help people manage work/life situations, and government emphasis on family, may seem unfair to childless workers, especially as the pendulum swings to fewer families with children. The problem isn't who's right or who's wrong, but who's going to resent whom. So what does that mean in the workplace?

To rid themselves of resentment by any group, every business, large and small, should become more sensitive and proactive to ensure "fairness" and "politically correct" procedures. Clear, precise goals, and universal policies on acceptable workloads, work hours, work locations, including virtual and actual, may more and more need to be cut in stone and followed to the last chiseled letter. Many businesses today, from large corporations to small Mom-and-Pop's, already strive to do this. Nevertheless, individuals can suffer in this "fairness game." The human factor often gets steam-rolled in the rush to become politically correct. The individual wrestles with specific, not general, issues. For instance, where does a company draw the line on family emergencies? Is it okay to let a mother take time off to rush her child to the doctor, but not allow a husband leave time to care for his aging parents or to nurse his wife who's recovering from an operation? What about the woman whose only family is her dog? Can she take emergency leave if Rover needs an operation? Deciding such issues would take the wisdom of Solomon.

Some believe national umbrella policies and court-determined solutions to grievances will solve the problem. But is that inviting Big Brother? The issue comes down to people working for people, to individual responsibility. If you're going to accept compensation from a company, give that company a fair day's work. Most people conscientiously do this. Many with children perform some of their work duties before their children wake up or after they go to bed, or on their commute to work, but they get them done. If you work for a company that understands this, and you perform the tasks you're hired to do, you probably face little difficulty. In this adventure, however, it did not work that way. The work didn't get done, and the employer couldn't allow the character to take work home, either. Neither personality appreciated the priorities of the other. Since all the communication in the world won't change that, you should try to understand the culture of a company before you accept a position.

Expanding Your Thinking

What can you learn from this story? "You" face many problems: your husband drove right out of your life, your son demands special care, your responsibilities overwhelm you, and your boss doesn't understand your situation and refuses to give you the raise you need. You feel vulnerable and alone. Other than that, you'd be the Queen of the Ball, right? Wrong.

You may not want to repeat many of the steps "you" took in this adventure. For instance, in Option A, you expect preferential treatment at work because you're the only one in the office with a child, even though the office culture doesn't allow for it. Denise chooses not to run her company with any "virtual" employees, or perceived part-time employees who take work home. You don't appreciate the pressures she's under owning her business, nor her right to run it as she sees fit.

In Option B, you feel sneaky seeking clients for your own business that rightfully you should have sold on The Art Factory. You foolishly take on a client without obtaining a deposit for expenses or a retainer fee. You leave your job after winning only one client, although one client, even if he did pay his bills, will never support you and Ryan. You don't do any research about owning a business and running it properly. You learn the hard way.

Things worked out well in Option C, but you took a huge risk when you encouraged someone to move into your home without testing how it would really work.

In Option D, you do everything wrong because you are too vulnerable, and don't use common sense. You're attracted to married man, who's a client of your office, and you take him to your Christmas party. You refuse to listen to your boss and co-workers who show their concern for your well-being. You step into water over your head when you quit your job to go to work for Carter, the same man who says he wants a divorce from wife number two but takes zero strides in that direction. Your situation progresses from bad to worse and, as one might expect, you feel like a fool with no place to turn.

In summary, then:

DON'T:

1. Expect preferential treatment in the workplace.
2. Expect to change a company culture to suit your personal needs.
3. Start a business without preparation and careful consideration of the time, money, and effort required.
4. Steal clients from your company to start you own business.

5. Think one client will cover all of your bills.
6. Assume there's only one way to solve problems.
7. Forget to share your good fortune with others who help you achieve yours.
8. Take someone in without checking references.
9. Disregard people's concerns for your welfare.
10. Make quick decisions when you've recently suffered a loss.

What positive lessons do you learn from this adventure? In Option A, you identify your problem: you need more income to support yourself and your son on a single paycheck. You try your best to communicate this to your boss, Denise, who recognizes your talent but doesn't see you as a conscientious worker. You offer to take work home to compensate for paying attention to Ryan's needs during work hours. Because Denise dismisses your ideas, you realize that you're at an impasse and should possibly consider working for a different company.

In Option B, you do a few positive things. When you decide to start your own business, you buy inexpensive business cards, call prospective clients, meet with Mr. Velasquez and prepare a presentation for him including designs for more than he'd requested to win the job. You enjoy dreaming up the scratch-and-sniff flyer to promote the idea of a taste-tempting enchilada. Mr. Velasquez hires you.

Your next plan, Option C, sharing your condo with someone who could watch Ryan, works out well. When you determined the age of the woman you'd like to share your home with, you placed notices on college bulletin boards and with university housing departments, and you followed up on references. Your choice turns out even better than you'd hoped when Janelle's interests and education in nutrition leads her to try a special diet that helps Ryan's condition. Your constant worry over Ryan lessens, and you perform well at work. You even get your raise and share some of the benefits with Janelle to show your appreciation.

About the only positive result of Option D was that you doubled your salary. Everything else in this option we'll relegate to the file marked "Poison."

Which of these positives can you use in your own life today?

DO:

1. Move on with your life as directly as you can after a loss.
2. Take responsibility for your future.
3. Ask for a raise when you believe you deserve it.
4. Define what you need in a work culture.
5. Communicate with your boss and understand her expectations.
6. Make sure you're carrying your load at work.
7. Offer solutions to problems concerning your work.
8. Go the extra mile when making a presentation.
9. Interview carefully and check references before hiring someone.
10. Listen to your gut reaction when others warn you that you're about to do something stupid.

Assessing Your Own Situation

If you encounter a similar situation to the one in this story, how can you help yourself or a friend discover the best decisions?

1. Ask yourself, "What are my main priorities right now?" "How much money do I really need to survive?" "What do I need to take control of first?"

2. If you feel that having children presents a problem at work, ask yourself, "Have I handled my personal matters discretely?" "Do I have my children call and stop by any time they please, and do others do the same in the office?" "Am I giving the impression that I don't concentrate on my work because of my child?"
3. Have you communicated your concerns with your boss? Ask yourself, "Do I assume my boss understands the degree of my child's needs, or that I just became a single mother?" "Have I reassured my boss I will accomplish my work, but would appreciate some leeway where I do it?" "Have I checked with my boss about her concerns and how I can correct them?"
4. Do you agree with your company's culture? "Am I happy with the company's work/family attitude?" "Is it an atmosphere where I can do my work and not feel pressured if something necessitates my being with my child?"
5. Have you planned back-up babysitters? "When my day care can't watch my child after a certain hour, have I found someone who can help out?" "Have I looked into co-op babysitting groups?"
6. If you want to start a business, ask yourself, "Is this an appropriate time?" "Do I have a clear picture of the time, money, and effort needed to get it going to the point where I can take home a salary?"
7. If you seek live-in help, ask, "Have I determined the best age person to share my home?" "Am I willing to take the time to follow up all referrals carefully?"

8. What questions can you ask yourself if you're looking for a new place to work? "Do I see pictures of children on other women's desks?" "Does my prospective boss display pictures of children or does she refer to them?" "Have I researched the background and policies of the company in every way I can?"

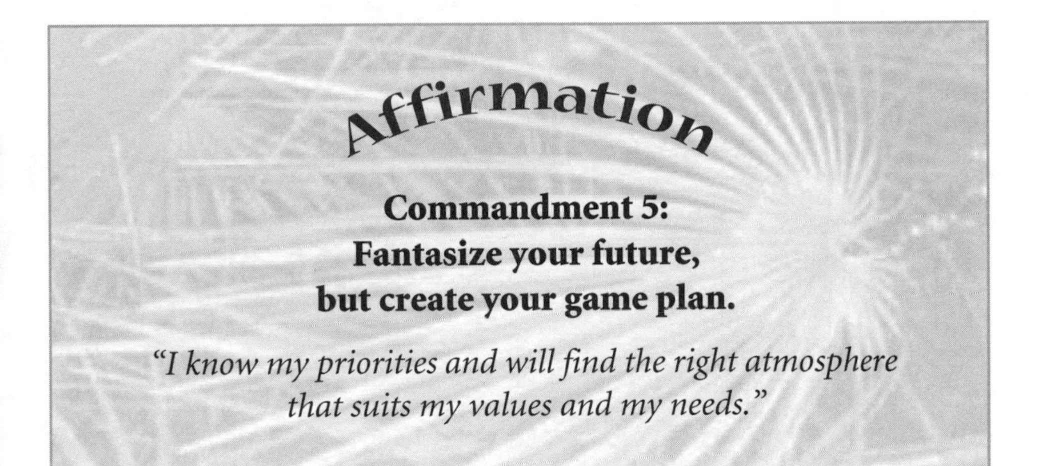

Affirmation

Commandment 5:
Fantasize your future,
but create your game plan.

"I know my priorities and will find the right atmosphere that suits my values and my needs."

ADVENTURE 12

HOW CAN I GROW A NEW BUSINESS ON A SHOESTRING BUDGET?

It's easy to start a business, but, given the fact that more than half of all start-ups fail within two years, it's harder to keep one growing. Do you long to start your own business but lack strong financial support, or do you already own one, but wonder how you can grow it on shoestring budget? If you or a friend faces this challenge, think how you would keep the bloom alive in No Shrinking Violets.

No Shrinking Violets

You're consciously making an effort to lose twenty pounds before your twenty-year college reunion in four months. You have put on a pound a year since you graduated from the University of Denver, and now you want to shed those extra pounds slowly, sensibly, and steadily. Other than watching what you put in your mouth, you try not to obsess about food. You've tried many diets before and found that they didn't work well because you focused on food too much. This time you plan to eat anything you want, only in small portions so you won't feel deprived, a technique your slim friends tell you works well. They suggest you eat six small meals of tasty but nutritious foods during the day, never continue eating once you feel full, and exercise regularly. To stay on track you've decided to record in your diary everything you put in your mouth during the four-month period. Hoping to put some fun in the program, after each daily entry you sketch a "flower of the day," complete with a full horticultural description of the plant. Since your interest in flowers has grown into more than a passing hobby, you're toying with the idea of turning your passion for flowers into a business, though you're not quite certain how to start and grow a business with your limited capital.

Every Thursday morning you meet your friend, Karen Franklin, at the gym and then join her for coffee at the Bean Stalk Cafe. Since Karen, too, wants to lose weight, you've formed a buddy system to keep you both inspired on days when you might otherwise backslide. Together over steaming cups of Colombian Decaf you review your week's progress. Karen marvels at your floral entries.

"I can't believe how much you know about flowers, Petula," she exclaims.

"My mother grew up in the U.K. Every little girl in England learns about flowers, their names, where they grow best. It's part of our education. My mum thinks it's a crime that girls in America miss this. I've inherited her love of flowers."

"You're a natural at arranging them, too."

"I've been doing that for years. It's a great hobby."

"You know, I love hiking with you. You teach me so much about wildflowers."

"It's fun, isn't it? Oh, did I tell you that I'm thinking about starting a business?"

"No! That's great. A floral shop?"

"Nope. I don't want to be stuck in one place all day. I have some ideas, but I haven't decided exactly what I want to do yet."

"You'll figure it out. With your knowledge and your design flare you could do anything."

"I know about flowers all right, but I don't know a thing about business, especially marketing."

"Oh, that's easy. Once you decide on a product or service to sell, you can identify your market. Ask, 'Who would buy this and why?' Just tell those people what you have to offer and how they will benefit from buying it. That's marketing in a nutshell."

"You make it sound easy."

"It is!"

"Well, maybe. But it sounds like a lot of work. I want to have fun with it, too."

"Let your passion guide you, Petula. See you next week. And remember, 'Busy hands are happy hands' because busy hands stay out of the refrigerator!" You both laugh as Karen waves good-bye.

You expect your new business to provide an income and joy at the same time, two elements you've lacked in your life lately. You know you can turn your passion for flowers into some sort of business, but you've seen great businesses fail for lack of funds and poor marketing. You're not sure what it will take to create visibility and gain the attention and the reputation a good business needs in order to flourish, but you know that without those guidelines no business can develop into a viable and rewarding enterprise.

Your husband, Scott, though he encourages you, sees your eagerness to start a business as a passing whim. He doesn't want you to deplete the family savings or build up credit card debt while trying to get your business up and running. You share his concerns, so you spend some creative time dreaming up four different, but viable, routes you can take to develop your business:

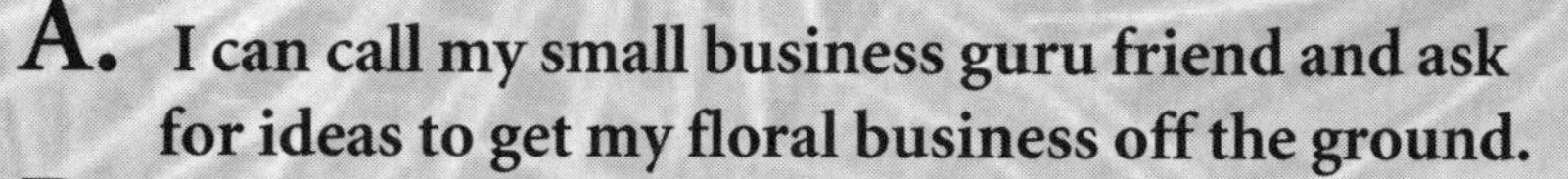

A. **I can call my small business guru friend and ask for ideas to get my floral business off the ground.**

B. **I can write articles and become a resource for people who want to know more about flowers.**

C. **I can turn my "flower of the day" concept into a line of greeting cards.**

D. **I can find a way to use my knowledge of flowers to help others.**

Turn to the option that most appeals to you. To learn the most from this adventure, read how the other options turned out, too. Then study the last three sections of this adventure: "Exploring the Issue," "Expanding Your Thinking," and "Assessing Your Situation."

A. I can call my small business guru friend and ask for ideas to get my floral business off the ground.

You call your friend Louise Stedman, a columnist who writes about small business issues, to ask her advice about developing your flower business. You've clipped most of her columns from the *Denver News* over the last year, and you've encouraged Louise to turn them into a book.

"Louise. I'm calling to pick your brain about getting my flower business up and running," you begin after brief greetings.

"Great, it's about time," Louise chuckles.

"I know. Finally I'm ready to sink my teeth into something."

"Have you decided what form your business will take? It'll make a difference how you market it."

"Well, I want to run the business from my home, designing flower arrangements for social functions and conferences. I certainly have the connections through my mother and all of her friends who sit on dozens of committees. My mother also thinks I could speak to her garden club and other groups about flowers and flower arranging. Actually, she's thinking of speaking together, as a mother/daughter dog and pony show, to add interest. You can guess who'll be the dog!"

Louise laughs, then adds, "Well, okay, Petula. That's a slow way to go, but it might make sense for you, especially if you want to develop it on a shoestring budget. Have you formalized these thoughts in a business and marketing plan?"

"Well, no. I thought I'd just let it evolve."

"Don't do it that way. Even if you don't currently envision a big business, and even if you plan to grow it slowly, you need to grow it smart."

"Well, I know you talk about that a lot in your columns, but I didn't think it would apply to me."

"Almost any successful entrepreneur will tell you that if she didn't start with a business plan, she wished she had. I know you don't want to spend money on advertising right now, but you need to realize just how much you spend on other things to get the best use of the big three: money, time, and energy. Look, why don't you work on a business plan, and fax it over to me for review?"

"Can you just talk me through it?"

"Yes, I could, but you wouldn't learn nearly as much that way. Plus, you need to do the basic thinking yourself. Envisioning the big picture is one of the main purposes of creating a business plan. For this reason you need to write one, even if you're not going to use it to raise capital."

"Okay. Where do I begin?"

"Every business plan includes specific details in four basic areas. I'll fax a list of them over to you so you can get started."

About fifteen minutes later you receive the following fax from Louise:

"Here are the four main parts of a business plan. Take your time and really think about them before you write down your ideas. When you finish, send the plan to me and I'll go over it with you. And remember, have fun!

1. The product: Why will customers want your product or service? What benefits do you offer? What needs do you satisfy? What problems do you solve? What makes your product different, better, more attractive than the competition? What exactly do you offer?
2. The market: Who will benefit from your product or service? How will you reach these people? Where can people currently obtain a similar product or service? Can you identify these direct competitors?
3. The financing: Do you plan to grow your business? When will you need your funds? How will you spend the money? If you plan to get a loan, how will you repay it? Will immediate cash flow cover expenses? When can you project a profit?
4. The people: Will you hire others to work in the business? Will you involve Scott or your mother in the business? If so, in what capacity?"

While you're working on your business plan, you give a few speeches with your mother to her garden club and other women's groups. Unfortunately, you find that you can't overcome your anxiety in front of a group. Though you know your topic inside and out, you get flustered and embarrassed giving presentations. Besides, your mother talks over whatever you're trying to say, which annoys you to no end. You realize that speaking is really your mother's ambition, not yours, verifying your assumption that you would play the dog in the show.

As you develop your business plan further, you realize more clearly that your business should focus on floral design, not speaking. You tell your mother that speeches stress you out too much and you want to concentrate on the design end. You revamp your business plan to include the four elements as Louise instructed. In a nutshell, it takes:

1. The product: I distinguish my floral designs from others' because I incorporate custom features such as my customer's artifacts into the arrangement.
2. The market: I offer floral decor for homeowners and centerpieces for luncheons, conventions, and parties. My mother markets to accounts through her contacts and her speaking engagements. She exhibits and describes my floral arrangements in her lectures.
3. The financing: I plan to finance my business from my savings and credit cards and my mother's investment.
4. The people: My mother is my partner, financially and physically.

You're glad you took the time to "preview" the growth of your business, and you think your business plan covers the issues Louise emphasized.

As you expect, your business takes time to grow. Still, you're encouraged that your efforts to promote yourself and your product have worked well, gaining good publicity in the local media. You have sent the brochure you designed to every association in Denver. The *Rocky Mountain News* has featured you and your mother in Home and Garden articles, How-to columns, and even in the business section of the paper. Since you send news releases to the local papers every time you supply flowers for an event, you eventually snag a write-up in the *Denver News* which includes a color photo of you standing next to the centerpieces you prepared for your college reunion. In the picture you look fabulous in your new size eight cocktail suit.

Louise continues to advise and encourage you, but you value most her insistence that you write a business plan. However, it turns out you failed to account for one variable when you worked on your business plan: working with your mother has changed your relationship with her. Today, the two of you enjoy a healthy business, but you don't enjoy each other's company much anymore. Your mother has taken the upper hand in running your business and she can't seem to treat you like a grown up. In the beginning, you welcomed her enthusiasm for your new business, but now you realize that she sees the business as her dream, not yours. You've become competitors rather than partners.

BENEFITS OF A:

- You seek advice from a small business expert.
- You rely on your mother to make connections with associations and clubs to promote your business.
- You try your skills as a public speaker.
- You recognize that your mother should perform the speaking part of the business.
- You write a business plan.
- You grow your business slowly, according to your plan.

- Your publicity efforts pay off with coverage in newspapers.
- You prepare the flowers for your college reunion and achieve your weight-loss goal.

DOWNSIDES OF A:

- You call only one person for advice about business when you also could have called the SBA or done your own research at the library and on the Internet.
- You count solely on your mother to make your connections.
- You feel uncomfortable giving presentations with your mother.
- Your mother takes over the business and treats you like a child.

B. I can write articles and become a resource for people who want to know more about flowers.

You've been toying with the notion of sharing your knowledge of flowers and developing a business through writing articles, but you haven't quite figured out the right angle on how to make your approach work. Then one weekend, driving back from a family outing in Durango, your son Jamie asks you to name some of the wildflowers growing in profusion along the roadside and blanketing the meadows. You teach him how to identify them as individuals and as part of groups, and about the different insects they attract. His questions spawn a great idea.

That evening as you undress for bed, you explain your plan to Scott, "I'll start by writing about the wildflowers in the Four Corners area, the ones that people see all the time but can't identify. Then I'll branch out to writing articles about the garden flowers that grow best here. What do you think?"

"Yeah, stories about *wild* flowers sound pretty sexy to me. Go for it."

"Hey, you just gave me an idea for the first article, 'The Sex Life of the Columbine.' How does that sound?"

"Sex sells, but do flowers really have sex lives?"

"Sure, getting pollinated is their primary purpose. They use colors and scents to attract insects and birds to help with the process. Did you know that insects can see ultraviolet colors but not red? Red flowers aren't pollinated by bugs, but by birds like hummingbirds. Flowers display colors on their petals like lights on landing strips for insects or birds." Scott laughs as you excitedly ramble on.

"I love it when you talk sexy," he whispers.

You decide to write to all of the editors in the Lifestyle and Garden sections of the local papers to offer yourself as a resource on the topic of flowers of the West. You send sample articles to newspapers. When the *Rocky Mountain News* picks up your article on the sex life of columbines, the article attracts so much attention that the garden editor contacts you to discuss further article ideas. Soon, your articles start appearing in the Sunday *Denver Post Magazine* as well. As a local expert, you now give quotes regularly in interviews, articles, and columns. The avalanche of letters you receive from those articles prompts you to start a newsletter about wildflowers and gardening in the West.

When you want to attract a broader base for your newsletter, you check with two major Sunday papers about the cost for placing a classified ad. Since a three-line business ad costs only $26 per Sunday, you elect to place an ad every other Sunday in one of the two papers. Two ads per month cost you $52. You plan to cover the cost of the ads by charging a subscription fee of $50 a year for your bimonthly newsletter. Within 4 months you spend $208 in advertising, with which you acquire 200 new subscribers. You calculate that your production and mailing expenses average $250 per month. When you include advertising in the papers, you find that your monthly expenditures amount to $458. Since you already have sold $10,000 worth of subscriptions, you estimate that you earned about $375 per month net after expenses.

Eager to increase your earnings, you look into advertising on a larger scale. In *Sunset* magazine, a small ad listed under "Books/ Publications" costs $17.10 per word, with a ten-word minimum and a three-issue placement. The outlay for three issues costs $769.50. You assume that if you managed to pull in 200 subscribers from the local Denver area in four months, you should easily cover the costs of the magazine advertising with new subscribers. Printing in larger quantities will lower the unit production cost of your newsletter as well. *Sunset* requires a three-month advance purchase of your ad before it runs, but during that time your ads in the Sunday papers attract even more subscribers.

You time your first *Sunset* classified ad to appear in the March issue which features wildflowers of the West. Within one month you receive more than 250 orders for your newsletter. You madly scramble to increase your publication run and get the newsletters sent out promptly. It pays off. Today, you feel you've found a viable means to earn money from your love of flowers. Your focus on your business has helped keep twenty pounds off ever since your reunion.

BENEFITS OF B:

- You listen to your son's questions about flowers and realize others will want to know about flowers, too.
- You choose a unique angle for your articles that makes them different and marketable.
- You offer yourself as a resource to editors.
- You run modest ads in newspapers before you try advertising in a magazine with wider circulation.
- You time your magazine ad to coincide with the wildflower issue.

- Your efforts pay off with little original capital outlay.
- You feel fulfilled by teaching others about the flowers of the West.
- Your focus on your business has helped keep your weight down.

DOWNSIDES OF B:

- You take a chance that newspapers will publish your writing without testing that assumption.
- The articles will not generate immediate income.
- You explore no other ways to get your writing published, such as books or pamphlets.
- You risk more than two months earnings from your newspaper ads on a broader campaign.

C. I can turn my "flower of the day" concept into a line of greeting cards.

You design your first deckle-edged note card with a pressed Colorado columbine in the center. Inside the front cover of the card you write: "*Aquilegia caerulea,* the buttercup family. The purple petals of this flower hang upside down until it goes to fruit then the petals turn upright. You'll find these delightful flowers in mountain and subalpine areas in late summer." You create two sets of six cards, each decorated with different flowers including snow buttercup, silvery cinquefoil, black-eyed Susan, wild geranium, fairy slipper, Jacob's ladder, wild rose, aspen daisy, shooting star, wild iris, and narrow-leafed paintbrush. Except for the description on the inside cover, you leave the cards blank for the customer to write her own message. You market primarily to women.

You purchase your paper supplies and printing at Joel's Print Shop south of Denver. He offers you prompt, reasonable service, and lots of hands-on quality control. You determine you can wholesale the cards with envelopes for $1.50 apiece.

After contacting several sales representatives with showrooms at the Denver Merchandise Mart, you find Abigail Cummings the most receptive to your ideas. She has developed contacts with reps in the Los Angeles and Chicago Marts. Your new "team" of reps call on gift stores and display your cards at gift shows in their areas. You feel you've developed a good distribution network, but you don't rely on your reps alone.

You also contact the Rocky Mountain National Park information office to set up an appointment with the gift store buyer. Her positive response encourages you to sell directly to national parks, museum stores, the Denver Botanic Gardens, floral shops, and local independent bookstores. You even find hospital gift stores want your cards. These combined outlets don't match what a national sales team of independent reps can accomplish, but you have found working with reps more challenging than you assumed.

Your continued efforts to develop your own direct distribution instead of solely counting on your reps works well for a while, but, deep down, you believe you can't grow without the exposure that only independent sales reps can provide. Still, you doubt that you can keep up with their demands. When they ask you to supply card racks and point of purchase displays for stores, as well as a color catalog of your entire card line, you consider the expense involved, but reluctantly agree. Also, instead of the standard terms 2%/10 net 30, (which means the customer gets an additional 2% discount if he pays in ten days with the normal payment date set at 30 days), your reps want you to extend the terms to 2%/15 net 60, with free shipping. Of course, your reps expect to receive their 15% commission when they place the order, not when you get paid. Some of your customers don't pay in 90 days, but you still must pay your printer in 30 days. You feel you've turned into everyone's banker.

When you use your credit cards to pay the printer and reps, you incur the additional financial burden of the exorbitant accumulation of interest. You're trying to compete with major greeting card companies with all the resources to provide the financial incentives and other benefits, such as display racks, to their customers. But you're a small business and simply can't continue to compete at this level.

Nevertheless, you've definitely gained some important sales and marketing knowledge from your reps. You've learned the importance of targeting a specialized niche with your pressed flower cards. You've expanded your product line to become more competitive by offering a broader price range of cards. Your terms include a minimum $36 order. You don't know what will happen in the future with your card business, but you know that if you don't continue using reps you'll have to find another way to reach your market. You feel damned if you do, damned if you don't.

"A true Catch 22," you mumble as you look over your accounts receivable, nibbling on your tenth Oreo cookie. You feel almost glad you long ago gave up on your weight-loss program and don' feel guilty about your cookie binge.

BENEFITS OF C:

- You turn your flower-of-the-day idea into attractive note cards.
- You research and find distribution through interviewing reps at the Merchandise Mart.
- You identify your market.
- You find a reasonable, reliable printer.
- You create your own line of distribution by contacting national park gift stores, museum shops, florists, hospitals, the Denver Botanic Gardens, and independent bookstores.
- You learn how to do business with reps selling nationally to retail gift shops.

DOWNSIDES OF C:

- You rely on such a wide variety of flowers in your cards, you could encounter supply problems.
- You contact only one printer and don't compare prices and services.
- You let your reps run up your business costs with their demands for expensive marketing tools.
- The expense of doing business through reps becomes a financial burden.
- You eat your way through your frustrations.

D. I can find a way to use my knowledge of flowers to help others.

You've been attending classes offered by the Denver Botanic Gardens, where you've discovered a keen interest in medicinal herbs. On your frequent trips to the Saturday morning farmers' market on Market Street between 16th and 17th Streets in downtown Denver, you search for the herbs that you studied in class. One morning you meet Leslie Love, a curly blond "Earth Mother" type, who sells medicinal herbs, salves, and flower essences.

"You can use flowers to create many effective potions," Leslie contends.

Though you're more analytical, you become fascinated with her ethereal outlook of "rescue remedies" and the vibrational power of essences. The fragrances of flowers certainly do soothe you.

Leslie continues, "My interest in floral essences began when I visited a friend twenty years ago in Germany who was being treated through her pregnancy and delivery with herbs from her immediate area. I then studied medicinal plants and natural healing for five years in India. Today, I work on body, mind, feelings, and attitudes with my flower remedies."

Leslie explains that aroma therapy began when a Swiss physician named Paracelsus pioneered the connection of chemistry to medicine in the sixteenth century. "He introduced many drugs and flower remedies to treat emotional problems. Much later, after World War I, a British physician, Dr. Edward Bach, began research on the effects of flowers. He's considered the founder of flower essences."

When you return home, you search the Internet for more information about flower essences. Soon you realize that herbs and flowers represent the tip of the alternative medicine iceberg. Expanding your research to include folk remedies, alternative medicines, marijuana and bee therapies, and acupuncture, you come upon the use of pure oxygen therapy in England and an assortment of other unusual therapies in Europe. Amazingly, you can locate no book, newsletter, or web site that analyzes these untraditional therapies, so you decide to hire a neurologist on retainer to consult with you. After much more research, you condense what you've learned and hire a web site specialist to design a web page with which you can market your findings over the Internet.

You know that you can't offer any medical advice, but you hope your research, based on your passion for flowers, will help others in need. It doesn't take very long for a book publisher to approach you about writing a book about your findings, offering you a $10,000 advance. You can't believe how your desire to help others has turned into your good fortune. You visualize your picture on the back cover of the book: the trim, twenty-pound thinner you. Researching health topics has reinforced your willpower to shed all those extra pounds.

BENEFITS OF D:

- You attend classes to learn more about plants and flowers.
- You go to the Farmer's Market to look for the medicinal herbs and meet an herbalist.

- You become interested in studying alternative therapies using flowers and herbs.
- You hire a neurologist to consult with you.
- You contact a web site specialist to help you develop a business over the Internet.
- Your web site attracts the attention of a publisher, who pays you to write a book.
- You visualize the new slim you on the back cover of your book.

DOWNSIDES OF D:

- You take an academic approach that may not result in a money-making venture.
- You incur the expense of hiring a consultant and setting up a web site.
- You only market on the Internet.
- Your web site doesn't pull in much income.
- Your efforts turn into more of a hobby than a business.

Exploring the Issue

You can make the best product in the world, but if no one knows about it, why bother? Some women find it easy to talk about their business and send out notes to update friends and customers about their progress, while others find promoting themselves disconcerting. No matter on which side of the fence you find yourself, you need to know what you can do to gain visibility for your business without spending a fortune. Many owners of small businesses don't budget for public relations or marketing. And what if you lack capital? You must resort to other means, but what exactly?

You must keep in mind that consumers need to hear about a product multiple times before they will take action and buy a product or service, even if they liked what they heard about it the first time. That's why repeated visibility is a must. Even if your company or product is well-established, you must maintain your visibility. For example, everyone knows of Wrigley gum; the company has been around for generations, but the owners still plaster billboards and the airwaves with ads. Why? They know that "out of sight" is truly "out of mind" even for a well-known product.

What can you do to get your product known? If you're willing to try creative ways to attract visibility for your business, but lack resources and ideas of what to do, relax. You can find effective ways to get your business known, some without spending a dime, though you always must spend time and energy. My "Low-Cost Marketing Strategy" that I use to promote my products (originally market umbrellas and now my books) and services (speaking and consulting) includes these ten tried-and-true components:

1. Write a business plan. Even if you have started your business, create a clear and compelling business plan. Not only does it serve as your road map, but it also can convince others to invest in your enterprise. A good business plan is a great marketing tool, and it only costs time and energy to assemble. Review the elements of a sound business plan in Option A, then think of it as a brochure or advertisement for your business.

2. Create a word-of-mouth chain reaction. Send notices about your business to everyone on your Christmas card list. Talk to strangers. Take every opportunity to open a short conversation with the person next to you on a plane, at a conference, even in the grocery store line. Ask these strangers what they do, and look for what they can teach you. You can then tell them about your exciting business. One person tells ten, those ten tell ten, and pretty soon 10,000 have heard about your business.

3. Become a public speaker. Talk to service groups such as Kiwanis, Soroptimists, and chambers of commerce. Speak to women's associations such as the Professional and Businesswomen's Association, and American Business Women's Association. You will find a list of professional and service organizations in your area by going to the library and asking the research librarian for her assistance. Call your local chamber of commerce for groups that hold meetings in your city. Consider not only what knowledge you can share with a particular group that would benefit them, but what you want from them in return. Do you want them to buy your book, use your service, or to give you referrals?

   Professional speakers stress these basics about becoming a good public speaker: know your topic, stay enthusiastic about your message, and emphasize solid information as well as entertainment. Speak to and keep eye contact with only one person at a time. In this way you may talk to a group of 4,000, but you maintain a personal approach and won't feel overwhelmed by the number in the audience. Don't focus on perfection in your presentation because you'll become flustered if anything goes wrong. If you can't think of a word or know you're saying the wrong word several times, simply ask the audience, "What's that word?" They'll be happy to tell you, and like you all the better for it, because they'll see that you're human.

4. Join organizations to network. Determine organizations in which you can participate to showcase your abilities so that others will want to refer people to use your product or service. Organizations such as Ali Lassen's Lead Club, headquartered in Carlsbad, California, specifically help women create their own "Old Girls' Network" and obtain viable leads and referrals for members' businesses. All business and professional associations provide a wonderful avenue to network.

5. Establish yourself as an expert in your field. If you don't want to hire (or can't afford) a PR agency, you still need to let the media know that your business exists. Write letters to the editor on topics that involve your expertise. Write a piece for the Opinion page. Getting quoted in an article gives you much more validity and power than writing one yourself. Write to newspaper editors and radio and TV producers in your local area to offer yourself as a resource in your area of expertise. How do you find these people? Call the newspapers, radio, and TV stations and ask them. All of these people need credible resources and will want to hear from you. For national exposure, go to the library and consult the *Bacon's* media guides, which list by state the names and addresses of radio and television programs and stations, daily and weekly newspapers and magazines.

   Keep people informed. Send press releases to the media whenever you launch a product, hire a new employee, land a huge account, or even when you plan to give a speech to a local organization. Keep your information newsworthy to the community's media by stressing its local relevance whenever possible. Use a standard format for your press releases and print them on your company letterhead. Choose either the upper right-hand or left-hand corner to write "Press Release" in bold capital letters. Directly underneath write "Date:" with the day you plan to send out the release, and below the date write "Contact:" followed by your name (or your publicist's) and phone number. (Make certain you include a contact name and phone number on every page of the release.) Two spaces below, center your catchy, informative title (or heading) using all caps. Do not use a period at the end of the title. Double space the body of your release and indent the beginning of each paragraph. The first paragraph must *briefly* include "who, what, why, when, where and how" information in such a fashion that grabs the reader's interest. Use the following paragraphs to expand on the information provided in the first paragraph. Include in the last paragraph a "Those interested in further information may call (800) xxx-xxxx" sentence. Preferably, your press release should not extend more than a single page, but if you must continue the release onto the following page, indicate that fact at the bottom of the first page by centering and writing, "—more—" in boldface type. Indicate the end of your message by centering in boldface type "—####–" or "–30–" or "–end–" under your last paragraph.

Be sure to enclose your business card with the release. Mail, fax, or e-mail your press releases to the appropriate print editor and TV, radio, or Internet producer. Prepare in advance a short biography of yourself, a black and white or color head shot of yourself, a color photo of your product, and a fact sheet about your product to send the media upon request.

6. On a more formal and far-reaching scale, you may want to consider direct mail campaigns. Many direct mail companies offer custom lists to reach a large variety of markets. The U.S. Postal Service offers free direct mail materials including a booklet *The Business Guide To Advertising With Direct Mail,* a binder with an overview of direct mail, case studies, samples of award-winning direct mail campaigns, research updates, and a computer program of advertising mail rates and mail profits calculator on a PC diskette. They send new information every few months to add to the binder.

7. Meet, and learn from, your customers. You can do what Debbi Fields did to get her cookies known. She stood out on the street corner with a plate of cookies in Oakland, California and asked every passerby to sample one. Yes, later her husband invested money to promote her product nationally, but in the beginning she got out there face to face with her customers. Build your business by thanking your existing

customers for their business. Ask them for referrals or for their input on how you can better serve them.

8. Hire independent sales representatives. Research whether your business would benefit from engaging independent sales representatives. You can learn a great deal about how to do business with a certain market, such as retail stores, from reps. I built up my umbrella business with the advice of good reps. They can help you pioneer your new product, determine what you can add to your product line, set up long-term agreements with customers, and, in general, act as wonderful collaborators. Your success is their success.

9. Advertise carefully. Research the cost of advertising in the Yellow Pages, local newspapers, coupon books, regional magazines, and on the Internet. You may think you can't afford to advertise, but do your research. Never blindly advertise. You will be approached by salespeople who will want you to advertise in coupons, specialized phone books, and local rags. Know your budget, and know exactly what you expect in return before committing to any advertising program.

10. Follow up every lead. If people show interest in your product, respond to them immediately. Keep their interest high. Prepare promotional materials in the form of brochures, post cards with a color photo of your product on the front, form letters that you can personalize, or anything that will keep your company name in front of a potential customer.

Expanding Your Thinking

In this adventure "you" discover many ways to get your business known with little initial capital outlay. Not everything progresses smoothly, however, and you make mistakes along the way. In Option A, you neglect to seek more than one person's advice. When you count on your mother to do much of the marketing, she assumes the lead role in your business. You try public speaking, but you're not comfortable speaking to groups and your mother overshadows you.

In Option B, you hope to get known through your writing for newspapers, but not in other ways. This limits you.

In Option C, you run into problems with the note card business when you try to compete with the big boys. You lack the resources to provide the same amount of sales materials and displays your reps recommend, let alone to carry the financial burden for late-paying customers. You eat your way through your frustrations.

Finally, in Option D, you rely on the Internet as the best means to promote your business but research no other means of marketing.

What negatives should you glean from this adventure?

DON'T:

1. Think that advertising is the only way, or necessarily the best way, to get a business or product known.
2. Assume you can't afford any type of advertising without researching it.
3. Spend your money on advertising until you know your target customer and what you can expect as a return on your investment.
4. Neglect preparing a business plan, even if you've already started your business.
5. Overlook the positive returns you can create from public speaking.
6. Wait for others to make connections for you.
7. Assume you can't serve as an expert in your field.
8. Ignore the benefits of joining associations to get yourself and your business known.

9. Think that "if you build it they will come."
10. Sit back and let someone you hire, a rep or a publicist, do all the promoting.

What works well for you in this adventure? In Option A, you call your friend and small business expert for advice and write your own business plan under her supervision. You try public speaking to promote your business, and you further promote it by sending press releases to newspapers. You enlist your mother to assist you in promotion. You create the centerpieces for your reunion and relish the photo of your trim self with your friends and your floral arrangements.

In Option B, you listen to your son's questions about wildflowers and realize that others would want to know the answers, too. You develop a unique and successful angle to attract attention to your writing, become a resource for newspaper reporters, develop a newsletter, find your market from the response to your articles, and take baby steps into advertising without spending a lot of money. When advertising in the Sunday papers pays off, you expand to a regional magazine, timing your ad to coincide with an issue featuring wildflowers.

In Option C, you expand your "flower of the day" concept into a note card business. You research and find several channels of distribution, some with reps and others on your own. You gain a great deal of marketing expertise from your reps.

You continue your education in Option D. You decide to research many alternative treatments using flowers as a remedy. You share that information on the Internet. Focusing on researching health issues helped you keep off the twenty pounds you lost for your reunion.

Points you might wish to remember on your quest to gain visibility for your business include:

DO:

1. Research and create a business plan.
2. Know your market before you try to create visibility for your product or service.
3. Seek advice from business experts.
4. Try promoting your business through public speaking.
5. Establish yourself as an expert in your field.
6. Think of an interesting and unique angle to present your information to newspapers and other media.
7. Send articles and press releases to newspapers and magazines.
8. Offer yourself as a resource to the media.
9. Experiment in low-risk advertising.
10. Look into hiring independent sales representatives if compatible with your business.

Assessing Your Own Situation

If you're trying to get your product, service, or business known, make certain you can answer these questions.

1. Ask yourself, "Where am I now with this business?" "What is my desired destination?"
2. If you were going to stand face to face with your customers, what would you tell them about your product or service? Ask yourself, "Can I briefly state three benefits about my product?"
3. If you want your business to become known, ask yourself, "Have I told everyone I know about my business?" "Do my friends on my Christmas card list know about what I do?" "What ways can I gain media attention?"

4. Have you thought of ideas to promote your business but nixed them without really looking into them? Ask, "If my accountant asked me to speak to her Soroptimist club, would I turn her down because I'm afraid to speak in front of a group?" "If I see an article about my field of expertise in the paper that I disagree with, would I take the time to write an opinion piece or send a letter to the editor?" "Have I learned how to write a press release?"

5. If you already have customers, do you keep in touch with them to cultivate business? Ask, "Do I send them thank-you's whenever appropriate?" "Have I asked my customers for referrals?" "Have I created an avenue for customers to contact me with feedback that could lead to improving my product?"

6. If you wish to generate free publicity, ask yourself, "Have I offered myself as a resource to the media?" "Do I keep the media informed of my business open houses, new personnel or promotions within the business, or any awards we've received?" "Have I developed a list of topics that will encourage the media to contact me for a quote?"

7. Even if you can't afford a PR agency, what can you do to promote your business? Ask yourself, "Have I asked everyone I know for advice to get my business known?" "Have I paid attention to what my competitors do to attract business?" "Have I read books on low-cost marketing strategies to learn about promoting a product or service?"

8. Have you looked around for non-mainstream distribution of your product or service? Ask, "Would someone sitting in a hair salon want to know about my product?" "Would museums, hospitals, bakeries, ski resorts, whatever, be willing to carry my product or a brochure describing my services?"

Affirmation

Commandment 6:
Get ready, get set, risk!

"I'm happy to share what I know and enjoy telling others about my business."

ADVENTURE 13

HOW CAN I DEAL WITH THE FRUSTRATION AND EXHAUSTION THAT COME FROM RUNNING MY OWN BUSINESS?

Have you ever suffered from "The One Woman Band" syndrome, where you feel you must play every instrument yourself? Do you feel compelled to put your personal touch on everything in your business? Maybe you **are** *your company and feel that only you can grow it properly, but even leading a band can create a lot of frustration and consume all your spare time. Can you imagine yourself* **Marching to a Different Drummer***?*

Marching to a Different Drummer

You thought that owning your own business would be the epitome of your career and make you feel like Julie Andrews in *The Sound of Music*. These days, however, you feel more like Jamie Lee Curtis in *Halloween Two*. "There's a thin line between a sweet dream and a nightmare," you tell yourself as you gaze out the window at another frosty day in Raleigh, North Carolina. The November chill weighs heavily on your mind as well as your body. Wiping your wire-rimmed glasses with the hem of your plaid Pendleton shirt, you shake your head wondering what miracle will enable you to finish the avalanche of public relations work for your three demanding clients—Shazam Software, MicroCrane, and Birch Power Drives—in just three and a half weeks before Comdex, the world's largest computer show held in Las Vegas.

Propelled by your determination, tenacity, and brains, you have spearheaded your personal campaign into the business world from your thatched-roofed beginnings in the Philippines. You and your younger sister enjoyed the good fortune to get farmed out to an uncle in North Carolina where you attended high school and college. You baby-sat and clerked in a variety of local retail stores during high school, and you sold student group trips for a travel agency during college. Immediately after earning your degree in Journalism from the University of North Carolina, you married Brian, a mature man and fine musician ten years your senior. While he worked nights and weekends, you wrote press releases and marketing plans by day for everything from an office furniture manufacturer to start-up software companies. Work always compromised your time as a couple, and within two years you separated but remain good friends.

One of your most successful campaigns early in your chameleon career catapulted the budding Durham Center for the Arts into a splendid home for the Raleigh-Durham Ballet Company. Riding the wave of your Center for the Arts notoriety, you started

Breath of Fresh Air Communications on a whim after skiing in Vail with friends. It was all music to your ears at the time.

Today, you hear nothing but sour notes. You're already exhausted and can't fathom how you'll survive the barrage of daily requests and client crises that will erupt before and during Comdex. Tracey Hunter, the receptionist/promotions person you hired to update your list of computer trade magazine editors, to type and send out pre-Comdex press releases, and to coordinate press conferences with your three clients, has arrived late with a migraine and a messy bag lunch. Your account assistant, Rodney Hoover, wants you to proofread his new product announcement for Shazam Software and stands fidgeting in front of your desk, as if expecting you to drop everything this minute. You realize that delegating anything but the most basic work ends up costing you even more time.

Just then the phone rings and the fax machine jams. You dive for the beeping fax machine as Rodney grabs the telephone receiver and yells, "Hello?"

You look at him and, with all your facial and body language, try to coach him to say, "This is Breath of Fresh Air Communications, may I help you?"

But he doesn't. He just shouts again, "Hello!" You shudder as you hear him explain, "Yes, yes, this *is* a communications company..." and you know exactly which client has called, your biggest one. Rodney shrugs. He doesn't understand what he did wrong.

"Didn't his mother ever teach him the importance of a proper, friendly phone greeting?" you wonder, wishing you'd thought of asking him if he knew how to answer a telephone when you interviewed him.

"He wants you to call him back, Lorna."

"For crying out loud," you scream, clamping a few scathing swear words between your teeth, and wishing you could afford to hire pre-trained, think-on-their feet employees. You take a minute to pamper yourself with a few self-pitying thoughts, then turn from the cleared fax machine to face the cold reality: you must impose strict deadlines on yourself or lose credibility with your hard-won clients.

Your two employees sullenly wait for guidance. You feel organizationally challenged and weighed down with your own perfectionism. As you sit down on the carton of press releases delivered from the printer yesterday, you pull a felt-tipped marker from behind your ear and jot down on the back on a large manila envelope four options that might help you regain your sanity.

What Would You Do?

A. **I will take a deep breath, get through the next few weeks, then devote time to planning growth, paying particular attention to training my current employees or replacing them.**

B. **I will call my travel agent to make plans to leave for Barbados the day after Comdex ends in order to regroup and reorganize my priorities.**

C. **I can accept the offer to work at MicroCrane as VP of marketing with a handsome salary.**

D. **I'll consider finding a partner to share the responsibilities.**

Turn to the option that most appeals to you. To learn the most from this adventure, read how the other options turned out, too. Then study the last three sections of this adventure: "Exploring the Issue," "Expanding Your Thinking," and "Assessing Your Situation."

A. I will take a deep breath, get through the next few weeks, then devote time to planning growth, paying particular attention to training my current employees or replacing them.

You feel like you're suffering from jet lag and you haven't even gone anywhere yet. You grit your teeth and tell yourself, "Okay, it's gut-it-through time for the next few weeks. I have no other choice, but I swear I won't get in this mess again."

You assign Tracey the task of collating the press releases and stuffing them into envelopes. When you ask her how much progress she's made in updating the mailing list, you hear the usual reply.

"I dunno. Uh, I need maybe another day or two," Tracey answers, popping an Advil Migraine pill.

"It's Wednesday. If you can finish the list by noon Friday, I'll buy lunch. With luck we'll get the majority of the releases out Friday afternoon." You turn to Rodney, who keeps jiggling his leg, and continue, "Rodney, give me twenty minutes to proof your Shazam announcement. While I do that, will you confirm with each client the rooms we've reserved for them? Ask if there will be any changes in flight plans, too."

You run your fingers through your blunt cut, raven hair, mentally vowing to take each day one hour at a time. Chiding yourself to keep calm, you manage to control your short-fused temper. Losing your cool now would just waste too much energy.

Finally the day comes when you fly to Las Vegas to hold your clients' hands and orchestrate their press announcements and conferences. During the show, you pull off a well-attended launch of Shazam's new investment software program, print up last-minute press releases, and wine and dine your clients and their top customers. The show goes extremely well, despite the fact that you feel mentally and physically exhausted.

You breathe a sigh of relief when you settle into your aisle seat on your Delta flight back to the Raleigh/Durham airport. After stretching out your legs in front of you, you open up your lap top and begin to write your thank-you notes and to list your follow-up tasks. An hour later you close your eyes, visualizing the expansion of your small business, if you can only land the two prospective clients you cultivated during the show. Then it hits you, "Here I go again, planning more growth before I can handle what's on my plate already. I have to do something about my office staff or I'll go crazy. I can't do it all myself. If I can't train my people to take the pressure off, I'll have to fire them and hire people who can."

You consider Rodney's skills. He writes well and has proved himself capable of bringing in revenue when he's motivated. Still, he keeps erratic hours and possesses few people skills. Is he salvageable? You don't know, but you'll try. Tracey puts no effort into her job and functions at a consistent C-level. She waits for you to explain everything she needs to do, when and how to do it. She initiates nothing. She's always sick. She's history. But who will you find to replace her?

When you return to your apartment from the airport, you listen to your messages, and one, from a woman named Jasmine Bassinger, catches your interest. She says she's a friend of your college roommate, Dana. You decide to return her call in the morning.

The next day, you discover that Jasmine is looking for a job. She says she has secretarial skills and has worked in a PR agency before. You make a hasty offer, "I need someone who can think on her feet whom I can trust to get the job done. My business is growing and I don't have the support system I need to develop it. I'm glad you bring a strong communications background to the job."

Three months later, you realize you've made a huge mistake. Jasmine, it turns out, needs even more supervision than Tracey did. The follow-up work after Comdex takes forever to complete, and you feel totally frustrated with Jasmine, though you worry about firing Dana's friend. But you decide that enough's enough already, and you tell her so late one Friday afternoon.

"Look, Jasmine, you haven't shown any of the communications skills you claimed to have, or you'd have been able to perform without me telling you exactly what to do all the time. This just isn't working. I suggest you start looking for a more suitable job."

To your astonishment, Jasmine stands up to you. "You know, Lorna, you should lighten up," she says firmly. "You're such a control freak, and such a perfectionist, it's no wonder no one can work for you. You pretend to delegate but you watch every move like a hawk then grab everything back if someone isn't doing it the way you would. You know what your problem is? You think you're the only one who can do anything right. You find fault in everything anyone else does, and rather than explaining what you want, you just criticize. I don't know how you've kept Rodney, because you scrutinize everything he does like a prison warden. You know I have no money and no other prospects, but now you're telling me 'it isn't working' and to leave. You're a terrible boss."

Her words wound you, but they make you think. Is Jasmine right? Or do you just have a knack for hiring the wrong people? You call your friend Dana to tell her you fired Jasmine, wanting to deliver the bad news before Jasmine can complain to her. To your surprise, Dana says that she never suggested Jasmine call you, that she knows nothing about Jasmine's work background or skills, and that Jasmine is only an acquaintance, not a close friend at all. You're stunned. You had put up with Jasmine for months because you thought Dana had recommended her.

"Great. Another lousy lesson," you mumble as you stare at the load of work piling up, "Check references."

BENEFITS OF A:

- You tackle your workload one hour at a time.
- You make clear requests of your office staff to complete work before the show.

- You perform well during the show and attract more prospective clients.
- You write thank-you notes and follow-up lists on the plane.
- You realize that while you visualize the expansion of your business, you must strengthen your office support.
- You evaluate your office staff and decide to make the effort to salvage Rodney and let go of Tracey.
- You immediately replace Tracey with Jasmine.

DOWNSIDES OF A:

- You seek new clients while you barely can handle current ones.
- You fire Tracey without a probationary period during which she might improve.
- You offer a job to Jasmine without checking any references.
- You feel Jasmine took advantage of you.
- You don't evaluate your own possible shortcomings as a boss.
- You still find yourself trying to run your company with an ineffective office staff.

B. I will call my travel agent to make plans to leave for Barbados the day after Comdex ends in order to regroup and reorganize my priorities.

"Hello, Janine? This is Lorna Dooley. Could you please check into a flight or package deal to Barbados for Thanksgiving week, leaving on Monday, right after the return flight from Comdex you booked for me? Find a great little hotel on a beach where I can plop down in the sand and bake."

"Got just the place for you, Lorna, the Smuggler's Cove. Want me to reserve a car for you, too?" Janine asks.

"Can you get a convertible?"

"How about a Jeep mini-moke? Looks like a little kid's peddle car, only it has an engine and a striped surrey top."

"Perfect. Include a broad-shouldered hunk to go with it, will ya?"

"Sure, no problem. I'll fax the schedule for your approval this afternoon."

When you get off the phone, you feel strangely exhilarated. You haven't taken one vacation since you started your business three and a half long years ago. Heck, you've hardly taken a full weekend off. No wonder you're on edge. All work and no play has made you boring and bored, not to mention exhausted and short-tempered.

After Comdex you fly to Barbados, drop your suitcases in your room at the lush Smuggler's Cove, close the wooden louvered windows to change into your bikini, and, as planned, forego the padded chaise lounges for a colorful beach towel to bake yourself on the radiant sand. After a strenuous swim in the turquoise salt water, you wonder why you haven't kept fit. You know the positive effects regular exercise has on your mind as well as your body. You lather SPF 30 sunscreen on your winter white body and try to doze. Sleep eludes you, however, because you can't turn off your mind. You've done remarkably well in just three years building your business, but now, just when it's become easier to win clients, it's lost much of its sparkle. You've proved that you can start a business and have enjoyed turning the concept into reality. Although your income exceeds what you'd hoped for, here you are in a romantic place on your very first vacation sitting all by yourself. What's wrong with this picture?

You feel too tense just to sit in the sun. You're not certain you *can* slow down. The pressured pace you live has become as habitual as those four cups of strong coffee in the morning. In the software industry, you barely get a news release written before the product becomes obsolete. The trouble with the computer world is that you can't stop or someone else will race ahead of you. What did you recently read? Some Boston-based consultant and former Boston University researcher who studies work/family issues reported that since 1975 the work year has expanded by 158 hours, approximately an entire month. In the computer industry, you bet the expanded hours exceed that. No wonder no one has time to squeeze in a personal life.

In the shower later that afternoon as you lather the foamy body gel over your sandy and slightly reddened body, you stop, momentarily stunned because your left hand detects a marble-sized lump near your armpit on your right breast. You wonder how long it's been there. You control your rapid fire mind and decide not to get overly upset until your gynecologist can check it out. You'll call tomorrow to make an appointment for the afternoon you return to Raleigh. You're surprised at how calm you feel when you land at the airport two days later.

At home you think about your whole life. Maybe your body is trying to tell you something that you already intuitively know: slow down, smell the roses. Your life has been so consumed by your business that you haven't come up for air in three and a half years. And for what? What are you trying to prove?

You start thinking about what you would do if you closed your business. When you ask yourself, "What would I enjoy doing most?" a neon sign in your mind instantly flashes, "Travel." You call Janine and ask what it takes to become a travel agent. The thought appeals to you so much, you seriously contemplate going that direction regardless of your health diagnosis.

The following Monday afternoon when you leave Dr. Thompson's office, you feel greatly relieved because the lump turned out to be only a cyst. Dr. Thompson aspirated it right there in the office. He noted that since there was no blood evident in the yellowish fluid, there was little to worry about, but he'd have the lab double-check his observation just to be on the safe side.

When you return home you find a fax from Janine who informs you that to become an independent travel agent you first need an appointment from the Airlines Reporting Corporation (ARC), which is available only to agencies with public premises, which means an office outside the home. Since you also must post a bond and work on a computer reservation system owned by one of the major airlines, Janine suggests you sign on with her as an outside agent. She encourages you to read books on becoming a travel agent, but she warns that if you expect to generate travel agent discounts, you must sell many tickets to qualify, and even so the special deals dwindle daily.

You're not exactly sure what you're going to do, but you know that whatever move you make, you will base it on more clearly defined priorities for your life.

BENEFITS OF B:

- You make plans to take a much overdue vacation.
- You soak up the sun on a sandy Barbados beach.
- You assess what running your own business means in terms of your overall life enjoyment.
- You consider the lump on your breast as your wake-up call to slow down.
- You imagine what else you would enjoy doing for a living.
- You start researching the possibility of becoming a travel agent.

DOWNSIDES OF B:

- You cannot relax because your problems keep surfacing in your mind.
- You've grown weary of your business because you don't relish building something you started.
- You do not realize that your problems reside within, not outside, yourself.
- Your idea to become a travel agent comes more as a reaction to stress than as a well thought-out plan.
- You still haven't identified or written down your priorities.

C. I can accept the offer to work at MicroCrane as VP of marketing with a handsome salary.

Andy Crane, owner of MicroCrane, has been wooing you to join his firm as VP of marketing since the day you met. You know his company needs your help because when you won his account a year ago and asked him the basic questions—Who's your target market? What are the demographics? What's the company philosophy?—Andy couldn't answer them. He just figured that if you got his name in the *Wall Street Journal* and *MicroAge*, customers would start beating down his door. However, you convinced him that his company really needed an identity, a message, and a thoroughly thought-out marketing campaign. He has wanted you to create a marketing plan for him ever since. Lately, you've been tempted to accept his offer, because you respect Andy, despite his ego, and see huge potential in the company. Its brilliant future could become your ticket to success.

Though you've enjoyed the prestige of owning your own business, you can't stand all of the personnel problems and related frustrations. They've taken a huge toll on your enthusiasm. Working for yourself requires that you be all things to everyone, and it's hard to find time to do what you do best, promote products and companies. The thought of working on salary again, a big salary at that, and letting someone else worry about payroll, taxes, and overhead sounds appealing.

You decide you'll talk seriously to Andy at Comdex, then tie up loose ends with your other clients right after the show. You won't be able to give Tracey or Rodney much notice or a severance, but hey, that's how the cookie crumbles. They haven't worked out well for you anyway. You'll schedule in a nice two to three week vacation before you change jobs, too.

Eighteen months after joining MicroCrane, you've not only created a successful marketing plan, but you've helped the company raise capital to expand and prepare to go public. You're glad you accepted a smaller salary in return for stock. You're excited about the impending initial private offering (IPO) in twelve months, which could make you a wealthy woman. You've never regretted for one minute your decision to pack up your own business and join MicroCrane.

BENEFITS OF C:

- You decide to join a company you know and respect.
- Your skills match the new job.
- You take a short but much needed vacation between jobs.
- You help MicroCrane grow and prepare for an IPO.
- You take shares and a smaller salary which will benefit you when the company goes public.

DOWNSIDES OF C:

- You avoid the hassle of fixing your own company's problems.
- You take the easy way out, when, in fact, your own management shortcomings may follow you to your new job.

- You risk working for someone with a big ego but without a clue about promoting his own company.
- You concentrate on changing companies while at Comdex when you should have been focused on all of your clients.
- You make arrangements to close your office right after Comdex with little notice to your clients or office staff.

D. I'll consider finding a partner to share the responsibilities.

On your flight to Comdex you sit next to Mary Jane Rice, whom you've met several times before, but have never taken the time to get to know. She owns her own PR company in Raleigh, too, and enjoys an excellent reputation. You aren't competitors, really, because she works for hardware firms, while you serve software clients. If anything, your client mix blends fairly well because some of the products and services interface.

You both laugh at how exhausted you feel, and you mention trying to get some rest, but you end up pouring your hearts out to each other during the entire four and a half hour flight. You had no idea other women felt the same way you do. The hours evaporate as you discuss the loneliness of running a business, and the difficulty of handling all the problems appropriately. You're not sure, but you suspect that the same thought crosses both of your minds—to merge your businesses. Maybe it's wishful thinking on your part because your lease runs out in four months. You know the landlord plans to raise your rent, and you could put this money to better use elsewhere in your business. Joining forces with Mary Jane may be just what the business doctor ordered. When you deplane in Las Vegas, you tell Mary Jane you'd like to meet her for lunch the week after Comdex, once you've both caught your breath. She eagerly agrees.

At lunch with Mary Jane two weeks later, you present your idea to merge companies, an idea she finds quite appealing. Agreeing to a four-month time frame gives you both time to work out details and write up a legal agreement for the merger.

Within a month, a lawyer has drawn up an agreement that satisfies you both. You both retain and handle your own clients, but share Mary Jane's office, the payroll, and all marketing expenses.

Despite the merger, however, you still feel overwhelmed by work. The constant struggle to build business and maintain the momentum with your core clients forces you to tears. Basically, you like building something from nothing, but lose interest when it comes to maintaining and growing it. Though your arrangement with Mary Jane certainly helps alleviate financial worries, and she runs the office skillfully, you feel like a second-class citizen, an addendum to her overall plans for success. You wish you shared her vision, but you don't. Now you feel hog-tied to your work, not only to please your clients and support your staff, but to hold up your end of the bargain with Mary Jane. You lessened your managerial and financial problems, but you have gained your own task master, Mary Jane. You seriously question your sanity when you suggested the merger, but now you're stuck.

BENEFITS OF D:

- You share your concerns with someone who relates to them.
- You find that you and Mary Jane could make good teammates.
- You meet her for lunch to discuss merging your businesses.
- You work out a legal agreement to combine your businesses.
- You lessen your financial and management burdens.

DOWNSIDES OF D:

- You do nothing to correct your own managerial shortcomings.

- You let your impending lease problem influence your thinking about merging your business.
- You do not explore whether or not your goals and Mary Jane's really match.
- You still feel overloaded with your work.
- You've treated symptoms rather than the real problem; you're bored now that your business is up and running.
- You feel more trapped now with a partner.

Exploring the Issue

Owning your own business can make you feel like a one-legged contestant in an Olympic decathlon. It requires that you become more resourceful than you've ever been in your life. Before you open the doors to your business make certain you know *why* you want to do it. Like everything else in life, you should carefully identify and weigh the trade-offs.

In this adventure we look at an overworked, disorganized, frustrated, exhausted woman who owns a monetarily rewarding business. And she doesn't have a husband and children to add to the demands on her time and emotions. What happens to her can happen to any woman who runs her own business, and can become even more problematic for the self-employed mother.

Most women who've ever owned a business will tell you that the number one question to ask yourself before you start a business is not "What will I do?" but "Why?" Once you have it up and running, you need to ask yourself that again and again and again.

It's always interesting to find out why women start their own businesses. Among the creative reasons I've heard: refusal to get locked into the constraints of the corporate ladder and an unwillingness to bang their heads against the glass ceiling; a desire to set their own challenges and goals; a longing for personal, professional, and financial independence; an abiding love for a product, a service, or an idea that they want to bring to fruition; a wish to control their own hours, call their own shots, prove to themselves or to others that they can succeed in business.

Why do some women close their businesses? The reasons include: they didn't plan properly and ran out of money; they got tired of the headaches of managing employees, cash flow, operations, marketing, production, and promotion all at once; they felt that they hadn't won their freedom from having to please a boss, because now they must please their employees, suppliers, and customers; they don't like their partners; their business took over their lives; or they accomplished what they wanted and no longer needed to prove anything to themselves or anyone else.

One woman said that she discovered, to her dismay, that she loved her reputation as a hard worker, but that she had taken it to the extreme. She cornered the market on fatigue and wore her haggard expression as the hard-won "badge" of an entrepreneur. She exemplified the Puritan work ethic run amuck. She lost track of what she was trying to accomplish, thinking, "If I work hard, then I'll get noticed, appreciated, and respected." Then one day she finally realized whom she was trying to impress, not herself or the business community, but her demanding deceased mother. Sick? No, not a rare occurrence when you don't know what *you* want to accomplish and end up trying to accomplish what you think someone else expects of you.

If you tend to take on too much, you know it. But do you know that by doing too much you effectively numb yourself to your own needs? You may lose your ability to distinguish between your wants and your needs. Being achievement oriented is great as long as it's not just for the sake of achieving without knowing why, being busy without real purpose, and staying active simply to fill a void.

You may be unconsciously masking a hidden issue by overbooking and overworking yourself. Overscheduling protects you from thinking, from asking the important questions, and from facing the answers to the questions you do ask.

Business ownership can be one of the most rewarding experiences of your life, spiritually and financially, as long as it doesn't replace your life. So ask yourself "Why" and "What am I trying to accomplish?"

Expanding Your Thinking

"You" in this adventure represents a typical, industrious, perfectionistic self-employed woman. You want to do it all yourself and believe only you can do it best.

In this adventure, you cannot easily delegate or trust others to do what you think you can do better. You don't take time to train your employees or express your expectations clearly, as evidenced in Option A. You offer Jasmine a job without checking her references. When you let her go, she's upset and hurt. You discover, much to your chagrin, that your college roommate hardly knows Jasmine and wouldn't have recommended her. You remain in your work dilemma without a strong support staff.

In Option B, you escape to the Caribbean, but once there realize you don't know how to relax anymore. When you find a lump on your breast, you decide you must radically change your lifestyle, including work. You realize that you feel bored with your business, but you haven't really assessed why you feel that way. You assume it's because you prefer the start-up phase, not the maintaining and growing phases. But are you being honest with yourself? Have you lost your spark? Does it take too much effort to keep your business going? Do you plan to quit too soon and use your health scare as an excuse? You look into becoming a travel agent, but that represents more of a fantasy than a well-thought-out reality.

In Option C, you decide to close shop when you get fed up with the responsibilities and deadlines of your own business. While you see a place to jump, you give little notice to your long-term clients or to your employees.

Finally, in Option D, you try to solve your problems by merging with another well-respected woman-owned PR company. While you thought you had found a kindred spirit, you find that she has grand plans for herself and the business that you simply don't share. You've solved some of your problems, but you've dug a deeper hole into a business you no longer enjoy.

What should you remember not to do?

DON'T:

1. Neglect to train and guide your employees.
2. Assume you can do everything better than anyone else.
3. Hire anyone without checking references.
4. Hire permanent employees if you can't take time to interview properly.
5. Put aside your need for vacations.
6. Wait for a wake-up call to examine your work/life objectively.
7. Make excuses to avoid taking time off.
8. Jump into other jobs without honestly asking yourself why you're leaving or quitting.
9. Create more problems by trying to find someone else to solve yours.
10. Dig yourself into a hole by merging your business for the wrong reasons.

Let's look at what worked well. In Option A, you visualize the expansion of your business, realize you need a stronger support staff, and analyze Tracey's and Rodney's effectiveness. You decide you'll try to salvage Rodney and let Tracey go. You hire Jasmine, who claims a sound communications background.

You realize you need to get away, to relax on a vacation, and to pull back and see your business objectively in Option B. You call your travel agent and book a week's retreat in Barbados. As you bake in the sand, you reassess why you want to own a business, and this particular business. You're unexpectedly forced to step back even further to see the big picture of your life when you detect a lump on your breast. Is your lump your wake-up call? Should you pay closer attention to your priorities in the future? You decide it's time to try something new, even though you aren't quite certain what that would be. You look into becoming a travel agent.

In Option C, you acknowledge that you wouldn't be deemed a failure if you closed your business and accept a lucrative and challenging offer at MicroCrane. You can separate your pride in your identity as an entrepreneur with the reality that you've accomplished what you wanted from your business: the thrill of creating something from nothing. You aren't afraid to admit you're bored with it. At MicroCrane you develop a successful marketing campaign and help raise money for the company to go public. In doing so you develop new skills, and you position yourself to make a great deal of money.

Finally, in Option D, you merge your business in the hopes of solving your lease problem, lowering the expense of office overhead, and easing the hassles of managing employees.

What can you learn from your character in this adventure?

DO:

1. Know why you want to own your own business.
2. Ask yourself periodically if you're accomplishing what you want to do.
3. Train and clearly direct your employees.
4. Find ways to relax.
5. Take vacations.

6. Weigh the quality of your work and your life.
7. Imagine what you would do for a living if you just wanted to have fun.
8. Acknowledge that it's okay to close your own business to follow a new challenge.
9. Give yourself credit for the things you've accomplished.
10. Respect your experiences and knowledge you gained from owning your own business.

Assessing Your Own Situation

If you feel like a One Woman Band, ask yourself some soul-searching questions.

1. If you feel you're doing too much, ask yourself, "Whom do I help if I'm exhausted, grumpy, and frustrated?" "What am I trying to accomplish by doing everything?" "Am I accomplishing my goals by overworking?"
2. If you feel exhausted, ask, "Do I trust my employees to do a good job?" "Have I given them clear direction so they can do their jobs well?" "Can I delegate projects clearly and oversee them from a distance?"
3. If you work alone, ask, "Have I tried to include personal time, or do I enjoy a reputation as a 'hard worker'?" "Do I believe I'll win respect from others if I do twenty things at a time?" "Am I too much of a perfectionist to trust others to do what I expect?"
4. If you feel overwhelmed, ask, "Am I in over my head, and if so, can I admit it and seek help?" "Have I hired the best people I can find?" "Have I written clear job descriptions then required my employees to fulfill them?"

5. Could it be that you're a perfectionist? Ask, "Do I carry the weight of the world on my shoulders, blaming myself for every detail that doesn't work out perfectly?" "Can I forgive myself for mistakes, learn from them, and move on?" "Am I too much of a perfectionist to trust others to do what I expect?"

6. Do you keep yourself fit? Ask, "Do I jeopardize the health of my business by not taking care of my own health?"

7. If you feel isolated, ask, "Do I meet with professional peers regularly?" "Do I feel I have to go it alone?" "Do I think I don't have time to network and find like-minded business owners?"

8. If you have a business and a family, ask, "What are the benefits of this business to my family?" "What do I take from my family when I overload at work?" "Have I reassessed my priorities lately?"

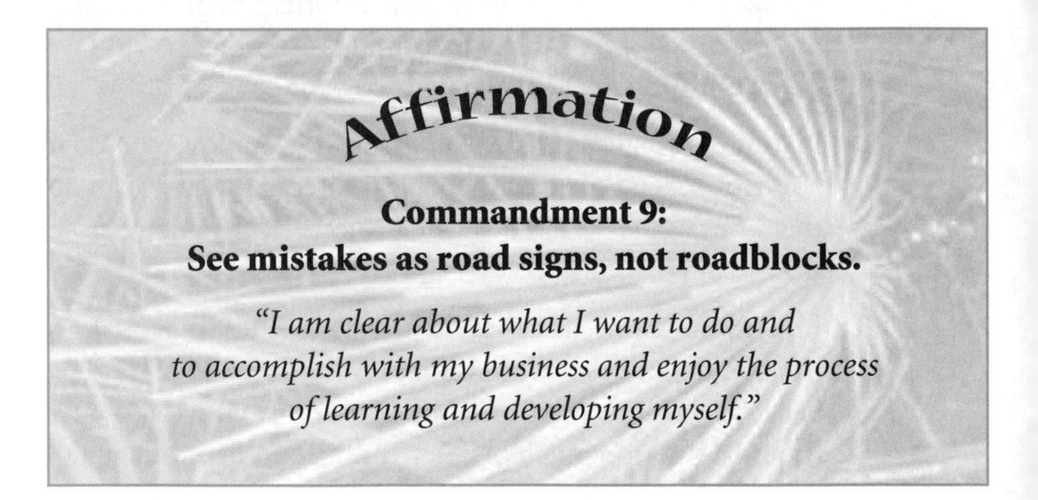

Part III

Love Adventures

Relationships, Family, and Balance

ADVENTURE 14

HOW CAN I LEARN TO TRUST AGAIN AFTER A BUSINESS ASSOCIATE'S BETRAYAL?

*Has a friend, a relation, or a colleague ever betrayed you? Sabotage, back-stabbing, lying and cheating may happen every day in business, but when it happens to you, the pain can make it hard for you to trust anyone again. If you've ever felt that way at some point in your career, imagine how you would handle being **Ripped Off by a Relative.***

Ripped Off by a Relative

"I never dreamed it would come to this," you confide to your lawyer, Susan Harrison, a personal friend since your days at Whitman College in Walla Walla, Washington.

"No one does," she confirms. "We're finished here. I can have the papers drawn up next week, just give me the nod. Come on, Hollie, I'll buy you a drink."

Susan holds the heavy glass door for you as you step outside her law offices on the corner of Kearny and Sutter Streets into a surprisingly cool, clear spring San Francisco evening. You walk to 19 Maiden Lane, the Iron Horse Restaurant, and find a table in a dark corner of the bar.

"You want to talk about it, Hollie?" Susan asks after ordering two kir royales.

Before you speak you reflect on what has brought you to this point, when you started suspecting betrayal, and what you should have done about it. Where should you begin, when your parents started their sewing business in their kitchen and named it Fredann's after their two first names? Or when they moved it to South San Francisco when they won a contract to make basketball and football uniforms for high schools? Or when you divorced Ben and went to work part-time for your parents at first doing bookkeeping ten years ago to support your kids, then ages one and three? Or, two years later, when you started working full-time and enjoyed helping the company grow into a nationwide sportswear manufacturer supplying merchandisers like K-Mart? Or should the story begin when you and your brother, Dominick, inherited the business after your parents perished in the fiery ten-car pileup on Highway 80 in the dense tule fog outside of Sacramento?

Dominick had been working full-time with your parents for ten years before the accident, you for only four years. The two of you inherited the company equally, but your strong-willed brother had claimed the presidency while appointing you secretary/treasurer. At that point, the business suffered cash flow problems, partly due to a failed experiment in overseas manufacturing which resulted in poor quality control, delayed shipments, and unanimous customer ill-will. You had scrambled to pay the inheritance tax on the company, then valued at $2 million.

Somehow, running the business with Dominick didn't feel right from the beginning. At first you noticed your brother's foibles, his tendency to utter insignificant half-truths and elaborate excuses for late deposits. Whenever you confronted Dominick about invoices that didn't look right, he only muttered, "Trust me. I'll take care of it."

You wanted to trust your big brother, but Dominick's heavy drinking after your parents' death concerned you and you wondered if he hadn't progressed into something heavier, like cocaine, but you couldn't bring yourself to think about it then. You hoped his wife could help him through it. You put his alcohol problem out of your mind, just as you had with your ex-husband, focusing all your thoughts on winning back accounts. Though you'd never sold anything in your life, not even a glass of lemonade from a roadside stand as a little girl, you single-handedly brought back customers with the promise of top-quality on-shore manufacturing and samples of your top-of-the-line women's running suits.

A year ago and nearly five years after your unexpected partnership began with Dominick, you thought brighter days had finally arrived. Dominick had kicked his substance abuse problems, and the company revenues had reached an all time high. Then you noticed a deposit to the company account you couldn't comprehend. Your old suspicions resurfaced in full force. This time you didn't confront Dominick. Instead, you asked the bank to send you a copy of the check, only to discover that it came from a bogus account, presumably set up by Dominick. Alarmed, you hired an outside auditor to call your customers and ask them to submit printouts of checks written to your company over the past year. Your accountant diligently followed the money trail, and after digging for nine months, he presented you with the naked truth: your own big brother meticulously and systematically had been stealing large sums of money from the business.

Deep inside you had suspected this for a long time, but you chose not to face it because, if it proved true, it would sever not only your business partnership but your last remaining family connection. You felt sick.

Your attorney, Susan, interrupts your reverie. "Hollie, do you want to tell me about it?"

"No, I don't think so, but I would like you to help me decide what I can do other than sue Dominick for embezzlement. It's so painful, Susan." You stifle a sob and add, "Here he's been ripping me off for years and I'm the one feeling guilty. Nuts, huh? How am I ever going to trust him again?"

"Believe me, Hollie, I've seen this sort of situation a hundred times. And, no matter how much pain you feel right now, you can find your way out of it. Here, let's sketch out some options."

Susan jots down these possibilities on a cocktail napkin:

What Would You Do?

A. I can force Dominick to buy me out, then I can forget this ever happened.

B. I can buy Dominick out and shut him out of my life forever.

C. I can confront Dominick and work with him to correct his wrongs.

D. I must find justice in order to let go of my anger and distrust and move on with my life.

Turn to the option that most appeals to you. To learn the most from this adventure, read how the other options turned out, too. Then study the last three sections of this adventure: "Exploring the Issue," "Expanding Your Thinking," and "Assessing Your Situation."

A. I can force Dominick to buy me out, then I can forget this ever happened.

The thought of suing your own brother makes you feel queasy. You know it's an option, but you also know that besides making you feel terrible and embarrassed, it will create bad publicity that would scare off customers. And rightfully so. Who wants to work with a company whose owners cheat each other? How would they know you haven't cheated them, too? No, there's too much competition out there to risk an ugly lawsuit, and you simply don't have the stomach for it.

Your meeting with Susan enlightens you, however, because it verified that you've gathered enough evidence to build a strong case. You'll use that information as leverage to force Dominick to buy you out quietly. You can't believe that Dominick would want a lawsuit and the subsequent public humiliation. He and his wife have two darling boys in grade school who don't need their daddy put in jail for embezzlement. Though you have a sneaking hunch that Madeline, Dominick's wife, has known about the ruse since the beginning, you only want your money and your freedom, not revenge.

With your accountant present, you confront Dominick in your office. Predictably, Dominick only smiles indulgently. No explanations, no apologies, no saying, "drugs made me do it," just that patronizing brotherly smirk. Your accountant places the figures squarely in front of Dominick, along with a financial statement that values the company at well over $2 million.

"You owe me half of the company, plus what you've stolen," you demand, your voice quivering with anger and fear.

Dominick picks up the papers and says, "These aren't legal documents. I'm not signing anything." He throws them back on your desk.

"Then I'll get the formal papers drawn up by my attorney tomorrow," you counter.

Dominick grabs his briefcase and pauses with his hand on the door knob, "You can't force me to buy you out, Little Sister."

"The facts don't lie, Big Brother. Don't make this harder than it needs to be."

That night you take out your nervous frustration by eating a quart of Ben and Jerry's Coffee, Coffee Buzz Buzz Buzz ice cream. You worry that Dominick may never pay you back and you wonder what you'd do if the company went bankrupt. You spend a sleepless night churning over horrible thoughts in your mind, and finally fall into a fitful sleep. At about 4 A.M., your phone rings. The

South San Francisco police inform you that your business has burned to the ground.

All of your evidence, save a few papers at your accountant's, went up in smoke along with the business. Of course it was arson. You recall the time when you were little and you and Dominick had argued over a sugar Easter egg with a village scene inside. You both had found it at the same time during the family Easter egg hunt. When your father flipped a coin, you won the egg, but at that point Dominick grabbed it from you and stomped it to dust saying, "If I can't have it, no one can." You have no proof, but you know who set the fire for the insurance money.

BENEFITS OF A:

- You avoid filing the lawsuit to keep from jeopardizing the reputation of the company.
- You hire an independent auditor to investigate the amount of Dominick's wrongdoing.
- ● You try to make the confrontation with Dominick as low key as possible.

DOWNSIDES OF A:

- You mistakenly think you can leverage the evidence against Dominick to make him buy you out.
- ● You fail to bring your attorney along when you confront Dominick.
- You offer no formal papers for the buyout.
- You take out your frustration by eating too much.
- You realize too late that Dominick might do something crazy.
- You have lost your business and your brother.

B. I can buy Dominick out and shut him out of my life forever.

Accompanied by your accountant and attorney, you present Dominick with legal papers in the conference room of your company.

"Hollie will pay you a fair price for your half of the business, less what you've misappropriated," your attorney, Susan, explains to Dominick.

Dominick sits there silently. He knows he's in a box. He agrees to the sale, at whatever price you name, but you want to be fair, perhaps fairer than he deserves, but feel that's beside the point. You just want to be rid of him. You can't give him one settlement check because you don't have that amount of cash on hand, plus you must clean up a few major financial messes in the business, thanks to your big brother. Though you feel guilty over this entire predicament, two other feelings sweep over you, relief and a sense of freedom.

You're amazed at how in control you feel, given the fact that Dominick has fooled you all these years. What a dummy you've been! Though you ran the finances of the company as treasurer, he still pulled the wool over your eyes. If you had blindly given him free rein over the company, you could let yourself off the hook, but he had insisted you work with the banks, pay the insurance, and deal with the payroll company. He made you believe you were doing a great job. Although you had suspected that something was amiss for a long time, you chose not to see it. You didn't want to think about it. Now, you can't believe he could have been so devious and you so afraid to face the truth. You're never going to forgive him.

You spend the next eighteen months working to repair the damage Dominick has done to the business. Every month, when you sign another check paying off Dominick, you try to let go of your anger, but you can't. Fuming with resentment, you funnel your energies into the company. First you bring in a business expert to advise you how to place safeguards and controls on every aspect of your operation. You install a new computer program that follows a transaction from order input and manufacturing, to shipping, and finally through invoicing and receipt of funds. The old system made it easy for someone to delete an invoice or change an amount without it showing up elsewhere. Once you get your in-house structure in order and set new incentives for your employees who want to ride out the storm with you, you look outside your company. Instead of hiding the fact that Dominick has left the firm, you call all of your vendors and customers. While you don't come right out and tell them that Dominick had been robbing you blind, you do tell them that he can no longer perform his duties with the company. Though you don't feel a need to be more specific about the cause of his departure, you feel strongly that everyone associated with the business knows you're going through a tough transition.

You work with your vendors, arranging for extended payment periods in return for a percentage point higher interest. You offer financial incentives to convince your customers to increase their orders. And you keep everyone informed monthly about the progress of the company, thanking them all repeatedly for their support. Your efforts pay off handsomely. Many vendors grant you the extended pay period without demanding the extra interest. Many of your customers pay their accounts sooner in order to help you with your cash flow. Everyone rallies behind you, especially your employees, who set all-time production records.

Six months later, you bring in two bright whiz kids, a hot-shot accountant and a marketing maniac fresh out of Stanford, offering them a piece of the action if they prepare the company for a lucrative sale to a larger sportswear corporation. The energy of the company switches from survival to full-steam-ahead growth mode. The swelling popularity of snowboarding opens up an entirely new market, which you pounce on like a hungry tiger.

At the close of a hectic year, you toast with your employees the sale of your company to Columbine Sportswear from Seattle for $18 million. While you never utter your brother's name during the party, you have secretly forgiven him, because if the ugly affair with him hadn't erupted, you never would have bought him out and built the company your way. Plus, there's no better retaliation than success. You've come to realize that although he cheated you, you weathered the storm and became one hell of a powerhouse. One bad experience, albeit painful, didn't taint your view of the world. It took time, but you feel that you've learned to trust your intuition more than ever.

BENEFITS OF B:

- You confront Dominick with the aid of your attorney and accountant.
- You offer to buy Dominick out and present a written legal agreement.
- You treat Dominick fairly.
- You feel relief at finally facing the issue.
- You funnel your energies into repairing the company.
- You hire a professional business consultant to help you put controls in place.
- You offer new incentives to your employees.
- You communicate with your vendors and customers who rally around you.
- You bring in new blood to boost sales.
- You grow the business and sell it profitably.

DOWNSIDES OF B:

- You let Dominick convince you that you controlled the finances while he plundered the business.
- You avoid the problem for too long by ignoring your gut feelings.

C. I can confront Dominick and work with him to correct his wrongs.

You collect the report from your accountant and march into Dominick's office. You sit down across from his desk, silently waiting for him to get off the phone. He smiles at you when he hangs up.

"What's up?" he asks cheerfully.

"That's exactly what I've come to ask you," you reply staring into those deep brown eyes that mirror your own.

"What do you mean?"

"You've been siphoning off money for years, Dominick. I've felt it, you must know that, but you always told me to trust you. I did, until recently. Here's the proof, this ugly money trail of your bogus accounts." You toss the report on Dominick's desk.

He leans back in his brown leather swivel chair. "I don't know what to say, Hollie."

"Tell me, or tell a judge."

"Look, you've been great to me, Hollie. You were the only one who finally confronted me over my drinking problem. You were patient when I went through drug rehab. You always stood beside me."

"So why steal from me, Dominick, and for years?"

"I got myself into debt, bad gambling debts. I always meant to pay the money back. I thought of it as a loan."

"If you thought I was there for you during your other problems, why couldn't you come to me with this one?"

"How could I? I have put you through too much. I've put my family through too much. I thought I could handle this alone."

"So why didn't you just pay off your debts without embezzling corporate funds?"

"I couldn't. I just borrowed a little and gambled with that to build up what I needed. Only I lost more. It got worse, not better. I couldn't stop. I'm sorry you had to find out before I could replace it."

"You've put the company in jeopardy, Dominick."

"I've put a lot more than that in jeopardy," Dominick swivels his chair away from you and puts his head in his hands. "I don't know what I'm going to do."

"Well, I'll tell you what we can do. You have to turn over all of your finances, personal and business, to my accountant. We'll work to get your debts paid off. You have to tell your wife the truth, and you *must* get counseling. You'll have to cut back everything, including your personal spending, to pay back the debt here."

"It'll take years, Hollie. Can you wait that long?"

"What choice do I have? Sue you, put you in prison, maybe lose the company, or work with you to rectify the wrongs? I see only one workable way where I can watch over you to insure progress."

"I'm so sorry, Hollie. I will make it up to you. I promise."

"I can't accept your promises anymore. You're not exactly trustworthy. Just *show* me." You want to hug him because he's so weak, but you're disgusted with him, and, to a great degree, with yourself. You could have nipped this problem in the bud, you saw it coming, but you refused to believe it. So you're in this mess together, and you'll have to get out of it together.

Three years later, you're glad you made that decision. The company teetered on the brink of extinction, but you pulled it out. Though it's been difficult and frustrating at times, you never wondered if you did the right thing. An interesting transformation has occurred in your relationship with Dominick as well. Instead of avoiding you, and always playing the upper hand, Dominick has become open and honest. You'd worried that this problem might break his spirit, but you sense that your love and support has given him a new resolve to better himself. He has poured tremendous effort into building the business. You hate to think where he'd be today if you hadn't given him the opportunity to right his wrongs.

BENEFITS OF C:

- You confront Dominick with proof of his stealing.
- You work out a way for Dominick to repay his debt to the business and keep working.
- You insist that Dominick get professional counseling and share his problems with his wife.
- You work out the company problems and regain a healthy relationship with your brother.

DOWNSIDES OF C:

- The plan could have backfired on you if Dominick had denied wrongdoing and resisted help.
- You shouldered responsibility for saving him from himself, when only he could do that.
- You regain a relationship with Dominick but you never know if you can fully trust him.
- You continue running the company with someone whose problems could resurface at any time.

D. I must find justice in order to let go of my anger and distrust and move on with my life.

An inner voice tells you to let go of your anger and get on with your life, but it also tells you to resolve the company's problems. Those conflicting impulses keep your head spinning. You've heard of women with worse problems—their husbands running off with the accountant *and* all of the money—but that doesn't make you feel any better about your own situation. How, you wonder, can you let go, get over your emotional and financial loss, and learn to trust again, when your company's plight worries you to distraction?

While you wait in your hairdresser's salon for a much overdue haircut, you read a magazine article on letting go of anger, trusting your intuition, and moving on after a betrayal. Isn't it amazing how, when you need help, information appears to you in the most unlikely places? You comment about that to your beautician, Cherissa.

"Happens to me all of the time, too. I've quit worrying about a lot things because I know I will get the answers when I need them," Cherissa says. "Say, what are you so upset about?"

"I've been really let down by someone I trusted. I know I have to let go of my anger to function well again, but I can't seem to break out of my depression. I feel so violated."

"That's an issue that my church group has been talking about for the last couple of weeks. I can give you the list of recommended reading if you'd like. Better yet, why don't you join in? We meet on Tuesday evenings at 7:30."

"Oh, I don't know. I'm not much of a church person."

"Doesn't matter. Just come and listen. You don't have to participate if you don't want."

"What are you? Catholic? Mormon? Buddist?"

Cherissa laughs, "This isn't a group that's going to proselytize. I just call it my church group because we meet in the Methodist Church. Anybody can come. So what do you say? Be my guest on Tuesday?"

"I'll think about it. Thanks."

You do think about it and conclude you stand little to lose, and, possibly, something to gain from Cherissa's group. At the meeting on Tuesday night you enjoy the people. The meeting doesn't deteriorate into a gripe session, as you had silently feared, but sheds a bright light on how to overcome a loss of any kind. You hadn't realized until that night that you were grieving the loss of your relationship with your brother, the last link with your childhood, as well as grappling with the issue of trust. The supportive group sends you home with a list of books to read and a few phone numbers in case you need a sympathetic ear.

Realizing that you're not the only one who's ever been deceived, and learning what others have done successfully to get over their betrayals and move on with their lives, you decide you must face your problems head on. Of course filing suit against Dominick distresses you and breaks your heart, but deep inside you know that you lost your relationship with Dominick long ago and that, were he not your brother, you would have had no problem confronting him much earlier. Though you're not certain when the courts will settle your case against Dominick, you do know that this unpleasant episode will eventually come to an end, and, with your support group's help, you will learn to trust again.

BENEFITS OF D:

- You open yourself up to information about overcoming anger and loss.
- You confide in someone who offers help.
- You keep an open mind to all suggestions.
- You attend a church group meeting even though you don't see yourself as a religious person.
- You feel connected with a supportive and understanding group.
- You discover through research that if you want to move forward, you must face your problems first.
- You trust that with support you will learn to trust again.

DOWNSIDES OF D:

- You don't seek professional help.
- You hope that anecdotal advice from magazines will give you answers.
- You look to others for answers.

Assessing the Issue

Business betrayal takes many forms: the promise then withdrawal of a promotion, unfair accusations of wrongdoing, acts of sabotage by jealous rivals, disloyalty, and broken confidences. Some acts of betrayal break ethical boundaries, others, like embezzlement, break the law. While financial betrayal seems to happen most easily to people who let others handle the money, it can happen to anyone. When it does, it not only violates your trust, it shatters your equilibrium. It's embarrassing. Even if you file and win a lawsuit, you must deal with feelings of vulnerability. Anyone who has been cheated tends to doubt the integrity of others for a long time afterward. But life and business lose their spice if you do not risk again, forever carrying the burden of distrust with you. Releasing yourself from that burden begins not simply with learning to trust others again, but with regaining confidence in your own intuition.

Renewal of your life after any sort of loss, especially the loss of trust, requires a lot of soul searching. What role did you play in the drama? What didn't you see? What did you ignore? What, if anything, could you have done about it?

In this adventure your emotions tell you that your brother wouldn't cheat you, while your intuition warns you that he would. The line between emotion and intuition may seem small, but they really can represent two distinct voices, one speaking from the heart, the other from the mind. Intuition is, after all, a deep-seated mental messenger. It tells you answers from deep inside, without the obscuring effects of your emotions.

We all employ both emotion and intuition when trying to solve a problem. How many times have you gone to bed wishing you could solve a problem, only to wake up the next morning having found the right decision? For instance, when my daughter was a teenager and wanted to go someplace out of the ordinary, perhaps to a party at a new friend's house, my love for her might encourage me to say yes, but I would always tell her I'd let her know in the morning. If I woke up feeling good about it, she could go. If I couldn't sleep or woke up worried about it, she needed to give me more information before I could decide. When that happened, she would laugh at me and tell her friends her mother needed to sleep on it, but she accepted my need to consult my intuition as a valid approach.

If you've suffered a betrayal, consider your role in the situation. Did you ignore your intuition because you didn't want to face unpleasantness? Did you fear breaking a family, business, or friendship connection? Fear of losing not only money but also an important relationship can keep you from listening to your inner voice. Fear of change or fear of loneliness can also deter you. Often we ignore seemingly small transgressions, thinking, "Oh, well, they're not really that bad," until they get out of control. In this adventure, your brother became more confident stealing from you because you became his silent accomplice. Whenever he said, "Don't worry about it. Trust me," you just left him alone. You shouldn't have enabled him to cheat by bringing your intuition to bear at the outset. However, it's not always easy to decipher your intuition's voice.

How do you know when your inner voice is trying to tell you something about a person? Pay attention to your reactions when you're with that person. Do you tend to withdraw from or avoid the person in question? Have you picked up on clues that make you feel uncomfortable? Think about how you react to a disturbing person. Do you take out your frustrations on yourself by overeating or drinking? Do you feel overly stressed around that person? Your body and your gut feelings call attention to your uneasiness.

What do you do when you distrust someone? Can you confront that person with your concerns, paying attention to his body language and to your gut reaction. In this case, when Hollie confronted her brother early on, he offered no explanations, just "Trust me." Deep down, however, she didn't trust him and only later found out why she felt that way. When someone causes an uneasy feeling that you don't understand, think about other people in your life who have brought out those same feelings. What did you do about it? Human nature causes us to react to threats to our well-being in one of these ways: you freeze, you flee, or you fight. In most cases of betrayal the third reaction accomplishes more than the first two.

To learn to trust again talk to others who have gone through similar situations. See a professional counselor. Educate yourself about protecting yourself from future betrayals, but avoid building a wall around yourself. Since your ability to judge who poses a threat to you has come into question, engage in some honest reality checks. Seek others' input. Understand that if you've suffered a betrayal, you most likely will find it hard to trust again, but don't let that get in your way of making good decisions. If trust has been shattered, gather as much information and new positive experiences as you can in order to reassemble your ability to trust again.

Expanding Your Thinking

In this adventure, "you" ignore your intuition and run into problems that you sensed ahead of time but didn't take action to correct until much too late. When you meet with your lawyer, you realize that you can sue your brother and probably put him in jail for a long time, but you also recognize that by doing so you could ruin the company. You hate resorting to such drastic tactics, especially with your own brother. Though you can't rely 100 percent on your intuition telling you what to do, you shut it out so completely that the situation can do nothing but deteriorate.

In Option A, you think you can leverage Dominick's behavior and make him buy you out of the company by showing him proof that he embezzled. He reacts poorly to your threat and leaves you wondering what he might do. You take out your frustrations by eating too much. You think you may have pushed Dominick to commit arson and now face a bigger problem than before.

In Option B, you realize that Dominick let you think that you controlled the finances, while he hoodwinked you. You feel that you should have listened to your intuition.

In Option C, you offer Dominick another chance, because you feel you can and should try to save him. You never know if you can really trust him, however.

In Option D, you seek information from different sources, but no professional advice. You hope that others will give you the answers you need.

What you should remember not to do:

DON'T:

1. Let a bad experience stop you from making good decisions again.
2. Set yourself up for failure by ignoring your gut distrust of someonc.
3. Accumulate too many doubts before you act.
4. Invite deception by not paying attention to your own finances.
5. Perpetuate feeling violated by retreating from others.
6. Abandon ship if you can turn it around.
7. Subsidize poor behavior by ignoring or condoning it.
8. Blame yourself by not seeing what others cleverly disguise.
9. Quit judging others by yourself.
10. Give someone else the power to ruin your life.

Let's look at what works best for you. In Option A, you confront Dominick with proof of his embezzlement and want him to buy you out. You figure that you can wash your hands of the whole issue and go on with your life.

In Option B, you buy off Dominick and proceed to rebuild the company. You hire experts to guide you and put new controls on your business. You offer incentives to your employees to work hard during the transition, and you communicate with your customers and clients, who work with you as well. Two sharp whiz kids from Stanford propel your company into high-growth mode. You build your business by tapping into the booming snowboard market, making it attractive for a larger company to buy. Once you release your anger at Dominick, you see that you never would have seized the opportunity to grow the company and sell it if you hadn't bought him out. Success is your best revenge.

In Option C, you design a way to work with Dominick that suits your sisterly nature, insisting that he get formal counseling and tell his wife the truth about his situation. You save the company and actually build a closer relationship with your only remaining family member.

You seek help to overcome your anger and distrust in Option D. You find helpful information serendipitously through magazines and your hairdresser. You follow up the suggestion to join a church group, even though you don't consider yourself religious, and you find friendship, advice, and resources. You learn that to move ahead you must confront your problems. When you face your problems, you release yourself from the burden of carrying them forever, which would hinder your ability to trust again.

Looking at the big picture, what positive points can you take from this adventure?

DO:

1. Your homework, if you sense deceit.
2. Get professional advice on how to deal with serious issues.
3. Listen to your inner voice.
4. Set up safeguards to protect yourself in the future.

5. Confront your problem, and move on with your life.
6. Look for a lesson in a bad experience, looking for what good can come from it.
7. Try to create closure on an ugly situation.
8. Conduct reality checks by getting input from others until your own confidence returns.
9. Talk to others in similar situations and gather a support group.
10. Choose to let go.

Assessing Your Own Situation

If you want to overcome a major disappointment or betrayal, ask yourself these questions:

1. Ask, "Could I see it coming?" "Has this event altered my view of the entire world or just this person?"
2. If you think you can see a bad situation coming, but ignore it, ask, "What am I trying to avoid?" "If I confront the issue now, what do I have to gain?" "If I wait, what might I suffer?"
3. If you ignore confronting people, ask, "Do I really want others to control this issue?" "Will I lose sleep over this?" "Why am I giving them such power over me?"
4. If you think something will get worse in time, but don't face it, ask, "What do I have to gain by avoiding the issue?" "Can I save myself embarrassment by getting to the root of the issue sooner rather than later?"
5. If certain people disturb you, try to figure out why. Ask, "Is this person reminding me of someone or something that upset me in the past?" "Can I identify the cause?"

6. If you have been badly hurt by someone's actions, ask yourself, "Can I ever forgive him?" "If I did forgive him, would it benefit me?" "Can I put this issue behind me?"

7. If you'd rather remain angry and distrustful for a while, ask yourself, "Okay, how long do I want to stay this way?" "Can I give myself a time limit and stick with it?"

8. If you can't get past feeling distrustful, ask, "Am I missing great new opportunities because I'm blinded by anger and resentment?" "When will I see the light of day?" "Who can I get to help me overcome my distrust and appreciate the rest of my life?"

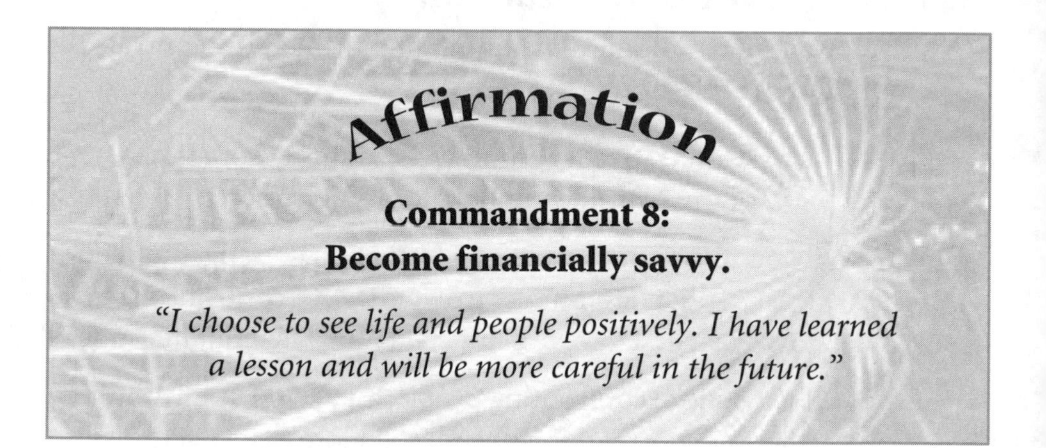

Affirmation

Commandment 8:
Become financially savvy.

"I choose to see life and people positively. I have learned a lesson and will be more careful in the future."

ADVENTURE 15

WHAT DO I DO WHEN MY HUSBAND SAYS HE SUPPORTS MY CAREER BUT DOES SO MANY THINGS TO SABOTAGE IT?

Has your husband or significant other professed his support, but somehow never quite delivered it? Lack of support takes many forms, from outright hostility or jealousy to subtle disapproval or ridicule. Whether in your personal or professional life, dealing with mixed signals can feel like ***Building an Empire on Quicksand****, as the following scenario reveals.*

Building an Empire on Quicksand

You feel you should appreciate living the life of a queen. Your husband, Jerry, makes good money as a sales representative for the Granite State Industrial Pipe Company. He covers the east coast from Bangor, Maine to Richmond, Virginia, traveling part of every week from your three-bedroom Tudor house set among the rolling hills of the Strathmore Vanderbuilt area of Manhasset, Long Island. Your two young girls love playing in your small backyard on the swing set or picking azaleas along the grassy slope of the front yard, fashioning garlands for games of The Two Little Princesses. You preside over this little kingdom as the dutiful wife keeping up the "show house" in the "right neighborhood" hand-picked by your image-conscious husband. But, instead of feeling like a reigning queen, you feel like a butterfly with pinned wings in a gilded display case.

Last year when the annual National Hardware Show and Convention convened in Chicago you begged Jerry to bring you along to enjoy the exciting corporate events. Although Granite State encourages salesmen to bring their spouses, Jerry denied your plea, saying, "Maybe next year. There isn't enough money for us both to go. Hey, Peggy, you know I deserve a break." His attitude makes you feel more like a suburban hostage than Queen of Azalea Avenue.

Despite his seemingly sensible thriftiness, however, Jerry always manages to find the funds for the fishing trips he needs to relax. Why can't he see that you need a break as much as he does? "We can't afford it this year," he claims. "When you bring in a paycheck, then we'll talk about it." Silently you swear to do it.

When Jerry left for the convention, he gave you a warm goodbye kiss and his typical patronizing farewell, "See you in five days, my little hothouse tomato."

Jerry often refers to pampered women as "hothouse tomatoes," by which he means women whose husbands take care of them and who couldn't hold a job if their lives depended on it. You have always resented the term.

Since Jerry refuses to spend money on day care, you tackle your new goal by researching jobs that could give you the flexibility you need. You earned a degree in early education from NYU, but a full-time teaching job wouldn't work under these conditions. Settling on real estate sales as an option, you discuss your idea with Jerry when he comes home, suggesting that you work a few nights and weekends when Jerry could watch the children. To your amazement Jerry wholeheartedly supports the idea. He even volunteers to take the kids to the Strathmore Vanderbuilt pool on weekends while he plays tennis. Thrilled, you enthusiastically jump into the world of cold calls and open houses.

That enthusiasm suffers a blow, however, as Jerry keeps throwing a monkey wrench at you every time you make a little progress. Your work never seems fit Jerry's plans. The night you plan to show three houses to a young couple eager to buy, Jerry insists that he has brought a lot of pressing work home and can't possibly work and watch the children at the same time. Another evening he can't take them to the movies or to a friend's house because he must prepare for a sales meeting. And, of course, he can't disrupt his usual Saturday morning tennis match by keeping an eye on the girls at the pool. He can't this, he can't that, he can't anything.

You tenaciously try to solve each problem, arranging for other mothers to pick up your children on weekends in return for your watching theirs after school. You prepare dinners for Jerry ahead of time so he needn't disturb his work schedule. However, twice you get tied up in long contract negotiations at the office and couldn't get home until 9 o'clock at night, which drove Jerry up the wall. "I thought you'd been in a accident," he moaned. But you know in your heart that he worries more about the disruption of the *status quo* than he does about your driving skills.

Not surprisingly, your business limps along for two years. When both of the girls reach the age when they attend school all day, you take full advantage of your expanded time to develop clients. Your work outside the home, however, absorbs the time you once spent housekeeping, shopping, and cooking. When Jerry complains about the messy house, you become even more stressed. You feel selfish, and you begin to doubt your decision to work, even though you have begun to make some serious, though not steady, money in real estate. You feel guilty sacrificing home time to earn that money. Yet, every time you make a sale, Jerry raves about your accomplishment, telling everyone how proud you make him. He does, in fact, like the extra cash you bring home.

Jerry also believes in pooling the family finances, but, to this day, it still "hasn't worked out" for you to join Jerry on trips. You're exhausted, frustrated, and sick of feeling guilty all the time. You don't know if you should quit your job or check yourself into a nuthouse. Wrestling with the dilemma late one night as you watch *Nightline* on television, you jot down a few options:

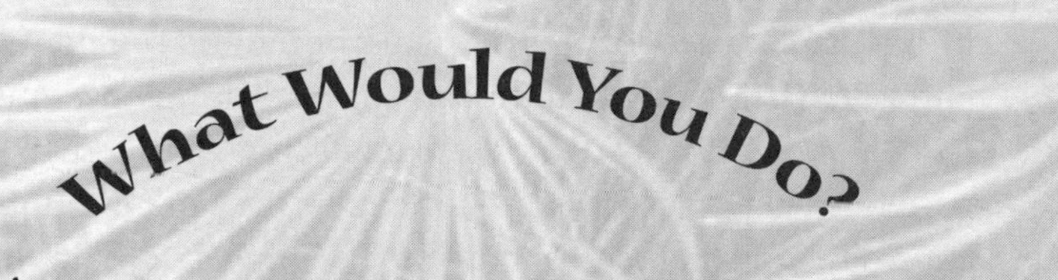

A. **I can contact a family counselor to find effective ways to gain Jerry's support.**

B. **I can try to find a way to include my husband in developing my business so that we can work as a team rather than at odds.**

C. **I can arrange a co-op babysitting program to give me more flexibility.**

D. **I can quit my job.**

Turn to the option that most appeals to you. To learn the most from this adventure, read how the other options turned out, too. Then study the last three sections of this adventure: "Exploring the Issue," "Expanding Your Thinking," and "Assessing Your Situation."

A. I can contact a family counselor to find effective ways to gain Jerry's support.

You've known Jerry since you were kids growing up in Brooklyn. You know he's possessive and likes to get his own way, but you understand his background, especially his struggles with his father's abandonment of the family when Jerry was only eight. You know he cherishes you and the girls and wants to provide everything for you, but at times you think he feels he owns you. That frustrates you so much you could scream, but again you understand his need to have his family around him and there for him whenever he's home.

The two of you started going together at fifteen, after that first date at Nathan's hot dog stand almost eighteen years ago. Unfortunately, Jerry often treats you like you're still fifteen, and he expects you to act like the adoring teenage girl walking beside her Prince Charming. He can be adorable and attentive, even generous, but he's very controlling. When you were younger you thought that meant strength, and found that attractive in a man. It made you feel secure and cared for. As you've grown older, however, it's become suffocating.

"That's the reason I'm here, seeking advice from a counselor," you explain to Samantha Culligan in her simple, understated office. "My marriage suffocates me."

You learned of Samantha Culligan from Molly, one of the women in your office, who loves the way her counselor has helped her resolve issues with her ex-husband. They had still been fighting over custody, Molly had explained to you. "He tries to control me even now, when we're no longer married."

"What can a woman do about that?" you had asked Molly.

"Get help. Don't even think of going it alone. I've got a great counselor. She's wise, she helps me see things clearly. It's made my life a lot easier. Wish I'd gone to her years ago. I'd strongly recommend her to anyone. She suggested that I read several truly helpful books. I can give you the names of those, too, if you'd like."

"Oh, yes. Thanks."

On your way home you stop by the Super Crown Bookstore and buy the books on Molly's reading list: *Women Who Love Too Much: When You Keep Wishing and Hoping He'll Change*, Robin Norwood; *The 30 Secrets of Happily Married Couples,* Dr. Paul Coleman; *Getting The Love You Want: A Guide For Couples,* Harville Hendrix; *Love Is Never Enough: How Couples Can Overcome Misunderstandings, Resolve Conflicts, and Solve Relationship Problems Through Cognitive Therapy,* Dr. Aaron T. Beck; and *Soul Mates: Honoring The Mysteries of Love and Relationship,* Thomas Moore.

As you read *Women Who Love Too Much*, you can't believe how much you relate to the examples. You pull Molly aside at the office the next day, wave the book dramatically in her face and exclaim, "This book was written about me! I've never seen my co-dependent pattern with Jerry before. I've always thought that if I played the dutiful, supportive wife, all would turn out fine, that Jerry would grow stronger, but instead he's become more controlling."

"That book shook me into action, Peggy. Have you read the section about the bell curve which illustrates all the things you do to hurt yourself when you're on your way down emotionally and feeling out of control. Then once you hit bottom it describes all the things you can do to get better on the upward swing?"

"Yes."

"Well, I realized it took me six years to hit the bottom of the curve, but when I finally got counseling and chose to take control of my own happiness, it took me only six months to reach the top."

"Guess I need to do something," you whisper.

"It's up to you to educate yourself and make your own well-thought-out choices." Molly gives you a hug and adds, "You'll be surprised how much strength you find when you're moving upward. It's not knowing what to do that makes you feel helpless."

After six months of counseling and reading, you've noticed a positive change in how you react to Jerry's demands. You've become more assertive in a non-threatening manner. You've found that problems in life do not come in stark black or white, but usually in a more manageable gray, where solutions need not suffocate you, or make Jerry feel abandoned. It hasn't been easy, or 100 percent effective, but it's opened up a new dialog between you and your husband, and you hope that it will continue. You're packing for your first trip alone together in years. You'll spend three days at a regional conference with him, then fly down to Bermuda for four days at the Sonesta Beach Hotel. You're both looking forward to it.

BENEFITS OF A:

- You seek professional counseling to overcome feeling suffocated by Jerry.
- You understand Jerry's background and truly want to make your marriage work.
- You follow up on a referral from a woman in your office who's found a counselor very helpful.
- You read the recommended books and stay with the counselor to work through ways to make your relationship with Jerry more satisfying.
- You spend time together as a couple, not just as a family.

DOWNSIDES OF A:

- You seek counseling only for yourself, not as a couple.
- It takes time and money to go to the counselor.

B. I can try to find a way to include my husband in developing my business so that we can work as a team rather than at odds.

Jerry is a master promoter, a truly successful salesman. You hope that he will become more interested in your working if you invite him to groom you for sales as your mentor. You haven't wanted to ask him for advice because you feared appearing as if you haven't learned anything in the year and a half you've been working part-time in the real estate office. You want his assistance as a respectful partner, not as a manager of a "hot house tomato." You try to think of the perfect way he could assist you that would stroke his ego, and get him personally involved with the success of your business.

The perfect occasion arises when you need to create a mailer to promote yourself and attract new listings. You've wanted to send out post cards to the community, but you'd hoped to find a really catchy way to attract people's interest. With your specific problem in mind, you approach Jerry after dinner.

"You know, Jerry, you come up with such creative ideas to get sales, I'm wondering if you could help me design a post card sales campaign?"

"What works with my customers won't work with yours, Peggy."

"I know, but you understand what motivates people to buy, no matter what the product."

"Well, let me take a look at what you have in mind. You know, a successful mailing stimulates only a 2 percent return."

"That low, Jerry?"

"Yeah. To pull it off you'll have to make the copy catchy and target your mailing list perfectly."

"What do you think will work best, darling?"

With Jerry's help, you list on the post card the houses in the area that sold along with the purchase price. When Jerry concocts a clever slogan for you—"We don't sell houses, we fulfill dreams"—you add it to the card even though you don't feel it matches your personality. In fact, whenever he suggests anything, you thank him, and congratulate him on his genius. If you question an idea, you discuss your concerns diplomatically, but you never question Jerry's creativity. The more you rave about his advice, the more he likes helping you.

When you start receiving a few direct responses from the post cards, you proudly announce them to Jerry over a "special" dinner. Even though he only nods his enthusiasm, you know he feels proud of your accomplishment. You do, too, because now he offers to help you even more, designing a chart to follow-up your cold calls, to track your sales expenses, and to plan more elaborate advertising.

You don't work as many hours as you would like because you still want to take care of the girls and Jerry, but at least you've released the tension over your budding career.

BENEFITS OF B:

- You ask Jerry to share his promotional talents with you to get him involved in your business.
- You praise Jerry for every idea.
- You reward him with a special dinner when you get responses to your mailing.
- You build your business but keep your priority at home while the kids are young.
- You quit fighting an uphill battle with Jerry over your career.

DOWNSIDES OF B:

- You manipulate Jerry into helping you.
- You accept advice that doesn't really make sense to you.

- You remain dependent on your husband and never assert your own preferences.
- You have skirted rather than tackled the central problem in your marriage.

C. I can arrange a co-op babysitting program to give me more flexibility.

You want more time to develop your real estate business, but the problems with the kids' schedules increase almost exponentially every year. You have tried to solicit more women to join the babysitting co-op to give you more flexibility, but with all the time you spend organizing everyone, you might as well be running a child care center yourself. You've been juggling schedules with so many kids, your own, your neighbors,' your children's classmates, that you've got to find a better way.

Though you know Jerry resists the idea of paying for day care, you now earn enough yourself to cover the costs. You talk to Jenny Page, the community outreach director of the Congregational Church in Manhasset, asking her about their day care program. To your surprise, Jenny tells you that the church has wanted to start a day care center, but needs a child care manager to set it up.

"Why don't you look into becoming our day care manager, Peggy?" Jenny suggests. "You'd be great. I've seen you teach Sunday school, I know you're great with children. And with all of the co-op organizing you've done, well, I just think you would be a natural at this."

"I don't know, Jenny. I'm just looking for a safe place for my girls."

"Well, you could build it yourself. Next year, you could keep them with you before and after school."

"Yeah, but I have to get dinner on the table, too."

"So hire some assistants. Work it out. Let me give you some of the literature that we've collected. Did you know there is a National Association of Child Care Professionals based in Christiansburg,

Virginia? Give them a call at (800) 537-1118. They will explain the self-study materials. Their accreditation fee for a licensed capacity of fifty or fewer children includes a $75 application fee, and $150 for validation. You should find out what qualifications you'll need, too. Hey, help yourself out by helping us out."

You had toyed with the idea of staying home with the girls and bringing in other children to watch as a business rather than dealing with the co-op system, but you know that you'd never receive licensing to do that in your neighborhood. The church location would do nicely for a lot of reasons. Before you mention anything to Jerry, you research what you would need to become qualified as a day care center manager.

You also call every day care center in the area and meet with the managers. You interview them to see what works and doesn't work. You find talking with other women who have succeeded in setting up well-run day care centers enormously encouraging. You listen to the problems and ask how they handle them.

Although you don't have a child care management background, you feel drawn to this business. It calls on your prior education, but, beyond that, it's a project that really matters to you. Though you like finding the right houses for people, you have found it basically a paper and numbers business with little to do with people's dreams. Making certain young children are in a safe environment, learning and playing together in a healthy way means much more to you. Plus, if you run the day care center, you can take care of your own children even while at work.

Eighteen months later, you have set up The Shepherd's Child Center at the Congregational Church. With the church's help, you have won accreditation for the center, and your self-esteem has hit an all-time high. Everyone, including Jerry, admires what a great job you've done. You're proud of your work, too, and, though you don't make nearly as much income as before, you don't care because the extra earnings you made in real estate came with too great a sacrifice in time away from your family.

BENEFITS OF C:

- You look into paying for day care to ease your load because now you can afford it.
- You consider a request to set up a day care center at the Congregational Church.
- You seek out information about developing day care centers.
- You research other day care centers and get inspiration from women who have succeeded.
- You gain valuable information about the need for day care centers and how they handle the problems they face.
- You find enormous personal satisfaction working with children.
- You become more self-confident.
- You earn a steady salary.
- You win Jerry's approval and support.

DOWNSIDES OF C:

- You don't tell Jerry about your plans to look for day care, fearing that it will upset him.
- You abandon a career that might have satisfied you in many ways, especially financially.
- You have not seriously faced the basic problem in your relationship with your husband.

D. I can quit my job.

You find it impossible to grow your real estate business part-time. You never know when you must drop everything to show a house at odd hours, or when you must stay late to get paperwork finished and faxed, and you can't live with the pressure of not knowing when the next listing will come in. The strict demands at home don't allow for ambiguity. Where real estate had looked like the perfect job that would allow freedom of schedule, you've found it more constraining because you not only find it difficult to work during specific times in the office, but you remain constantly at your clients' beck and call.

You look at what you've accomplished in the year and a half since you started your real estate career. You had done some smart marketing, sending out post cards and calling strangers for business. Word of mouth has spread as you've helped home buyers secure their dream houses, but your data base still looks skimpy. A paltry few names reside in your computer. To complete your mailings, you rented costly mailing lists which resulted in a modicum of interest. You only attended one women's business networking event because meetings conflicted with family time, so you've had little opportunity to promote your business that way.

The only places where you can comfortably tell people about your real estate business are your children's school and at church. Even there, you've been reluctant to press your card at people. In general, you're a little embarrassed and shy about confiding what you do, because you don't do it full-time. You don't feel successful, and you know it shows. So who would want to work with you?

What an unrewarding experience! You've spent more money than you've earned, so your effort has done nothing to alter Jerry's attitude about "hothouse tomatoes." If anything, he's seen the lack of results as proof that you belong at home, not in the business world. He disdainfully refers to your predicament as "tomato soup."

You feel like a failure and that maybe you really are a "hothouse tomato." You thought having a job would help you feel good about yourself, but it's bankrupted what little self-esteem you held in reserve. You wonder how other mothers juggle it all. Why can't you find someone to guide you to a better career choice? Frankly, you've lost both the energy and the desire to seek help.

Fed up with struggling to develop your business, you decide to quit your job; but instead of feeling relieved, you feel more trapped than ever. During the long afternoons at home waiting for the children to return from school you take solace in alcohol. You withdraw from your husband, you spend a lot of time brooding about your failure, and you find your temper flaring when your children demand your time and attention. The only person who seems unaffected is Jerry, and you resent him for it.

The panacea of vodka doesn't last long. Over the course of two years, your self-destructive behavior escalates into full-blown alcoholism which ruins your health, alienates your daughters, and terminates your marriage. Jerry files for divorce. As you sit in court, you hear the words "unfit mother" and can't fathom how far you've fallen from grace, and when, if ever, you will get your life together.

BENEFITS OF D:

- You realistically evaluate the progress of your business.
- You muster the courage to quit when you feel you're hitting your head against the wall with your business.

DOWNSIDES OF D:

- You list only what went wrong in developing your business.
- You don't seek professional guidance for a more appropriate job or to deal with your marital problems.
- You let one poor career choice crush your self-confidence.
- You accept Jerry's "hothouse tomato" assessment of you.
- You feel like a failure and take that resentment out on your family.
- You turn to alcohol for solace instead of facing your problems.
- You ruin your relationship with your family and end up divorced and emotionally paralyzed.

Exploring the Issue

Many women will tell you that their husbands or significant others offer a lot of encouragement and support. Others will say that their husbands pretend to support them, but in reality do everything they can to undermine their efforts. This adventure focuses on that dilemma. What causes a man to act this way? He can feel insecure or threatened by his wife's business or her success. Counselors hear dozens of reasons for this, any of which can cause a man to become manipulative and controlling. In this adventure, Jerry's own father had abandoned him as a young child, which later attributes to Jerry's need, even as an adult, to control Maggie's whereabouts by undermining her career. Lack of clear communication may be a primary factor in such behavior, but usually there's more to the issue than conscious sabotage.

Look at what you may be doing to contribute to the problem, what's *your* role in this drama? Every woman in this situation should ask herself the following questions:

1. "What do I want to accomplish by working (or volunteering)?" Are you seeking fulfillment? Adventure? Appreciation? Financial security? An escape from boredom? Your answer may be as simple as "I like working." But what if your eagerness to fill your day with work or volunteer commitments stems from a desire to run away from a problem at home? In that case, even if you develop the most successful career in the world, you won't solve your problem. Why? Because you're running away from it. Taking the time to identify your purpose in working/volunteering is as important as identifying whom you're trying to please. That purpose should complement the "big picture" of your life's purpose.

   For me, nothing has given me more enduring pleasure or fulfillment than bearing and raising children. I adore being a mother. And I believe that the confidence I gained through my different careers has made me a better, and more appreciative, mother. Luckily, during my checkerboard career, I had a great deal of "home" time. I view working as a wonderful way to express creativity, expand skills, develop new interests, meet interesting people, and challenge your mind, as well as earn money. In my own experience, I doubt that I would have become nearly as self-confident or daring had I not charged out into the working world, often in jobs for which I had zero training or background. Those experiences and challenges have changed the way I view myself and my own capabilities.

Judge Bonnie Crane Hellums of the 247th District Court in Houston, Texas, says that she believes the "non-religious" definition of sin is "Having a talent or a gift that you don't develop or use." Go out and use your talents, share your gifts, and challenge your capabilities, but don't use work as an excuse to avoid your problems. Your problems will follow you into the work arena. Face the real issues that trouble you.

2. "Do I unintentionally belittle my spouse when he offers helpful suggestions?" Your spouse may not realize that usually a woman wants simply to be heard while she talks through a situation, and, in fact, doesn't want him to "fix it" for her. On the other hand, a man, operating in a solution-based world, feels honor bound to create the correct answer to solve her problem. While he would probably be relieved to find out that she doesn't expect him to solve the situation for her, he feels hurt and offended when his wife rejects his suggestions.

3. "Have I become tired and snippy over work issues, taking it all out on my family?" Are you taking care of yourself? Remember the safety tip flight attendants announce, "If you are traveling with a child and the oxygen masks drop down in front of you, place a mask on yourself first." We are not much good to anyone else unless we take care of ourselves.

4. "Am I hoping and wishing to change my husband?" If so, what about him would you change? Why? Probably you've noticed that it's nearly impossible to change someone, so what attracted you to your spouse in the first place? Has he changed since you married him, or have you? Understand that the only person you have a prayer of changing is yourself. Judge Hellums, who not only presides over her family court but also holds a degree and license as a marriage and family therapist, says that couples often marry "their shadow" the first time in hopes of feeling complete. For instance, a quiet woman may purposely seek an outgoing mate. However, Judge Hellums notices that when people love and respect themselves and work through family-of-origin issues, they tend to seek a partner who "mirrors" them. They don't count on their mate to make them feel whole.
5. "Do I communicate clearly?" Can you say what you mean in a way your husband appreciates and understands? A woman may behave in a covert manner to accomplish her goals, fearing she would seem pushy if she were to come right out and ask for what she needs. Though she can't make herself clear, for whatever reason, she expects her partner to read her mind. If he doesn't act in a way that she perceives as supportive, she's upset with him. Even when he tries to act supportive, he may discover that his wife interprets his behavior as controlling and manipulative—a terribly frustrating experience for all concerned.

Judge Hellums, who, by the way, won her election with the slogan "Give 'Em Hellums," sees family disagreements that could have been ironed out with clear communication, escalate into ugly divorces. She shares this example to illustrate the importance of understanding what different messages a man and woman give even when they say the exact same thing:

"When a man sees his wife sitting alone in a room, he asks, 'What's wrong?' The wife answers, 'Nothing.' When a woman sees her husband sitting alone in a room, she asks, 'What's wrong?' The husband answers, 'Nothing.' Are the man and woman saying the same thing? Definitely not. The woman says nothing is wrong because she doesn't want to burden her husband, but she wants him to ask again, to probe, to listen, and give her a supportive hug. She feels abandoned when he takes her at face value and doesn't get the metamessage (the underlying meaning of her words). He is merely following through on what he would like done to him when he's asked the same question, but the wife is hurt at his lack of sensitivity when he accepts her answer, leaves the room, grabs the clicker, and blithely settles in front of the television. On the other hand, when the husband gives the same answer, he means that he isn't sure he wants to talk about it and just wants to decompress, grab the remote control, and 'veg out' in front of the television. The wife, however, does to him what she wants done to her and follows him, probing and encouraging him to talk (our way of achieving intimacy). He invariably feels nagged and wishes she would just let him be. What we need to do is do unto others what *they* want done to them, not what we want done to us."

If you have assessed your own role in your situation and still can't see how to make it work, seek help from a professional counselor who will ask you about the step-by-step process that led to your decision to work. She'll most likely want to know your husband's role in this decision and his response. Does your husband feel conflicted about his wife working? Does he desire to have a wife at home taking care of the children, but also likes the idea of her earning extra money? He may feel guilty that he doesn't earn enough income—or fear that others may think that he doesn't—to provide comfortably for the entire family. He may have been raised by a mother who made cookies with him after school and wants that experience for his children. He may feel stressed when the morning rush of scrambling to prepare school bags and lunches sends the house into chaos, and resent his wife's need to work outside the home. Though you may find it difficult to cope with such conflicts, it's not a sin if a man feels ambivalent about these issues.

When you and your husband re-explore why you both thought it would be a good idea for you to work outside the home, and when you both agree that it can go more smoothly, then you can decide together how to manage it better. Start by prioritizing what's most important to each of you individually. Clarify what you both have to do to keep functioning on the job (there may be some evenings you work late, or you may have some travel). Discuss what you both need from one another. You may need only six minutes of his time in the morning to see that the children have their school backpacks ready. He may suggest you prepare lunches for the children and set out their clothes the night before. What must get accomplished varies per household and by the ages of the children, but talk out your needs specifically. Don't assume your husband knows what you want him to do, or *vice versa.*

It's hard to know what to do if someone, supposedly in your camp, behaves more like an enemy. Trying to survive, let alone thrive, in such an atmosphere takes considerable stamina. Women must recognize what they can deal with and what they can't. It's helpful to talk to other women and especially to seek out professional advice from those trained and experienced with the complexities of such a situation. A support group of like-minded women can do wonders for your sense of balance. If you're faced with a similar situation as the one in this adventure, reaffirm your priorities and purpose. Seek a win/win solution through clear communication, which can also help you identify and overcome hidden issues that lead to disagreements about family roles and expectations. But whatever you do, don't put off confronting the issue with clarity and conviction.

Expanding Your Thinking

The "you" in this adventure grapples with her husband's need to control and her need for freedom. You understand why he is the way he is, but that doesn't make him any easier to live with. Still, you love him and feel committed to your relationship.

Some choices work better than others in this adventure. In Option A, you probably could have benefited more from the counselor if you had included Jerry in some of the sessions.

In Option B, you try a new way to attract Jerry's attention that makes you feel like you're manipulating him. You feel your ends definitely justified the means.

In Option C, you go behind Jerry's back to look for day care for your girls. You don't tell him you're considering that as a field to pursue, either. This makes you uneasy because you still haven't found an effective way to communicate.

You give up altogether in Option D. You don't look at what you learned, only at what you didn't accomplish in developing your real estate business. You gain nothing positive from the experience, you give in to Jerry's nasty appraisal of your abilities, and you take out your resentment on your family. Your self-destructive drinking problem gets out of hand and you lose your family and your self-worth.

Don'ts you may want to remember include:

DON'T:

1. Let anyone convince you that you can't do things.
2. Give up before you try, in a relationship or a job.
3. Believe if you try once and fail, you can never try again.
4. Change your thinking if you know it goes against your inner voice.
5. Let small sacrifices turn into huge personal deprivations.
6. Take care of everyone else without concern for your own well-being.

7. Allow others to divert your personal goals.
8. Let others determine your fate.
9. Fence yourself off from contact with others.
10. Try to drown your problems with alcohol.

What works for you in this adventure? In Option A, you seek advice from a friend who suggests you read helpful books and seek professional help to learn how to deal effectively with Jerry. Your counselor helps you choose how best to react to him, not how to change him. This works pretty well for you. As your communication improves, so does your relationship.

In Option B, you attract Jerry's interest in your business by complimenting his talents. You ask him for his assistance, listen to him, and praise him. You win new clients and Jerry's interest. It may seem like a game to you at first, but it pays off. You also feel more in control, keeping your focus on home in the foreground while you develop your business, which makes you all feel good.

In Option C, you look into paying for day care rather than going crazy juggling the co-op business. In doing so, you discover your church needs a manager to set up a day care center. You research the resources the church administrator gives you, and conduct your own investigation into other day cares in the area. You discover that more day cares are needed, learn about common day care problems, and realize that running a day care center appeals to you. With that information, you continue educating yourself on what you need to qualify as a day care manager and set up the center for the church. Running the day care provides a steady income and keeps you available for your children even at work. Jerry learns to appreciate your accomplishments.

In Option D, you choose to quit your job, which at least allows you to turn your focus homeward.

From this adventure you may wish to take away these positive points:

DO:

1. Accept responsibility for your own happiness.
2. Seek professional help with tough work-family issues.
3. Make sure you don't contribute to the problem by making your husband feel left out or jealous about your time with your business.
4. Keep up your network of friends from different parts of your life.
5. Use praise as a powerful tool.
6. Open up new lines of communication.
7. Look for opportunities for personal growth outside the home.
8. Give yourself permission to quit something without beating yourself up as a failure.
9. Face difficulties as personal challenges.
10. Know your priorities and make sure *you* are one of them.

Assessing Your Own Situation

If you relate to the situation in this adventure, you aren't alone. Take stock of your own life and work by asking these questions:

1. If you think your husband sabotages your career, ask, "What specific instances or events make me think this?" "Do I react with anger or understanding?"
2. When you feel sabotaged, ask, "Is there some way that I have contributed to this?" "What am I doing that seems threatening?" "Can I find a simple way to alleviate this situation?"

3. If your husband says he supports you but acts as if he doesn't, ask, "Does he do this to me in other matters besides my career?" "Is there a way to communicate better so I don't send or receive mixed messages?" "Am I the only person he treats this way, or is it a pattern of behavior?"
4. If you feel beaten down by negativity, ask, "Where can I go for help?" "Do I think I deserve this ugly treatment?" "Do I think this is my lot in life?"
5. If you don't like how you're being treated, ask, "Am I providing a good example to my children?"
6. When you want to throw in the towel, ask yourself, "What are my priorities?" "How can I reach them?" "How important is it to me to complete this?"
7. If you have acquiesced to control before and want to break the habit, ask, "Have I tried to control little things in my life?" "What if I try taking back some control?"

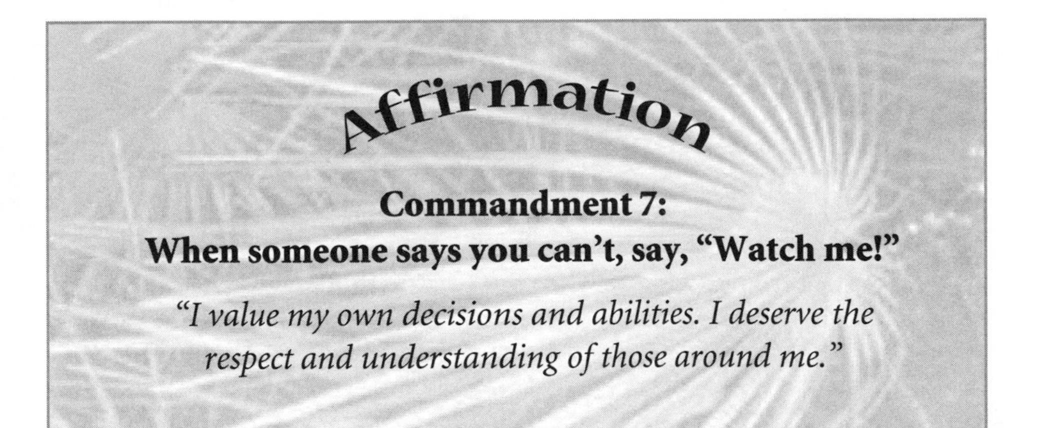

Adventure 16

What should I do when my husband encourages me to help out in his business but shuts me out of the big decisions?

Do you help out in your husband's or significant other's business? Perhaps you have gladly given your time, energy, and even your money to develop his business, only to discover that your spouse doesn't ever intend to include you in making the big decisions. He simply doesn't want to hear your opinions. What would you do if you found yourself ***Running Up the Down Escalator****?*

Running Up the Down Escalator

The exquisitely dressed audience rose to a standing ovation after your presentation in Palm Springs to the packed auditorium filled with members and guest architects of the American Society of Interior Designers (ASID). A top designer, you possess all the prerequisites of power in this industry: brains, talent, flair, and a fundamental grasp of marketing. Your lecture, "Designs to Make Rooms Sing," showcased all your skills. You own the top of the mountain.

Only one other presenter could have followed your stunning act, Paolo Costas, the devilishly handsome and charismatic architect of Luxury Resorts Worldwide (LRW). Paolo launched his career in a large prestigious South African architecture firm, where his rise to almost legendary stardom began when no one else in the firm would volunteer to draw preliminary sketches for a prospective client's entirely new hotel concept. Who in that starched white Oxford-shirted office would waste their talents on such a project when there were so many skyscrapers and shopping malls to design? Paolo, that's who. After sketching out ideas in his free time, he took them to the client, who, it turned out, controlled a billion-dollar family fortune. He loved Paolo's drawings and stole the young architect away from his employer at double his salary. Within a few years LRW had mushroomed into a hugely profitable global enterprise.

You met Paolo ten years ago and you've bumped into him periodically at conferences, but you haven't seen him for two years, not since your marriage of twenty years dissolved in a quagmire of financial finagling and unbridled bitterness. Your first marriage to Wilson Summers, fifteen years your senior, turned into one of convenience, though it started out burning with passion. Early on, the flame fizzled when it became apparent that Wilson's high profile, multi-national re-insurance company was his mistress. Childless, you busied yourself with decorating your homes. You developed your natural talents in design and color by studying interior design at UCLA. Yet, neither you nor your business blossomed until after your protracted and painful split from Wilson. You fought hard to rebuild your self-confidence by burying yourself in your work. It paid off, in all ways. By the end of that trying time you had won a solid business reputation and been granted a small fortune from your divorce decree.

Paolo, in the meantime, had split from both his wife and his business partner. His financial state had eroded sharply, but not his overriding optimism and charm. Your relationship with Paolo had always been professionally proper until the week-long conference in Palm Springs. There it developed into something much deeper. Ten months later, the ASID trade journal heralded your wedding as the "the design partnership of the decade."

Now, as you celebrate your first anniversary of your marriage and your business merger with Paolo, the flush of the "design partnership of the decade" has begun to fade. Far from operating as equals, you and your husband function more as master and slave. Your frustration escalates to outrage during your work together on the Landsdale project, a huge equestrian resort. Paolo habitually encourages your input, but finds fault in your drawings, correcting what he calls "spatial inadequacies" and your "grossly over sentimental, overstuffed style." You're not even sure what language he's speaking, but you certainly understand its meaning: he's closing you out. Whatever happened to all the respect he once bestowed on your talent? The ultimate put down occurred two weeks ago when Paolo insisted on presenting the project plans to the Landsdale board by himself, though you had conceived and developed the plans together over the last nine months.

"Men want to buy from men, Rosilyn," he had insisted, waving away your protestations.

The crowning blow came when you discovered he had reinstated into the final plans all of the "design faults" he'd so sternly criticized, seeing their value and claiming them as his own during his presentation. You hadn't been prepared for such treatment from the man you love. You know you could sell circles around him but choose not to fray his fragile ego. Why did he ever encourage your input? To cover his own inadequacies? Or should you chalk it all up to Old-World chauvinism? You've been paying for all of the business expenses, plus the down payment for your lovely Spanish villa in the Hollywood Hills. Your "partnership" has meant little more than his plundering your divorce settlement and stealing your design ideas, all for his own personal glory. You feel like a woman running as fast as she can toward a dream but falling further and further behind.

Nevertheless, unwilling to give up on your marriage and engage in the misery of another divorce, you consider ways you might rebuild your relationship, both personally and professionally.

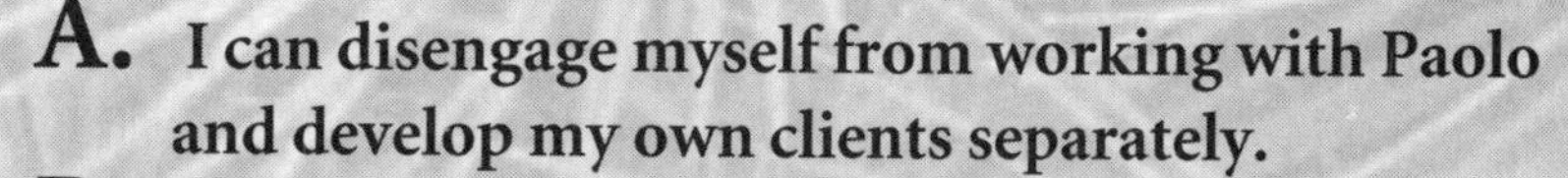

A. I can disengage myself from working with Paolo and develop my own clients separately.

B. I can assume a different role in our business, managing rather than designing projects.

C. I can ask an accountant to set up a fund for our business, but keep my settlement separate.

D. I can contact the ASID and volunteer my services to instruct classes and not compete with Paolo at all.

Turn to the option that most appeals to you. To learn the most from this adventure, read how the other options turned out, too. Then study the last three sections of this adventure: "Exploring the Issue," "Expanding Your Thinking," and "Assessing Your Situation."

A. I can disengage myself from working with Paolo and develop my own clients separately.

You had turned down several projects of your own, one big one—a health spa, with a favorite client, Josephine Baker—in order to work on the Landsdale project with Paolo. The thought of working together sounded so exciting that you'd put all of your own projects on hold indefinitely. You didn't mind. In fact, you couldn't wait to see how you and Paolo would inspire each other and raise the level of your individual work by combining your talents. While you believed you'd complement and enhance each other's work beautifully, it didn't turn out that way at all.

Over the years you've become adept at the fancy footwork needed to dance around inflated male egos, coddling the fragile ones and coping with the overpowering ones. Whatever the personalities involved, you've always found a way to stay on the dance floor to complete a project. But you're not willing to dance backward with Paolo's ego in your own home and business. Now, you can see that continuing to work with Paolo risks ruining your otherwise promising marriage. You don't agree with his business tactics and can't accept his chauvinistic attitude. True, he's a brilliant architect who doesn't need your input; he can certainly design his own projects.

You call Josephine Baker to see how her health spa project has turned out.

"Don't ask, Rosilyn. It's turned into a complete and utter disaster. Why did you abandon me? This nincompoop we hired comes up with outrageously creative ideas, but he hasn't a clue how to turn them into practical results. I should have known we were in trouble when he talked about knocking out a weight bearing wall to install a beveled glass window that would 'thrust a cascade of dappled sunlight across our massage therapy salon.' Total hogwash, but I fell for it. Of course, the contractor didn't, and it's been like that every step of the way. Miserable. By the way, how's your Landsdale project going?"

You think, "Into the sewer." But you say, "On top of the world."

"So maybe you have time to salvage this mess? Tell me you will."

"As a matter of fact, I've got some free time. I'll be over tomorrow at 10:00 A.M.."

"You're a life saver, Rosilyn darling. See you then."

You've always enjoyed working with Josephine, a funny and flamboyant character who pays her bills promptly. You designed her Palm Springs 10,000-square-foot home two years ago with surprisingly few glitches. She thinks you walk on water.

With her major project as a base, you make a few more phone calls, securing enough business to separate yourself from Paolo's clients. You don't even feel tempted to bounce ideas off of him. Besides, he's busy moving ahead with the Landsdale project. He seems to feel that his all-male approach won him the contract, so you let him think that. You don't want this open wound to fester. Better to allow time for your relationship to heal, rather than rip it apart by proving your point. Anyway, Paolo has apologized to you for using your ideas, saying he reconsidered their usefulness but was too embarrassed to tell you at the time. Since he had never mistreated you that way before, you grudgingly accept his apology, thinking you'd want him to accept your apology were the tables turned.

Two years later, you're glad you embarked on a course of "separate by equal." You never involve yourself in "his" projects, and he stays away from yours. Today, you both enjoy strong separate identities in the design world, and you've built a loving and non-competitive relationship at home.

BENEFITS OF A:

- You decide to separate yourself from working with Paolo.
- You call your old accounts and reinstate your own separate design business.

- You work with people whom you enjoy and who appreciate you.
- You don't make a big deal out of your situation, even though you're hurt, but set up a way to avoid making it worse.
- You accept Paolo's apology as you would want him to accept yours.
- You enjoy a good business of your own and a satisfying relationship with your husband.

DOWNSIDES OF A:

- Your fantasy of working together as a team disintegrates.
- You feel hurt and disappointed.
- You have to scramble to recreate your business that you had put on hold to work with Paolo.
- You may be putting a Band-Aid on a much bigger wound than you expect.

B. I can assume a different role in our business, managing rather than designing projects.

You can't believe Paolo's tactics, using your brains and stealing the show. His behavior has hurt and confused you. Hadn't Paolo whispered to you time and time again during your whirlwind courtship, "I love you because you're brilliant, talented, and beautiful"? The chemistry between you could have rocked buildings four blocks away. You fell in love with him for much the same reasons, but you also felt that Paolo needed you, something your ex-husband never did.

Your confident air became a magnet for others. You knew Paolo never would have been attracted to a less confident and independent woman. That's why when Paolo began to undermine your efforts, even put you down in front of others, you dismissed them as exceptions rather than the rule. You tried to work around those exceptions, demurring to his wishes to avoid his sudden temper. But Paolo would blame you whenever he himself screwed up. Of course, he'd apologize later for his thoughtlessness and bestow you with expensive jewelry and trips to the Costa del Sol. You thrived on his attention, which you worked hard to earn, despite the increasingly larger affronts to your self-esteem.

Before you realize what has hit you, however, things take an ugly turn for the worse. The ugliness began, you later realize, when you decided you couldn't do design work side by side with Paolo during the Landsdale fiasco and proposed, instead, that you spend your time and efforts on the management side of the business. Paolo liked the idea, though again, he kept finding reasons to fault you. When a hurricane at sea delayed one important shipment of marble, it set back the project for a week, costing thousands of dollars. Paolo flew into a rage and shoved you against the office wall. Since then, that behavior has grown more and more predictable and, you don't know why, but you've come to accept it as normal. Just when you begin to worry that it's not normal, he follows an outburst with gifts, apologies, and tender lovemaking, promising he can't live without you, and that he'll control his temper better in the future.

You have never admitted to yourself that you've become an abused woman, until you call and cancel a lunch appointment with your friend Kate and she asks, "Has he hit you again?"

Her question stuns you. You didn't think anyone knew. You always offered a logical explanation for a bruised arm or blackened eye. After all, you work around construction projects all the time. Finally, you must look at yourself honestly. You've rationalized and tolerated your husband's abuse, partly out of love, partly out of fear of losing him. All that fear has blinded you to the stark reality that your relationship with Paolo has deteriorated from psychological to physical mistreatment.

Kate calls you back a few days later to see how you're doing. Fighting back tears of anger at her for breaking your code of silence, you suddenly realize how stupid you've been. You wanted your marriage to work out, and you certainly didn't want to go through another divorce, and in that frame of mind you have slowly learned to tolerate abuse. You even began believing you caused it all, that it was all your fault. Kate encourages you to seek professional help.

"Rosilyn, get info off of the Internet. Just type in abused women, battered women, domestic violence. You'll find a ton of information. And call a professional counselor. Do it today."

Tears well in your eyes. You know she's right. You never believed an intelligent, talented, and once self-confident woman could become a battered wife. Now you know it could happen to any woman if she overlooks little abuses and doesn't stand up for herself from the beginning. But it's insidious, and even now you're afraid to leave Paolo. That's why you've never kept your appointments with a counselor.

A few weeks later you inadvertently leave a message from the counselor's office confirming an appointment on the answering machine. When Paolo hears it, he hits the roof. In a fit of rage he flings you like a sack of rotten potatoes through the plate glass French door onto the patio decking where you fall in a heap of fear and pain. Paolo stands over you, shouting, "Don't you ever tell people about our private lives. Ever! Do you understand me?"

Paolo forbids you to seek medical attention even though you're unable to remove all of the slivers of glass from your back. But after hours of unbearable pain and sleeplessness you sneak out of the house and drive yourself to the hospital emergency room before the sun rises. A caring intern who patiently removes the pieces of glass from your swollen back, surprises you when he warns, "Don't go the route my mother took. I never could convince her to leave my stepdad even though he used her as a punching bag. One time, well, she just didn't recover. Go to the police. Get a restraining order. Get as far away as you can. Now."

You followed his advice, and two years later, you still feel indebted to the young doctor who forced you out of denial. Today, the restraining order and subsequent divorce proceedings seem like a nightmare in another lifetime, yet tears of anger smart in your eyes when you talk to your psychiatrist about the abuse you accepted from Paolo. You're willing to endure the painful process of revealing and reliving your abusive relationship in order to purge yourself of the fear and disgust you harbor toward him. Confident that you're well on your way to repairing your damaged soul, you look forward to finding joy again.

BENEFITS OF B:

- You realize that you can't do design work with Paolo and offer to manage projects instead.
- You want to make your marriage work.
- You listen to your friend and face up to your status as an abused woman.
- You seek medical attention to repair your physical wounds.
- You take action to protect yourself by getting a restraining order.
- You seek professional help to repair your wounded soul.

DOWNSIDES OF B:

- You slowly learn to accept Paolo's abusive behavior.
- You allow him to hurt you mentally and physically.
- You let him buy back your trust.
- You lie to your friends about your bruises.

- You hide the truth from yourself.
- You don't keep your appointments with a counselor.
- You wait until you're badly hurt to leave your abusive husband.

C. I can ask an accountant to set up a fund for our business, but keep my settlement separate.

After a year of marriage, you feel that Paolo has taken advantage of you financially and professionally. With the large Landsdale contract only an inch away, according to Paolo, you'll need to fund your fledgling company even more. You hadn't bargained for his uncontrolled spending "for the company." You know that under California's community property law commingling funds would benefit Paolo in the event of divorce, so you contact an accountant to help you set up a corporation. You know you shouldn't fund your business with your personal assets any longer, because doing so puts you too much at risk. On the advice of your accountant, you contact an attorney and incorporate your company. You discuss with Paolo how much money you will put into the account when, not if, the Landsdale contract comes through. You know the contract will stipulate certain benchmarks of completion for payments to become due. Usually, the first progress payment comes at 25 percent completion. So you'll need enough cash in the company account to cover expenses until that first payment. You and Paolo settle on $250,000 in the account, $200,000 to cover contractual agreements and a $50,000 cushion. Paolo would have preferred more, but you make certain he knows that you will invest these funds and not a nickel more. Any extra funds the business must generate itself.

In your past marriage your ex-husband always kept you in the dark about financial matters, and you probably would have ended up without a penny if you hadn't hired a shrewd attorney who followed the money trail, and won you a huge settlement. You vowed then and there to become financially savvy. Though Paolo has barred you from presenting the proposal to Landsdale, you insist that you participate in all contract negotiations. This way you'll know exactly what cash flow to expect. The business now operates with a proper "division of labor." Paolo may be the Chief Executive Officer, but you're the First Financial Officer, and that means no matter what Paolo decides, you control the purse strings.

To protect yourself further, your accountant also advises you to set up a managed account, either by a brokerage firm or a bank trustee, for your settlement funds. That way your money will be tied up if Paolo argues that the business needs more capital. You don't think Paolo married you for your money, but it never hurts to install a few safeguards.

After working with Paolo for another year in your new position as financial officer, you can certainly see why his last partnership fell apart. Paolo seems to have little money sense, and, if not tightly reined, he could gallop through a fortune mighty quickly. Though he chomps at the bit relentlessly, together you have developed your design business far beyond expectations. Paolo loves to kid you that you're a "mean money miser," but he says it with the smile of one who knows his own limitations and who appreciates the talents of another.

BENEFITS OF C:

- You do not commingle your personal funds with Paolo's business.
- You contact an accountant for advice.
- You have an attorney incorporate your business to separate it from your personal assets.
- You set limits with Paolo on how much you're willing to fund the business.
- You establish a managed account to protect the rest of your settlement.

- Your safeguards give you peace of mind.
- Your business prospers.
- Your husband respects your money-management talents.

DOWNSIDES OF C:

- You feel your husband has taken advantage of you, financially and professionally.
- You feel overly sensitive to financial matters because of mistakes you made in your first marriage.
- You have to rein in your husband's spending habits.
- Your husband thinks you're a "mean money miser."

D. I can contact the ASID and volunteer my services to instruct classes and not compete with Paolo at all.

You don't really *have to* work anymore, so why go through all this stress? You decide not to compete with Paolo, and certainly not continue working with him since he's turned into such a difficult partner. Since you love interior design, however, you consider a new career track, perhaps teaching others about it.

With that in mind, you contact your alma mater, UCLA, and inquire about design programs that could use outside speakers. When you learn that UCLA hosts a student chapter of the ASID, you call the ASID to find out about other such student chapters. It turns out that Brooks College in Long Beach, Cal State at Long Beach and Northgate, and Woodbury University in Burbank all participate in the program.

You've been inactive in the Los Angeles ASID chapter for many years, but decide to call and find out about the next meeting. You're surprised to find yourself chatting over the phone with Libby Kaplan, the current chapter president. You've known Libby for years.

"Did you know I'm Rosilyn Costas now? You probably remember me as Rosilyn Roberts."

"Rosilyn! Great to hear from you. Yeah, I heard you got married. It was in all the trades. How's it going?"

"Great. Say, look, I'm calling because I'd like to come to the next ASID meeting. I know it's been forever, but I'd like to get involved again."

"Oh, shoot, you just missed one last week. There won't be another until after summer vacation. Is there something I can help you with? Why don't we get together for a drink anyway? How about tomorrow around 5 at the Blue Whale?"

You meet Libby at the LA Design Center, nicknamed the Blue Whale because it's so huge and painted blue. After pleasantries you confide your interest in teaching design informally and wonder if she can help you get in touch with the director of the student ASID chapters at the Southern California colleges.

"Not only can I put you in touch with the student chapters, but we really need someone to help with our scholarship fund that disperses the trust left by Howard Grieve. Howard Grieve was the production designer for the first Ben Hur film, to name just one. He was known for designing famous movie stars' homes. Some give him credit for founding ASID. Anyway, he left a charitable trust to the Los Angeles chapter of ASID to be used for scholarships for student members of ASID in LA County to study Interior Design. It would be right down your alley. What do you say?"

You're thrilled. Libby's right, this would be perfect. You spend the summer contacting all of the appropriate people, setting up meetings to promote the scholarship fund, and scheduling a speaking tour of the campuses with student chapters, as well as other colleges.

By the end of the year, you're totally engrossed in your chapter, the scholarship fund, and you love occupying center stage speaking to groups everywhere, from classrooms to auditoriums. You include

Paolo at some of your larger talks and you work like a magnificent team on stage. Finally, you find a platform where you complement each other instead of compete. You're pleased that Paolo feels the same way, and that he enjoys feeling like king of the mountain in his own business, working with only a few select clients. Best of all, you feel content because your relationship flourishes.

BENEFITS OF D:

- You decide not to compete in the design business with Paolo.
- You explore teaching what you know about design as a volunteer.
- You contact the LA chapter of ASID and get involved.
- You promote the scholarship fund and enjoy being center stage.
- You find a platform to complement rather than compete with Paolo.
- You find pleasure in having separate but supportive careers with your husband.

DOWNSIDES OF D:

- You abandon your dream of working with Paolo when he proves difficult.
- You put starting your own business on the back burner because you don't want to compete with Paolo.
- You don't actually teach as much as raise awareness and funds for the ASID scholarship.
- You let Paolo run the business you thought you would operate together.

Exploring the Issue

The situation in this adventure encompasses some of the issues that arise in any family-run business. No matter how much the family partners may believe in equity, one person tends to dominate the other. In the case of a wife and husband team, this can lead not only to rivalry, jealousy, and arguments, but to a stressful, even abusive, marriage. In this particular case the male ego takes over and the female ego suffers. Her opinions don't matter. The plot thickens when he uses her talents and her finances to his personal advantage.

Plenty of women gladly assist their husbands in their businesses, but sometimes the lines of authority blur. If a wife devotes her time, efforts, and resources to what *she* considers a family business, she naturally wants a say in the big decisions. In her mind, she's become a full partner, but has she become one in her husband's mind? When a dilemma like this arises, there's often more going on than a communication problem.

Imagine you're the wife. You want to support your husband, but where do you draw the line between supporting him with your love and supporting his business as a non-paid employee? If you share responsibility for developing the business, worrying about the problems, helping out with finances and banking, you want a voice in the company as well. If your husband doesn't see you as a partner, but encourages you to help out in his business, what can you do?

One, look for the big picture. Identify the underlying reasons behind his actions, not just the symptoms. In this adventure there's a much bigger issue looming behind whether or not Rosilyn and Paolo see eye to eye in their business partnership. Paolo felt attracted to a bright, independent, successful woman, but then he wanted to clip her wings to maintain the upper hand. Why was he using her? Did he feel threatened? Insecure? The fact that he felt he could steal her ideas and leave her out of the presentation because "men want to buy from men" showed great disrespect for her. But was it just her, or all women?

Two, ask questions to determine what's really going on. When someone needs your time or money, but not your input, ask why. Perhaps you're better off letting him run his own business with outside capital, while you invest your time and money elsewhere.

Three, communicate. If you've forgone your own livelihood to assist him, you have a huge commitment that needs to be recognized. Many people who own businesses think of them as their baby. If you're helping your husband with his business, does it become your baby, too, in his eyes? You may have mentally adopted it, but where are the legal papers? Does your husband know how you feel?

Four, set limits. Know how much time and money you're willing to invest. Have you discussed with him how much time and money you're willing to contribute to "his business?"

Five, set up safeguards. Women who inherit or win a large sum of money in a legal settlement often feel vulnerable, especially when they remarry. They wonder, "Is it me or my money he wants?" Seek legal and financial counsel.

If working with your husband still leaves you feeling left out, gracefully decline to help, but continue to provide emotional support. Focus your energies on your own projects. Earn your own money. Spreading the risk, rather than putting all of your family eggs in one basket, can take the pressure off of your relationship.

Though this adventure focuses on working with your spouse, I include the issue of abuse in Option B because I've seen too many intelligent, attractive, otherwise successful women feeling trapped in abusive relationships. Abusive behavior knows no boundaries and exists in relationships of every creed, every race, and every socioeconomic group. If you or a friend face this problem, don't hesitate to go to the authorities for help. It may frighten you or make you feel embarrassed, and, unfortunately, there is no guarantee you'll have complete protection, but notifying a judge or a police officer and obtaining a restraining order are important tools to insure your own safety. Protective services can change, and maybe even save, your life.

Expanding Your Thinking

In a situation like this, "you" face few easy choices. Much is at stake, your new marriage, your reputation, and your pride.

Some things don't work out as well as you had hoped. In Option A, you turn away from working with Paolo, which shatters your dream of creating designs by the two of you, the team so brightly heralded by the industry. You feel you had to do this or put your marriage at risk. Since you can't work comfortably with Paolo, you just back out and reinstate your own separate business.

In Option B, things go from bad to worse. Still wanting to work with Paolo, you offer to manage rather than design projects. First, you give up what you like doing best. Next, you stay under Paolo's thumb emotionally. Your self-confidence erodes the longer you put up with his abusive behavior, sugar-coated by protestations of love, gifts, and apologies. You further your isolation by lying to friends about your bruises and canceling social engagements. You cannot accept the fact that you're a battered wife, because in your mind that couldn't happen to a woman with your education and intelligence. You're dumbfounded when the medical intern who removes the glass from your back after Paolo throws you through a glass door warns you not to follow in his own mother's footsteps but to seek immediate police protection.

You deal with money issues in Option C. You can see that Paolo plans to use your money as the golden goose for his business. You didn't mind that at first, especially when you thought you were full partners, but you come to see the need to protect your assets.

In Option D, you give up your design work altogether because of Paolo. Not wanting to compete with him in business, you let him run the business you assumed you would build together.

The options in this adventure offer some clues about what not to do:

DON'T:

1. Assume you're a business partner with your husband when he simply asks you to help out.
2. Try to compete with your husband in business.
3. Quit your usual livelihood to work with your husband without clear goals and expectations.
4. Give up your own interests to help out someone else unless you're certain they need it, and will recognize and want it.
5. Subjugate your personal feelings when trying to make a relationship work.
6. Pretend you're not abused, if you are.
7. Avoid talking about difficult differences of opinion.
8. Feel you have to stay in an abusive situation.
9. Fake happiness without admitting the truth to yourself.
10. Think you cannot overcome difficult situations.

What worked well for you? In Option A, you want to work with Paolo because you're excited about combining your talents. When that appears unlikely, you decide to develop your own client list again and start working with people whom you enjoy. Since Paolo usually doesn't treat you so poorly, you reluctantly accept his apology and go on with your life and your relationship.

In Option B, you try a different tack with Paolo, offering to work with him in a different capacity, managing projects. When that, too, brings out the worst in Paolo, you listen to your friend Kate , but you seek professional counseling and police protection only after Paolo throws you through a door. You find that taking charge of your life and your own protection allows you to work on creating a better life for yourself.

In Option C, you set up a different kind of agreement with Paolo, a legal financial agreement that gives you control over your money. You also set up a managed account for your settlement money. The safeguards afford you peace of mind and turn out to be a wise move that helps you and Paolo make your business profitable.

In Option D, you win recognition in your field without competing with Paolo. You help young people learn about Interior Design and promote the ASID scholarship fund. Your old self-confidence reemerges.

Lessons to take with you from this adventure include:

DO:

1. Be a helpful spouse, but clarify expectations when working together.
2. Speak up when you feel out of sync with your husband's business goals.
3. Take pride in the fact that your husband wants your help, but ask him how much he really wants.
4. Communicate your expectations and set your limits.
5. Keep lines of communication open, even if you disagree.
6. Stay actively involved, if you invest your money in a business.
7. Get professional advice about how to safeguard your finances.
8. Look for a satisfying job separate from your husband's, if you feel uncomfortable working together.
9. Take any abusive treatment seriously.
10. Seek professional counseling and police help, if you're abused.

Assessing Your Own Situation

If you or a friend finds herself in a similar situation, you'll find no easy answers to questions about what you or she should do. That's why a smart woman asks herself many questions before she takes action.

1. If you imagine developing a great business with your husband, ask yourself, "Does he feel the same way?" "Is this his business, mine, or ours?" "If I want his help with something I'm doing, am I asking him to be my partner?"
2. If you have assumed a role in your husband's business, ask, "Does he see me as his equal?" "Have I expressed my interest in becoming his partner?" "Are all of the facts out on the table?"
3. Ask yourself why you want to work with your husband, "Am I bored with my own job?" "Do I think he needs my help because he's not doing a good job himself?"
4. Do you communicate clearly with your husband in your personal and business life? Ask, "Do we speak to each other one way at home and another in the office?" "Do we seem to shift roles when we talk about personal matters as opposed to business matters?" "Have we discussed this with each other?"
5. Have you given up a part of yourself to please your husband? "Have I given up my work, my painting, whatever, in order to please my husband?" "How much am I willing to give up before I feel completely drained?"
6. Do you keep secrets about how your husband treats you at home? Ask, "Who am I trying to protect?" "Do I make up excuses about my appearance?" "Am I covering up his bad behavior out of embarrassment?"
7. Do you feel isolated? Ask, "Have I pulled away from many of the people I used to see?" "Do I turn down invitations from friends?"

8. What do you want? Ask, "Do I want to work through this?" "Am I making a mountain out of a mole hill?" "If I can't figure this out by talking to my husband, am I willing to get professional help?"

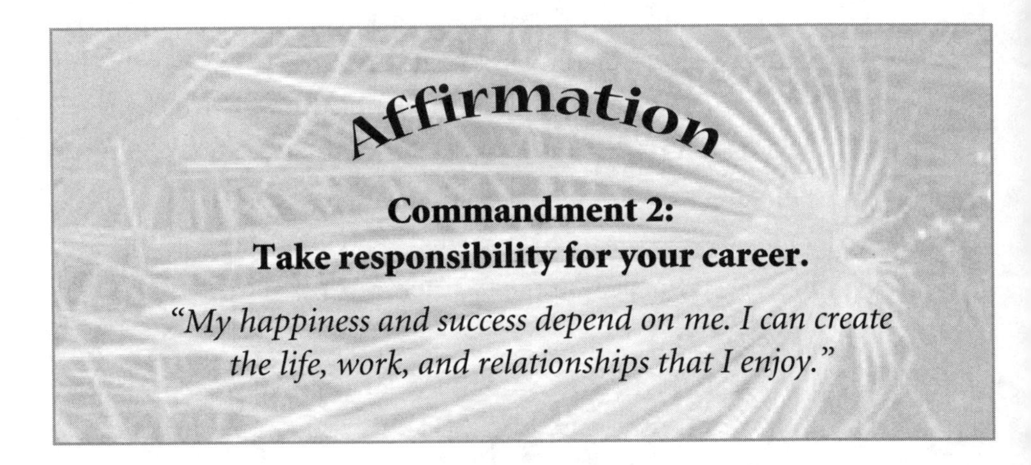

ADVENTURE 17

HOW DO I, AS THE MAJOR BREADWINNER IN OUR FAMILY, HANDLE THE FACT THAT I WANT TO SPEND MORE TIME AT HOME WITH OUR BABY?

Do you wish your career consumed less of your time and energy so that you could spend more time with your growing family? Many working women, especially those whose incomes largely support their families, worry that they may be shortchanging their children or themselves. Some women feel added pressure from their spouses who insist that they continue working full-time. If you personally can relate to this dilemma, think how you would handle **Heartburn in Heaven***.*

Heartburn in Heaven

Returning to your fast-paced trouble-shooter position at Quick Response Computer Networking Company six weeks after Nanyka's birth broke your heart. Your particular *post partum* blues came less from hormones than from separation anxiety about the baby you had dreamed of bringing into this world for five long infertile years. Nanyka is the miracle baby your gynecologist thought you could never bear. And now, you must leave her with strangers every day from 7:30 A.M. until 6 P.M. while you desperately long to apply for an extended leave with no pay. Jefferson, your husband of eight years, insists that you can't afford to do that.

You recall only too vividly the mental and physical pain you suffered from the endometriosis that rendered you infertile for years. During that time, Jefferson displayed extraordinary patience with your "female" problems, though you know he resented your frequent fear of intimacy and felt guilty and angry when he caused you pain. Only after meeting with Dr. Davenworth, your reproductive endocrinologist who proposed surgery to correct the condition, could you see a ray of hope. An endoscopist performed the laparoscopy to remove pelvic adhesions surrounding your ovaries, tubes, and uterus, but you knew that even with this your chances of getting pregnant remained a paltry 43 percent. Still you prayed for a baby. Your prayers were answered when Nanyka blessed your life, a blessing that filled your heart to overflowing with joy. No wonder your heart aches so much when you trudge off to work every day.

You met Jefferson at Howard University in Washington, DC, and from that moment the two of you began building a bountiful life together. When you earned your degree in computer science you were immediately recruited by a large computer software company based in Austin, Texas. Jeff had planned to land a job with a Big Three accounting firm after graduation, but for that he needed a masters degree. Putting that goal temporarily on hold, he married you and moved with you to Austin, where he settled for a lackluster position as purchasing agent for an industrial farm equipment company. You joined Quick Response four years later with a sizable salary increase that enabled you to make the down payment for your 2,400-square-foot, three-bedroom home in the hills of West Austin.

Now you want to cut back your work hours so you can nurture Nanyka while she's still a baby. You ache every day when you drop her off at day care and she reaches out her eighteen-month-old arms for you and cries. But trying to communicate this heartbreak with Jefferson proves impossible, like struggling to hear through hopelessly crossed wires. He simply refuses to budge from the comfortable, two-income lifestyle you've shared for eight years, blackmailing you with accusations that you'll ruin your family's welfare if you allow your income to drop.

"Why should we scrimp just so you can stay at home with the baby?" he demands. "If you quit your job, we'd have to move to a lousy area with poor schools. Do you really want that for Nanyka? Think how that would hurt her, Valerie."

"Nanyka's outgrowing dresses that I've never had time to put on her, Jeff," you lament.

"What? We should give up a good neighborhood for a dress? Come on, Baby, you know this is the life we talked about, we built together. You don't want to wreck everything we've worked so hard to gain."

"Maybe I could job share, and save some money on day care."

"You wouldn't earn enough and couldn't save enough. No, you'd really be hurting all of us and you know it."

You feel trapped. "There must be *something* I can do," you mutter as you wander into the kitchen for a note pad. An hour later, you've come up with four options:

What Would You Do?

A. I'll ask a Realtor to find a nice house in a good neighborhood we can afford if I work half-time.

B. I don't want to upset Jefferson, or appear selfish, so I'll keep doing what I do now.

C. I can become a portfolio worker, performing several jobs from home to earn enough money to maintain our lifestyle yet keep me near Nanyka.

D. I can look for another company with on-site day care so I can spend more time during the day with Nanyka and still earn the money we need.

Turn to the option that most appeals to you. To learn the most from this adventure, read how the other options turned out, too. Then study the last three sections of this adventure: "Exploring the Issue," "Expanding Your Thinking," and "Assessing Your Situation."

A. I'll ask a Realtor to find a nice house in a good neighborhood we can afford if I work half-time.

You're sick of the stalemate with Jeff. He seems so incredibly closed-minded on this issue. You've always expected him to display more understanding of your needs, just as he had through all those years you struggled with endometriosis. You're surprised and hurt at his insistence that you keep working full-time. To you, your income doesn't seem nearly as important as your time with Nanyka. But how can you convince Jeff of this?

You contact Polly Braverman, the Realtor who sold you your dream home. When you meet with her the following day during your noon hour at her office not far from yours, you confide the reasons why you're considering a move.

"Polly, I'm committed to living in a good area, but if I work part-time, we'll need smaller mortgage payments. Jeff worries about downgrading. He loves our present situation, but I'm hoping you can come up with a compromise that will make us both happy. Tell me I'm not crazy."

"Not at all, Valerie. You're smart, and you know it. Actually, this may be an excellent time to make a switch. In the last four years your home has appreciated in value 15 percent, and right now interest rates are lower than they've been for decades. There are several ways you can go. You can sell your place at a nice profit and buy another more reasonably priced house with a larger down payment, locking in a lower interest rate mortgage. Your monthly payments would drop considerably. We can figure out exactly what your savings will be when we find a replacement house."

"Can we find a decent place in a nice neighborhood?"

"Of course. You're in a premium neighborhood right now, but there are fine areas for young families that might suit you even better, with playgrounds nearby and excellent schools. Terrytown, just west of downtown, has charming older homes that might provide a more convenient commute to work than where you live now. You'll like the area, I'm sure. But I would also suggest that you consider staying where you are and refinance your loan. That could cut down on your monthly costs, and you wouldn't have to go through the expenses of moving, not to mention closing costs. But only you and Jeff can decide which alternative will work best for you."

"I could live with either choice. Jeff, I don't know. Any cutbacks will upset him."

"Would you like me to show you a few homes, just to give you a feel for the area?"

"That would be great. Can we do it during my lunch hours?"

"I'll set it up for the next two days, Valerie, if that works for you."

"Yes, thanks, I want to get going on this."

Over the next two days you discover some choices that you believe could work well. Excitedly, you discuss them with Jeff. You also mention that if he prefers to stay in the West Austin house, it might work out through refinancing and cutting back on non-essential expenses. "Jeff, you know we could cut back for a while without really hurting our lifestyle. We only use the Explorer when we're taking the dog with us somewhere so we don't get the BMW dirty. We could replace the Explorer with a smaller car. But it might make more sense financially to sell the house. We really never use the upstairs, so why pay the big mortgage every month for something we don't use? I'm not saying we need to downsize forever, but I think we could be using our money more wisely by tapping the equity from our current house and moving to a more modestly priced one in a family neighborhood."

You show Jeff your financial calculations, hoping to convince him that either approach might satisfy both of your needs. You also tell him that your employer feels optimistic about arranging part-time work for you. To your surprise, Jeff replies, "What do you really think you're doing, Valerie? You talk about 'satisfying both our needs' when you're just talking about yourself. You know exactly how I feel. Look, I'll say it again. I'm not moving, I'm not selling *my* Explorer, I'm not going to take any more of this scrimping crap from you. So get over it."

Defeated, you get up to check on Nanyka in her crib. As you look down on her angelic face, you scare yourself when you wonder, for the first time, what life without your husband would be like. In the following frustrating months, you wonder about that a lot.

BENEFITS OF A:

- You check out your options with a Realtor.
- You find that you could relocate to an acceptable, more affordable neighborhood or refinance your present home.
- You calculate the effects of a reduced income and a few spending changes and share that information with your husband.
- You feel happier and less stressed with the possibility of working less and spending more time with your baby.
- You think researching ways to alleviate your problem with Jeff will convince him to see things your way.

DOWNSIDES OF A:

- You take the entire responsibility on yourself.
- You've never suggested to Jeff that he help figure out a way to keep the lifestyle he wants.
- You're disappointed that your husband will not budge an inch.
- Your problems with your husband turn out to be greater than you thought.
- You start fantasizing about what life without your husband would be like, thinking that if you can't convince him, dump him.
- You don't consider talking to a marriage counselor for professional help.

B. I don't want to upset Jefferson, or appear selfish, so I'll keep doing what I do now.

You try your best to stifle your disappointment over Jeff's insistence that you continue to work full-time. There's a side of you that understands—that likes your lifestyle, too—but there's another side that warns you not to ignore your maternal instincts. You believe you could live anywhere, with less income, provided you spend these crucial early years with Nanyka. But, you just don't want to continue fighting with Jeff over it. You've found dealing with this issue so stressful that you've not only been unable to lose your "baby fat," but you've added another fifteen pounds.

You try to pour your energies into Quick Response, losing yourself in the hubbub and daily crises, but you come home drained. You particularly hate days you must work late, when Jeff picks up Nanyka and you get to spend even less time with her. Take yesterday, for instance. When you walked in the front door at 7:30, what you saw made your blood boil. The baby was crawling around in dirty diapers, Jeff was glued to the television watching Monday Night Football, and you were expected to fix dinner. It hit you like a lightning bolt. "Is *this* why I've been working myself to exhaustion? I'm not spending one more day in this hell."

Instead of screaming, you calmly walk over to the television set, turn off the game, pick up Nanyka and put her in Jeff's arms, saying, "Change her. I'm going to order a pizza and take a bath before it comes."

"Whoa, must have been a rough day at work," Jeff grinned.

"No, it turns out it was a great day, my last day at work. It's time for you to figure out a way to keep us going without my damned paycheck."

"Hey, now..."

"Not now. I'm too tired."

After your bath, a pepperoni pizza, and some picture book time with Nanyka, you walk back into the living room to talk with Jeff.

"Look, you've made me feel guilty ever since Nanyka was born, saying that if I cut back at work, *I* will ruin *our* lifestyle. Well, just what do you contribute to *our* lifestyle? You barely pick up after yourself, let alone help with the baby or fix dinner on nights I work late. I've been continuing to work full-time because of you, but I see no effort on your part. It's as though you're punishing me for finally having a baby. I don't get it. We should be really happy, instead we just fight. I'm fed up with it all."

"And I'm fed up with your put downs, Valerie. I'm going for a walk." He storms out of the house.

Again, you've accomplished nothing by your outburst, except hurt feelings. You think you should see a shrink, or a marriage counselor. Instead, you go to the kitchen and eat three large bowls of butter crunch ice cream.

BENEFITS OF B:

- You try to keep your lifestyle intact by working full time.
- You enjoy losing yourself in the demands at your office.
- You try to communicate with Jeff.

DOWNSIDES OF B:

- You never enlist Jeff's help when you work full-time.
- You acquiesce to Jeff's wishes until it hits you that you're being used.
- You get frustrated and seethe with anger.
- You can't communicate with Jeff when you're both angry.
- You threaten to quit your job.

- You haven't resolved anything.
- You eat your way through your anger.
- You don't seek professional help.

C. I can become a portfolio worker, performing several jobs from home to earn enough money to maintain our lifestyle yet keep me near Nanyka.

Before you can convince Jeff that your plan will work, you study ways you can shift from a salaried job to working at home as a portfolio worker. What will it take for you to switch from an office job to a career as an entrepreneur juggling multiple projects? On the plus side, you take care of multiple problems simultaneously already. On the minus side, you'll need to learn how to market yourself and win projects. However, you believe your ability to troubleshoot computer problems for a variety of manufacturers, coupled with your programming ability, should form a sound basis for your own portfolio business.

You had become interested in the portfolio concept of work ever since you read Charles Handy's book, *The Age of Unreason*, in 1990. Back then, the idea sounded like an *avant garde* concept for professionals, though tradespeople with skills in plumbing, carpentry, and such hourly jobs had been, in effect, doing portfolio work for years. Today, career gurus, like Tom Gorman, author of *Multipreneuring*, consider it a smart way to work and make good money. You like the concept and think of it not so much as starting your own business, as adapting your structured office to a home-based environment. You ask your co-workers and friends for their opinions about what you do particularly well, looking for skills you can add to your portfolio. Though you can't match your income or benefits from Quick Response, you will gladly trade those for greater flexibility and more time with Nanyka.

You try to help Jeff understand that with the arrival of Nanyka, it makes no sense to cling to your pre-baby lifestyle. The fabric of your life has changed so dramatically, you both must rethink your needs and roles. Even if you bring in exactly the same amount of money you always have, you still must cough up $100 a week for day care. If you both agree that change has already taken place, then you can look at your roles and needs together, rather than fighting about it.

You explain to Jeff that if you keep Nanyka in day care only half-time, you'll be saving $200 a month right there. You identify other effects of your proposed career shift. Certainly, you would not know your exact income every month. You'd lose health and retirement benefits. However, you can get on Jeff's health plan, though you'd have to look into that because of your pre-existing condition of endometriosis. The main obstacles you foresee? Convincing Jeff that your plan will work and getting those first essential clients.

When you talked to your boss at Quick Response, she first expressed her shock that you'd think of going out on your own, but then she offered you a great suggestion, "Why don't you consult for us? The company has been thinking of hiring independent contractors to help with the growing number of accounts, but we've hesitated until now. You could be our guinea pig."

"Hey, what an offer. I've never been a guinea pig before," you laugh.

As you discuss the details of how the program might work, you fall in love with the notion. After all, you'd simply be doing what you know best, but on your own time. You know you'll pick up more clients through word-of-mouth once you start. Jeff worries how it will all turn out, but he does like the idea that you'll continue to earn an income throughout the transition.

By the time Nanyka reaches age three, you enjoy a hectic but rewarding life. You still live in your dream house, though you're pulling in about three-quarters of what you earned full-time at Quick Response. You save some money on day care and you've been surprised at how other small savings, such as not needing an office wardrobe, fewer dry cleaning bills, and greatly reduced transportation and parking costs, have made up the difference. You've also saved because you no longer spend as much on take-out foods, which you believe has helped you shed some of your extra weight. Your taxable income may have fallen, but all those small savings have really added up. Even Jeff seems to appreciate that the new lifestyle isn't worse than the old, just different, partly because he's made changes in his life, too. In another year he'll finish his MBA night school program at the University of Texas, then he plans to go after his dream of working for a Big Three accounting firm at last.

BENEFITS OF C:

- You determine that you possess a variety of marketable skills.
- You look into portfolio work.
- You ask friends and co-workers for their input about your particular skills.
- You calculate savings, from day care to transportation.
- You discuss the concept with your company and win a contract for outside consulting work.
- You find portfolio work a rewarding life/work choice.
- Your husband supports the transition and continues to better himself to provide more income in the future.

DOWNSIDES OF C:

- You take a financial and marital risk starting you own portfolio business.
- You live on uncertain monthly income.
- You juggle more jobs than ever.

- You don't consider the possible detrimental side effects from working at home.
- You now have the added expense of your husband's MBA program.

D. I can look for another company with on-site day care so I can spend more time during the day with Nanyka and still earn the money we need.

You remember reading that National ProComputer, IBM, and Xerox provide state-of-the-art child care for their employees. The thought of changing jobs doesn't bother you as long as it can help alleviate the separation anxiety you feel every time you leave Nanyka at day care. You hope to solve Jeff's concern over income. You feel resentful, however, that you're the one making all the changes. Why can't he go to school nights to earn his MBA or look for a higher paying job? You really wish he had gone to graduate school, but it's never too late.

You contact the National ProComputer office in Austin and talk to the HR director, Audrey Alverson. You possess remarkable and highly desired skills that impress Audrey. You raise your concerns about day care.

"You know that National ProComputer was listed in 'The Ten Best Companies for Working Mothers' in a *Working Women* magazine article?"

"No, but I had read about National ProComputer offering day care."

"Oh, the program is a great success. The child care nursery takes children from just after birth to five years old, and it's located next to the cafeteria. Mothers join their babies in the cafeteria for lunch. It's very popular."

"It does sound great. I guess the next step is to get a job at National ProComputer," you laugh.

"Actually, the next step is to fill out an application and come in for an interview. Give me your address, and I'll mail you an application. You can tour our child care center when you come in for the interview."

Though you would prefer working part-time, you love the child care set-up. While you will miss your friends and co-workers at Quick Response, you have enjoyed a good four years there, and it just may be time to move on, and up.

You spend a few days updating your résumé.

When Audrey tells you her company has no current openings that would call on your troubleshooting expertise, and that you would have to take a pay cut if you accepted a training job, you discuss the pros and cons with Jeff. It would require a lot of changes on your part, but he would also need to change a few of his own habits in order to save money as well. His response surprises and delights you. "I can probably make a few changes," he promises. You don't know why he's changed his tune, but you're not going to question it. Though you'd have to accept a different position than you'd hoped, you don't mind because you enjoy learning new skills. You're eager to work for a company that provides the sort of child care that will allow you to eat lunch with Nanyka every day. With Jeff's blessing, you accept the offer at National ProComputer.

Three weeks after you start working at National ProComputer Jeff surprises you again when he announces, "I didn't want to tell you until I landed it, Valerie, but Landslide Equipment Inc., a competing industrial equipment company here in Austin, stole me away with an offer I couldn't refuse, a 20 percent pay increase," Jeff smiles.

"Oh, honey. That's great news. How did it happen?"

"I met the marketing director of Landslide at the Farm Equipment Expo six months ago, one thing led to another, and now you're looking the new accountant of Landslide Equipment."

Your heart swells with pride as you hug your handsome husband who suddenly seems much taller.

BENEFITS OF D:

- You research computer companies that provide on-site child care.
- You're delighted National ProComputer operates a facility for infants and toddlers.
- You're willing to accept a lower position to make it all work.
- You discuss the plan with Jeff.
- You look forward to seeing Nanyka more each day.
- You're proud of your husband's quiet efforts to find a new job.

DOWNSIDES OF D:

- You must change positions and take a cut in pay.
- You're the one instigating most of the job changes.
- You must start all over at a new company with new co-workers.
- Your husband promises to make changes but you have no guarantees that he will before you change jobs.

Exploring the Issue

Successful women often attract men who don't mind their wives earning more than they do. This doesn't apply to women of any particular race, color, creed, or career. And it needn't be all bad. The husbands of many women with high-powered careers take care of the household and the children. Others truly share those duties fifty-fifty, or more. Communication, appreciation, flexibility, and acceptance make these marriages work, as they do in any marriage. However, when a dominant bread-winning woman can't control how she spends her time or money, problems arise.

The character in this adventure faces such a dilemma. She loves her husband and enjoys the lifestyle they've worked hard to attain, but when their "miracle baby" arrives, family loyalties and lifestyle issues become unexpected bones of contention. The pressure rests squarely on her shoulders, a more and more common twist to the work/family dilemma.

Couples with two jobs, two cars, and a nice home before the baby arrives, often find that along with their bundle of joy comes dissension in the home that leads to other problems. It's not just the sleepless nights that cause irritation either. When the woman contributes more income to the family than her husband, there's added pressure on her to keep the lifestyle going. Plans that may have seemed logical and practical before the baby arrived change dramatically when it wails in anguish every time it's left at day care. This dilemma plagues many working women who have worked hard to get ahead in their careers, but now want to spend a lot of time with their babies.

If you accept a disproportionate share of both the financial and emotional side of your relationship, does that role fulfill you, or not? If not, you might:

- Assess your behavior. Are you the type of woman who can't say no, who takes on more than you should? Do you like to fix things in people's lives and shoulder responsibility for their well-being, but don't like to ask for help yourself? Do you expect a lot of yourself and others? Record your findings.
- Notice how you feel. When you take on too much, do you feel burdened, resentful, exhausted? Read everything you can to learn about what others have done in your situation.
- Get ideas from friends and relatives. Stay open and not defensive. If you don't like what you're hearing because it strikes a painful chord, seek professional help to sift through your feelings.

- Set limits for yourself. Respect your own needs. The more you do for others, the more they will let you do and eventually expect you to do. It's a breakable cycle, but like every spinning thing, it will take some strong resistance on your part to stop it.
- Look into part-time or portfolio work. Whether for primary or supplemental income, you'll find more opportunities available than ever before. According to the U.S. Department of Labor, almost 18 percent of us work less than forty hours a week in part-time jobs. Until relatively recently, part-time positions didn't include professionals such as attorneys, accountants, doctors, and computer analysts. When contemplating part-time or portfolio work, first approach your current employer. Can you spell out the advantages for them? Many companies have toyed with the idea, but haven't set it in action yet and would prefer to start with people who already have a track record with the company. Many companies contract out work because doing so saves them money on benefits and other full-time employee costs.

Though you may not feel it at the time, you do have choices. Think them through, communicate them, and work toward the happy life you want.

Expanding Your Thinking

In this adventure, "you" develop a sense of urgency about spending time with your baby that differs from your husband's priorities. He doesn't want to disturb his comfortable lifestyle. Although you try many ways to handle the conflict of interests and needs, many of them didn't work out as well as you had hoped. The biggest problem remains communication. Jeff's rigid desire for you to maintain the lifestyle to which he's become all too comfortably accustomed clashes with your needs. Trying to cope with this, you do all of the research and make all of the major changes. The fact that you're willing to take on that burden makes you vulnerable to stress and depression. You find it difficult to cope with your recalcitrant husband.

In Option A, you conduct all the research and perform all the calculations to prove that you could maintain a reasonable lifestyle even if you downgrade your income so you can spend more time at home with your baby. You never suggest that your husband might help figure out a way to keep the lifestyle he wants and feel disappointed since he will not budge an inch. When you realize that your problems with your husband may be greater than money issues, you fantasize life without him. You neglect contacting a marriage counselor for professional help.

In Option B, you never consciously plan to enlist Jeff's help after the baby comes. You assume he'll behave as understandingly as he did during your struggle with endomitriosis. When he doesn't, you cave in, staying in your full-time job until you seethe over his selfish behavior. When you threaten to quit your job altogether, you argue with Jeff. He storms out of the house, and communication ends because you're both angry. You're unable to resolve anything and take out your frustration by bingeing on ice cream. Again, you don't seek professional help.

In Option C, you take a financial risk starting your own portfolio business at home. Your husband does not fully back your efforts, and you find your new juggling act as hectic as your old job. You ignore the possible detrimental side effects your working at home might produce. Although you're pleased that your husband has chosen to return to school, you now have the added expense of your husband's MBA program.

In Option D, you find a company with an on-site day care center, but you must change companies and move back down the ladder. Again, you do all of the research and make all of the changes. You must start all over with a new company with new co-workers, while your husband promises to make changes even though you have no guarantees that he will.

What problems could you avoid?

DON'T:

1. Let maintaining the *status quo* rule your life.
2. Assume your husband understands what role you think he should play in child raising without communicating with him.
3. Enable your spouse to take advantage of you.
4. Acquiesce to demands without checking out your options.
5. Make threats you're not prepared to act on.
6. Go along with something you dislike then take out your frustrations on others or yourself.
7. Expect incomes to remain at the same level throughout your career.
8. Avoid seeking professional counseling.
9. Ignore the possibility of home-based or portfolio work.
10. See yourself stuck in one job, when many others may support the lifestyle you seek.

What about the positives? In Option A, you take charge by researching other housing solutions. You talk with your Realtor and learn about attractive alternative areas and refinancing. You calculate different financial scenarios which all require some change in current spending habits, and you explain the choices to your husband. Meanwhile, you talk to your employer and find that you can work part-time, which will permit you to spend more time with your baby. You hope you can convince Jeff to see things your way because of your research.

In Option B, you try to uphold the *status quo* by working full-time. You enjoy losing yourself in the demands at your office. You realize that keeping your husband in *his* lifestyle is wearing you down, so you try to encourage him to change his habits.

In Option C, you look into the possibility of portfolio work. Your array of marketable skills makes this feasible. You calculate what you can save on baby care, transportation, and eating out. Your employer likes the idea and becomes your first client. Not only do you find this a rewarding alternative, but Jeff supports it as well. To your delight, your husband returns to college to earn his MBA to increase his own marketability.

In Option D, you identify a different computer company that provides on-site day care. You contact the company's Human Resources Department and apply for a job. You're willing to accept a lower position to make it all work, plus you enjoy learning new skills. With Jeff's encouragement and blessing, you accept the position and look forward to seeing Nanyka more each day. You're proud of your husband's quiet efforts to find a new job, and you respect him more.

DO:

1. Research different options for supporting your lifestyle.
2. Know that your choices all require flexibility and communication.
3. Keep your priorities straight, updating and aligning them with your husband's.
4. Calculate hidden expenses you could save were you to work at home or part-time.
5. Check out the availability of part-time work with your own employer before going out on your own.
6. List and expand your skills.

7. Ask friends and co-workers what they think you do particularly well.
8. Look for alternative companies that provide flexible work arrangements and on-site day care.
9. Realize that lifestyles change throughout a marriage.
10. Keep in mind that your children are only young once.

Assessing Your Own Situation

If you find yourself relating to this situation, ask yourself some serious questions.

1. Why did this situation occur? Ask, “Have I enabled my husband to expect me to provide too much?” “Have I sat down with him to discuss what I need and expect concerning his role in the family?” “Do I feel resentful but fear saying anything?”
2. Do you feel guilty? Ask yourself, “Why do I feel guilty?” “What could I do to alleviate this guilt?”
3. Do you feel like the only one bending to make things work? Ask, “When did the balance shift to my side?” “Do I actually enjoy the role of main provider?” “If I earn the most money, do I have a say in how we live?”
4. If you give in to requests you don’t agree with, ask, “What is the worst that would happen if I just say no?” “If I’m willing to force a change, am I aware of the consequences and willing to accept them?”
5. Have you actively searched for a variety of solutions? Ask, “Have I looked into alternatives for housing, work, and child care?”
6. Are you trying to go this alone? Ask, “Have I talked with others who’ve solved similar dilemmas?” “Should I seek professional counseling?”

7. If you can't seem to reach your husband, is he jealous of the baby? Ask yourself, "Have I gotten so wrapped up in the baby's needs, that I've ignored my husband?" "Have I tried to include my spouse in my new mother role and do I compliment him whenever he does great father things?"

8. Have you set limits for yourself? Ask, "Am I caring for the people in my life or carrying them?" "Have I accepted the lion's share of the emotional and financial load, but don't want to keep on doing that?"

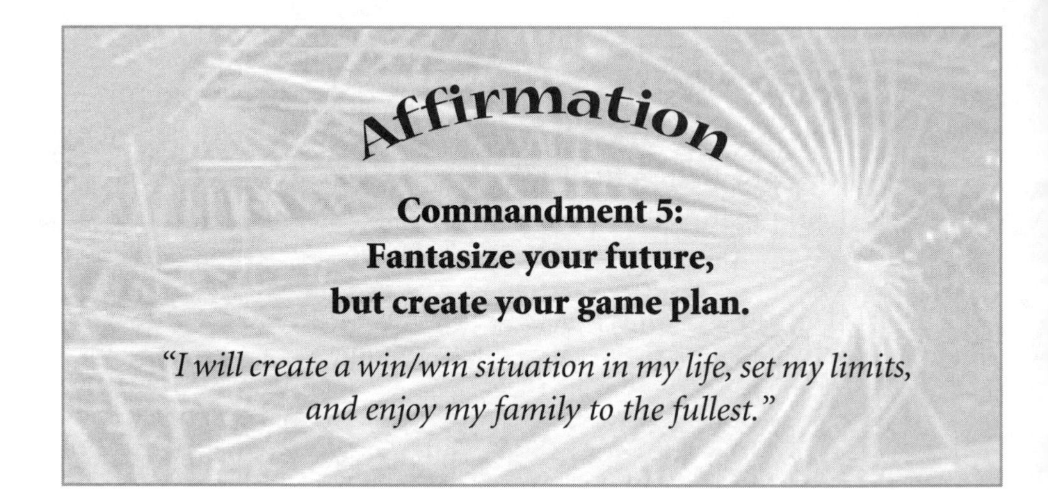

ADVENTURE 18

HOW CAN I FIND A MOMENT FOR MYSELF WHEN I MUST JUGGLE A CAREER, JOINT PARENTING, A SIGNIFICANT OTHER, AN AGING PARENT, AND MY OWN HOT FLASHES?

Whatever your age now, you will most likely find yourself one day in "The Sandwich Generation," those folks responsible not only for their own lives but for the well-being of their children and aging parents. How does any woman find time to care for herself with all that responsibility? How would you solve this dilemma if you're the woman who left this recording on your answering machine: ***"Leave a Message, I'm Either away from My Desk or out of My Mind"****?*

Leave a Message, I'm Either away from My Desk or out of My Mind

You smile as your children, Sam, fifteen, and Megan, fourteen, pile out of your white Volvo station wagon with their bags full of new back-to-school clothes and supplies, then check "school shopping" off your list. School starts in a ten days. What a break this year, both kids going to the same school, Maryvale High, not far from your home on the west side of Phoenix. "I'll save at least forty-five minutes driving time a day," you mentally calculate. Lately, every second counts.

When you enter your bedroom the blinking answering machine light indicates five messages. You flop down on your Laura Ashley quilted bed, grab your note pad and pencil, and press the "New Messages" button.

Message 1: "Hey, Helene. Jack here. What did you find out about Labor Day weekend? Is it a go? You're gonna love Cabo San Lucas. We're booked on the 5:15 P.M. America West flight on Friday. We'll be walking the beach under the stars by 9:30. Call me." Your heart skips when you hear Jack's deep resonant voice booming with boyish excitement. A few months ago your boss introduced you to Jack Gilbert, the new man in your life, a stock broker five years your senior. Jack's the kind that's hard to find and you want to keep him. A widower with no children, Jack offers you a wonderful future, provided you can create enough space for him in your harried schedule. Jack wants to take you to Mexico over Labor Day. You desperately want to go and have been working feverishly to keep all your "responsibility balls" in the air long enough for you to run off for the weekend and then slip back in time to catch them all before they drop and hopelessly scatter.

Message 2: "Helene? This is your mother. Uh, I hate these machines. Are you there? Is my podiatrist appointment this Monday or next Monday? Can you still take me during your lunch hour? Oh, and the light in my bathroom burned out. Call me, Dear, when you get in. Uh, this is your mother." Your eighty-year-old mother lives alone in her deteriorating family home thirty-five minutes away. She suffers from an array of ailments, none life-threatening, but her osteoarthritis restricts her severely. She shuffles around the house in her slippers, leaning heavily on her walker with the yellow day glow tennis balls on the back legs to prevent scuffing her hard wood floors, maneuvering gingerly around the piles of plastic vegetable bags secured with paper clips and rubber bands that contain all her important papers, semi-current bills, and favorite recipes. You want her to move to an attractive retirement complex where people her age live in their own apartments, go on outings in the facility van, sit with friends in the auditorium to enjoy afternoon entertainment, and play bingo in the activity room after dinner. However, your mother refuses to give up her "independence," though she's terribly lonely, can't leave the house alone, and counts on you to help her with everything she can't do herself, which includes changing light bulbs and getting her prescriptions filled.

Message 3:"I know it's my weekend over Labor Day, Helene, but I'll be in New York working on a huge case. Sorry." Leonard, your ex-husband, father of your two children, and the most undependable man in the solar system, leaves you stranded again. He can't seem to grasp the concept that when it's his weekend for the kids, he should find a sitter if he can't fulfill his responsibility. As usual, his schedule becomes your problem.

Message 4: "This is Dr. Kellerman's office confirming your appointment on Friday at 4:30. See you then." Your hot flashes have elevated your dry cleaning bills more than 400 percent over the last two months. You must do something soon before you dissolve your entire wardrobe. You've waited six weeks for this appointment.

Message 5: "Helene. Looks like the merger is on. Need you to work late all week and into the weekend. I know, I know, it's Labor Day, but it can't be helped. Thanks." The on-again, off-again, long sought merger between your radio station and the second largest in the greater Phoenix area seems to be going through at last. At least Jacob, the station manager, says "thanks," but you know he counts on you, as office manager. Your job pays the bills comfortably, and, at age forty-eight, you don't know where you'd find a less stressful job that would.

After you delete your messages, you drop your head in your hands. With all this hullabaloo in your life, how can you possibly set aside some time for yourself? You desperately want to spend the weekend in Mexico with Jack, but you feel so overwhelmed, you don't see how you can manage that. Feeling squashed in the center of a sandwich, you take a moment to list ways you might juggle everything before you lose your mind.

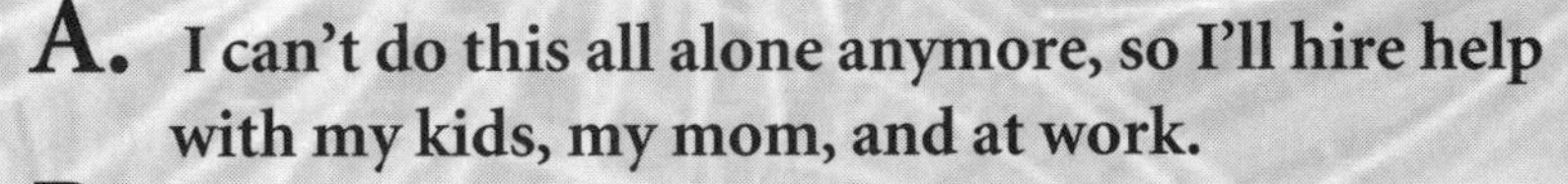

A. I can't do this all alone anymore, so I'll hire help with my kids, my mom, and at work.

B. I can put my relationship with Jack on hold because I don't know where else to cut back.

C. Whatever I do, I must deal with these hot flashes before they become even more debilitating and embarrassing.

D. I can continue as best I can because I just don't know what else to do.

Turn to the option that most appeals to you. To learn the most from this adventure, read how the other options turned out, too. Then study the last three sections of this adventure: "Exploring the Issue," "Expanding Your Thinking," and "Assessing Your Situation."

A. I can't do this all alone anymore, so I'll hire help with my kids, my mom, and at work.

As you contemplate your messages, your emotions race from frustration to anger, the latter directed at yourself for allowing so many people to depend on you for so much. Something has to give before you lose the last few tattered shreds of your sanity. "No more," you vow. "I'm getting help." No, you're not going to ignore the people you love, but you're going to quit ignoring yourself. Immediately you embark on a mission to find the help you need.

You contact Maryvale High School for a list of child care providers and mothers' helpers. You also talk to several other mothers who routinely hire someone to take care of the kids while they're away. It only takes a couple of hours to obtain six names of qualified candidates. Surely you can find a reliable older woman who can stay with the kids when you're out of town, and to help out a few days a week when needed. Leonard, your ex, can hire this same woman whenever he can't take the kids as scheduled, rather than dumping the problem in your lap.

Next, you tackle Mom, consulting the phone book for Elder Care Services. When you type "Elder care, Phoenix" in your computer's search engine, you're delighted to discover that the Internet provides information for elder care services for all fifty states, including the Phoenix area. You'd love to find a service that could pick up your mom and help her shop, replace her burned out light bulbs, and take her to her doctor's appointments. Some geriatric social workers, you discover, not only assist older people, but locate permanent help. You had no idea there was so much available, but you had never looked. Your mother won't like it at first, of course, but you assume she'll form an attachment to one of her "helpers," freeing up your time so that the time you do spend with her will focus on having fun together rather than on running around checking off her list of errands. You've come to realize that the more you try to help your mother get settled, the more "emergencies" she can dream up. Her needs have become a black hole, sucking every bit of energy out of you. You're not going to let it happen anymore. When you learn about other elder services that offer planned social events for people your mom's age, you hope this will alleviate some of her loneliness and provide introductions to people her own age for conversation and companionship.

At work, you discuss with Jacob, your station manager, the wisdom of hiring an intern or a part-time assistant. You know that he's trying to keep expenses low during the on-again off-again merger talks, but his frugality has increased your workload threefold. You think you're valuable enough to demand assistance. You've never asked for such help in the past, which in itself explains why your boss blithely piled so much work on you.

Pleased with the resources you've found to help you accomplish your goals to find the right help for your family and at work, you then turn your attention to your own health problem. You'll call the doctor's office and reschedule your appointment for after your vacation with Jack, because, hey, it'll be so hot in Mexico, your perspiration from hot flashes will look normal. You still don't know if you'll get it all coordinated in time to take off for Cabo with Jack, but you're going to give it the old college try.

You miraculously pull it all off, and enjoy a wonderful, but not necessarily worry-free, weekend in Cabo with Jack. Your worries prove well-founded when you discover upon your return that the highly recommended woman you hired to watch your children has spent every last cent of the "emergency" money you'd left her on delivered meals (since she decided not to cook), and on a shopping spree that included buying an outdoor bug zapper, of all things. You hate hearing bugs fry. Furthermore, the service you employed to assist your mother while you were away sent over a different caregiver every day, which not only completely annoyed and confused your mother, but racked up many "case management" costs. You didn't realize that in order for the service to assist your mother, she becomes a "case" for which they can send as many people as they wish to call on her whenever they deem it necessary, and they will charge you $60 an hour for their "service."

With that kind of help, you'll all be headed for the poor house. Luckily, you didn't miss anything at work because, at the last minute, the merger talks halted altogether.

"Well," you think, "at least I got away." You have some major fine-tuning to do on your help arrangements, but you feel it will simply take time to iron out the bugs. Then again, maybe you could zap them.

BENEFITS OF A:

- You decide to hire help with your family.
- You conduct a search through the phone book, the Internet, the school, and through friends.
- You're pleasantly surprised at all of the help available for elderly people today.
- You plan to find a mature woman to watch the kids and insist your ex-husband hire her when he can't take them.
- You convince Jacob to hire an assistant or an intern.
- You feel more in control coordinating a team of helpers than you did trying to do it all yourself.
- You enjoy a wonderful weekend with Jack in Cabo San Lucas.

DOWNSIDES OF A:

- You incur heavy and unexpected costs hiring help to watch your children and mother while you were away.
- You have no one you can insist that your ex hire while he's away.
- Your mother's needs were not met.
- You face much more trial and error to perfect your back-up systems.

B. I can put my relationship with Jack on hold because I don't know where else to cut back.

Although you'd much rather do it face-to-face, you decide to call Jack because you just can't wait any longer to solve your problem. You've convinced yourself that you just can't devote the time it takes to develop a deep, lasting relationship, but it breaks your heart to turn your back on this delightful, loving man.

"Jack? It's me," you begin.

"Helene, I was hoping to hear from you tonight." As Jack's voice embraces you, you realize this is going to be a lot harder than you hoped.

"Jack, can I tell you the truth? I don't know if I have the courage to do it in person, or even over the phone, for that matter."

"What is it, Helene?"

"This sounds horrible, because I think the world of you, but I can't..."

"Whoa, wait right there, Helene. I'm coming over. Okay?"

"Okay," you sigh. Both kids have gone to friends' houses for the evening, part of the last hurrah before school starts.

Jack shows up twenty minutes later with a chilled bottle of Robert Mondavi chardonnay and a bag of salted peanuts roasted in the shell, your favorite snack. You escort him into your well-lit dining room and sit across from him with two glasses and a bowl for the shells. As you try to explain your reasoning, your stress level, and your overwhelmingly demanding responsibilities at this time in your life, you try to sound reasonable and coherent, though you catch yourself talking in circles. Jack listens intently, sipping his wine, never taking his gaze from your face.

Finally Jack says, "You know, Helene, if you told me you don't care for me, or if there were something about me that drives you nuts, I could understand that. But from where I'm sitting, I think our feelings for each other are mutual."

You nod, tears running down your cheeks. You excuse yourself to grab a box of Kleenex. When you return, Jack continues.

"You think I can't see what you're trying to juggle here? You're amazing, that's one of the reasons I adore you. But, Helene, don't put off your own happiness till sometime in the future. I'm not trying to take you away from your responsibilities, I just thought a weekend away would be good for you. I still do, but I'll never pressure you."

"But if we can't spend much time together, what future can we build together?" you whimper, knowing you're losing the battle you so desperately didn't want to win.

"Step back, Helene. In four years your two primary concerns, Sam and Megan, will be off to college. Those years go by quickly. I'd like to be part of them in whatever way I can. I don't know anyone I'd rather spend the rest of my life with."

"Oh no, are you asking me to marry you?" you laugh.

"Not at this moment. I know your answer would be no. But I want you to know how I feel. Now, what do you say we reschedule the Cabo trip for later in the school year, when your life has settled down a bit?" Jack walks over to your side of the table and takes you in his arms. "Or tell me you want me to leave and I will."

"I can't," you whisper. You both feel relieved.

Over the next ten months, Jack finds useful ways to become part of your lives. Since he leaves his brokerage firm early every afternoon, he helps out by picking up the kids after school or taking them to soccer practice. Three nights a week he comes over and prepares dinner for "his favorite people" or takes you all out for pizza, including your mother, who adores him. Jack slips into your life with such ease, you honestly don't know how you ever managed without him. When Jack asks you to marry him, you plan a very short engagement.

BENEFITS OF B:

- You confront your problem.
- You take action, rather than procrastinating.
- You find that Jack appreciates your honesty and that he's sensitive enough to realize you're overwhelmed with responsibilities.
- You feel relieved when Jack convinces you that you should continue your relationship.
- You find Jack slips into your life more smoothly than you could have imagined.
- You plan to marry Jack after a short engagement.

DOWNSIDES OF B:

- You were fooling yourself thinking you can put a relationship on hold.
- You never really wanted to let go of Jack, but put your needs last.
- You were hurting yourself and your future happiness by choosing to put your relationship with Jack on hold.

C. Whatever I do, I must deal with these hot flashes before they become even more debilitating and embarrassing.

As you finish writing down the messages another "power surge" sweeps over you. Your upper body, especially your face and neck, burn. Perspiration beads form rivulets down your forehead, cascading past your ear before you can catch them. "This is it," you say to yourself. You may not be able to make that appointment next Friday with your doctor, but you've heard of some alternative symptom relievers, and you're going to look into them today.

"Kids, I'm heading out for the health food store. Anyone want to come?"

You hear two muffled "No's," over the thundering downbeat of their music bulldozing its way down the hallway.

As you drive to the strip mall near your home, you wonder if you're a candidate for estrogen replacement therapy. Your family history makes taking it inadvisable, because your maternal grandmother underwent a double mastectomy, your mother fought uterine cancer, and your own cystic breasts have been diagnosed as atypical hyperplasia. You know you're long overdue for a complete physical exam by your OB/GYN, including a Pap smear, a progestogen-challenge test to rule out endometrial cancer, a bone density test, a urinalysis and hematocrit and other blood tests—the full protocol to determine where you are now and what you should or should not worry about.

When you arrive at the store you ask the sales assistant questions about remedies one of your friends at the radio station has extolled. "I have a friend who raves about Vitamin E to fight her hot flashes. What do you know about it? Also, I've heard about people drinking ginseng tea because it's considered an estrogen plant."

The young woman nods enthusiastically. "Yes, let me first tell you about Vitamin E. A lot of women do find it helpful. Start with 400 IU daily. You can slowly increase the dosage until your hot flashes are relieved, but don't exceed 1,600 IU daily. Now, ginseng is a pretty potent plant. When you take it, you do not know for sure how much estrogen you're getting, and you wouldn't be cycling it with progesterone. There's also a cautionary note in our resource book that says people should not use ginseng if they have hypoglycemia, high blood pressure, or a heart disorder."

"I'm not sure I should take estrogen anyway," you admit. "I was just curious."

"I would recommend that you take a multivitamin and mineral complex that contains 400 IU's of Vitamin E and a calcium supplement. If you want to increase your Vitamin E levels, you might want to do it through diet. Eat more dark green leafy vegetables, nuts and seeds, legumes, and whole grains. The next best sources are brown rice, cornmeal, eggs, milk, soybeans, sweet potatoes, watercress, and wheat germ. You probably have some of these in your kitchen."

"You know, that reminds me, I've also heard that soy milk is good," you mention.

"Soy milk, soy beans, and soy powder are all good. Studies have shown that Japanese women experience fewer menopausal symptoms, possibly because they consume more plant estrogens, the phytoestrogens found in soybeans, tofu, miso, and dates. These plant estrogens act like estrogens produced in the body. But you know, your best bet is to quit smoking, get regular exercise, watch your fat intake, avoid salt because it helps deplete calcium, and drink at least two quarts of water a day."

You laugh, "I'll just take the multivitamins and the calcium supplements for now. Thanks for your help."

"One more thing, do get a check up with your doctor."

"Oh, don't worry, that's on the list."

You head home with your purchases, soy powder and vitamin E capsules, and hope to see a quick response to alleviate what ails you.

On your way home you analyze the foods you keep in the cupboard and refrigerator and realize you your diet hasn't been helping you one bit lately. You stop by the local supermarket and buy vegetable burgers, kale, brown rice, sweet potatoes, non-fat yogurt, and wheat germ. Neither Sam nor Megan object to the tasty "vegetarian" dinner you prepare with your groceries, as long as they still get their dishes of vanilla ice cream with chocolate syrup for desert. While they do the dinner dishes, you take a brisk walk around the neighborhood as part of your new health regime.

During your rescheduled appointment with your OB/GYN six weeks later, you admit that you've observed a noticeable decrease in the severity of your menopausal symptoms since you started exercising and watching what you eat. To your delight, your doctor encourages you to continue your new routine. She'd much prefer that you avoid estrogen replacement therapy drugs, considering your family history. You concur. You feel you can minimize your hot flashes, and with that control, you feel happier and more confident, which enables you to handle your other responsibilities with less stress.

BENEFITS OF C:

- You seek information about natural remedies for your hot flashes.
- You don't go overboard with products, but stick to vitamin and mineral supplements and vegetables.
- You start cooking healthier meals and exercise daily.
- You get a complete physical and consult with your OB/GYN, who encourages you to keep up your new health routine in order to avoid estrogen replacement drugs.

DOWNSIDES OF C:

- You seek quick fixes for a long-term problem.
- You have not done any research of your own through reading and research.
- You have done nothing to solve your schedule problems.

D. I can continue as best I can because I just don't know what else to do.

As you sit in the waiting room of your mother's podiatrist late Monday morning, you notice another woman waiting as well, another daughter about your age escorting her mother. You share knowing smiles.

"I can see you're spending your lunch hour the same way I am. You're here with your mother?" you begin.

She's about to speak when the receptionist interrupts, "Are both of your mothers from Phoenix proper?"

You both nod.

"You should know about the new service available for seniors, Drive U. Their small vans pick up senior citizens at their homes and take them to their medical appointments. It's not expensive, especially when the service can combine several clients from one area. Your mothers would have to be a little flexible about time, of course. Would you like more information?"

You both jump up and grab the information sheet with a huge "Thanks."

The other waiting woman beams. "I'm going to call and see how this all works. It certainly would be a God-send for me," she says. "I've had a really hard time saying no to my mother, but, right now, I don't have a job, I just got divorced, and Mom's my entire life." She turns to her mother sitting next to her and pats her hand. "But we had a great heart-to-heart talk. She brought it up, bless her heart, because she was worried I was ignoring my own life. I don't have much of a life right now, but I do need to start building one again."

"That's really thoughtful of you," you say to her mother.

"I'm sure your mother feels the same way. Why don't you talk to her about it?" the elderly woman urges.

You wonder if your mother would actually feel that way. You could see that these two women can talk realistically about their problems. You know you need to be more realistic, too. All your commitments have accumulated slowly and insidiously, until now you feel stuck with an impossible schedule. You never take time to relax anymore. You can't remember when you last read a magazine, let alone a book. If you aren't going full speed ahead, you drop dead-tired into bed. Of course, that doesn't mean you can sleep. Too many stresses plague your weary mind. Your night sweats don't contribute to a good night's sleep, either.

On Monday night, you lie awake rehashing your life. Your stomach churns with a jumble of emotions. You know you must slow down or completely lose your sanity, but where can you cut back? Then it hits you. You can't cut back right now, but you can approach your life with a different attitude. There's a side of you that's proud to be there for those who need you, so why worry about it? Your kids will both head off for college in four years, you'll be over your hot flashes by then, and who knows what will happen with your mother's health. Why not enjoy your family now? Crazy as it may seem, you realize you've been lost in organizational minutia rather than appreciating what and who you have in your life. Unlike the woman you met at the doctor's office whose whole life revolves around her mother, you live an incredibly rich life.

You also realize that lately you've become overly tired, overwrought, and overly sensitive, making you less than an ideal daughter, mother and lover. The antidote? Get away, refresh yourself. So you pick up the phone and call Jack. "Hey there, I've been thinking about the Cabo weekend. It's sounds wonderful. I will find a way to make it work."

Jack must have picked up the tension in your voice. "You know, Helene, though I really want to take you away to Cabo over Labor Day, if the pressures at home are too demanding, we can plan something here, with the kids. We can go to Mexico together anytime. You call the shot. You don't have to decide until the day before. I don't want to complicate your life, Helene. Whatever works for you will work fine for me." You hang up the phone, feeling for the first time that the light you see at the end of the tunnel isn't a runaway train bearing down on you.

BENEFITS OF D:

- You share your experiences with another woman, less fortunate than you.
- You obtain information about a company that can drive your mother to medical appointments.
- You see the need to be more realistic about your time.
- You resolve to maintain a more positive, appreciative attitude.
- Jack proves more sensitive and understanding than yo had even hoped.

DOWNSIDES OF D:

- You doubt that your mother would worry that you're ignoring your own life.
- You make no concerted effort to try to lighten your load.
- You think you can easily change your behavior by changing your attitude.
- You remain sandwiched between heavy responsibilities.

Exploring the Issue

This story doesn't tell a tale about overwork, or even overcommitting, so much as it does about a woman honoring many roles, as mother, daughter, lover, nurturer, and career woman. I say *honoring* because while we're juggling multiple schedules, many of us don't want to give up anything, even though the pressures can crescendo our lives into craziness. We want to be there for everyone. If we can't be there, we often feel guilty. That's the rub. We cannot easily say no.

The character in this adventure feels "sandwiched," stuck in the middle taking care of both kids and parents. When she tries to juggle everything to get away for the weekend, it all comes unglued. If she can only arrange things for this one weekend, perhaps she can get a handle on the rest of her life as well, better managing her time and relying on any new systems she sets up. Can you relate to that?

When we're mired under a multitude of personal and professional responsibilities, we can scarcely find time to comb our hair, let alone find perspective. If the title of this adventure looks all too familiar to you, you know exactly what I mean. Life does that to us, piles on responsibilities periodically, but these periods ebb and flow, depending on whatever stage of life we're living.

I see myself going through life like an inchworm with extended periods of time when I feel compressed, with zero time for myself, and with other periods when life stretches out and I have plenty of time for myself. When I remarried, moved my two children into my husband's and his four sons' home, set up new household operating procedures, sponge-painted the walls, learned to cook for an army, and continued to run my division at work, I felt totally compressed, especially during the first two years when my new husband accepted a job 400 miles away in Los Angeles and commuted home only on weekends. Now all of the children have finished college, save one, and my husband and I enjoy great expanses of time. How did I survive that crazy period? And, actually, I must have been crazy then because I truly thought I could do it all. I look back now and realize I fully *enjoyed* the challenge, trying to do everything for everyone, and feeling like I could. Though I felt pressured and pulled and often frustrated, I wouldn't have missed it for the world. It's like childbirth, you forget the painful parts. Certainly I could have done some things differently, or better, but I did the best I could with the knowledge I had at the time. I've learned to give myself credit for what I accomplished, though I didn't at the time, and to forgive myself for what I wished I'd done, but didn't.

During "compressed" periods of our lives we relegate time for ourselves to the bottom of our priority list. And no wonder, that's the easiest thing to do. But, in actuality, we are doing what we want to do: everything. You can cope with it all because you know it's a special period in your life that won't last forever.

However, wise women do manage to find a moment's peace for themselves. Many wake up early before the circus begins. They watch the sunrise while savoring their private cup of Java. They read the paper, do a crossword puzzle, or watch the morning news, alone. Others construct a refuge late at night. If they can't easily fall asleep, they take that time to soak in a hot bath, read a magazine, sip a cup of herb tea. Still other sleep-deprived women find that peeking in on their slumbering children dissipates any frustration they feel. When they see their children fast asleep, looking sweet and angelic, they forget for a moment all the "I should do's" in their lives.

One day when I gave a talk to a Women in Science group, someone asked me when she would get rid of all the "should's" in her life. My short answer? "Get really old." Everyone laughed, but they also saw the truth in that answer: being busy beats the alternative of having absolutely nothing to do, or even caring if you do anything. With further probing, I learned that the woman who asked that question still had a sixteen-year-old daughter at home. She felt she couldn't put aside her responsibilities and say, "It's my time now," so she felt guilty and frustrated. She suffered from the "should's." But was she really suffering, or was she just asking how other women let go of feeling guilty? We women hate to appear selfish, or feel selfish, so we pile on the "should's" at the expense of ourselves. Replenishing our energy and emotional spirits makes us less resentful of others' demands and more patient so we can look for the good and appreciate the moment.

Expanding Your Thinking

The "you" in this adventure leads a good life, only you're too buried in it to notice. You have a home; a job you enjoy; you have two healthy children; a loving mother; and a wonderful boyfriend. Yes, you suffer from hot flashes, but that's normal for a woman your age. Your ex-husband reneges on his responsibilities with the kids, but he doesn't give you any major grief otherwise. On a certain level, you count your blessings. However, when you juggle all of your different roles—mother, daughter, lover, career woman—you can't find a spare minute for yourself.

When you feel everyone else controls your schedule to the point where you've become a pawn in the chess game of your life, you try to regain control. Sounds easy, doesn't it? Let's look at the ways you tried to gain control that didn't work out as well as you hoped.

In Option A, you gather the information you need to make informed decisions about hiring assistants for your family and office, but when you try a couple of them while vacationing, you incur heavy and unexpected costs. The service you hired for your mother didn't meet her needs or yours. They billed you for "services" you didn't request. Since the woman who watched your children went on a spending spree with the emergency fund you'd left, you still have no one you can recommend that your ex hire when he's away. You must face much more trial and error to set up reliable back-up systems.

In Option B, you want to put your love life on hold. However, you're fooling yourself to think you can put a good relationship on hold, and by trying to do so you cheat yourself. Of course, you never really wanted to let go of Jack, but feel the only way out of your dilemma is to put your needs last. By choosing to put your life on hold you squash any hope of developing your future happiness.

In Option C, you're forced to pay attention to your hot flashes and seek a quick-fix answer at a health food store because you'll have to cancel your doctor's appointment. You don't do your own research but rely on a co-worker and the sales assistant in the store to supply you with vital health information instead. You hope to find relief through vitamins but do not consult your doctor first. While focusing on your hot flashes, you've done nothing to solve your schedule problems.

You take the ostrich approach in Option D. You don't make any decisions, hoping that your problems will somehow work themselves out. After talking to the older woman in the doctor's office, you wonder if your mother would worry that you're ignoring your own life. Since you think you can easily change your behavior by changing your attitude, you remain sandwiched between all of your heavy responsibilities.

What might you remember not to do?

DON'T:

1. Sacrifice your personal life completely.
2. Think you have to do everything alone.
3. Assume you can't afford help.
4. Let scheduling hassles cause you to ignore those around you.
5. Assume no solutions exist before you do your homework.
6. Disregard what your body tells you.
7. Put medical appointments second to other priorities.
8. Take on everyone's responsibilities.
9. Hurt your mental outlook by neglecting your own needs.
10. Leave your future to fate.

What about the many things you handle well in this adventure? In Option A, you decide you no longer need to play superwoman and research ways to ease your responsibilities minding your children, transporting your mother, and hiring an assistant at work.

You're pleased with the resources available through friends, the phone book. and the Internet, especially concerning senior citizens. You haven't put all of the pieces together yet, but you're determined to do it. You know where to get assistance, and you schedule appointments to interview prospective helpers. Your plan to find a mature woman to watch the kids helps not only when you need her, but will also work when your ex-husband can't take the kids. When you find people to take care of your family members and to assist at the office so you can get away with Jack, you feel more in control of your life than when you try to do it all yourself. Because of your efforts, you enjoy a wonderful weekend with Jack in Cabo San Lucas.

You almost blow it in Option B by thinking you should put Jack on hold, but at least you're trying to confront your problem. Luckily, he sees through your exhaustion and frustration and convinces you to keep the relationship alive. Jack appreciates your honesty and you appreciate his seeing that you're overwhelmed with responsibilities. You feel relieved when Jack convinces you that you should continue your relationship. He cooks dinners and helps with the children after school, efforts which allow Jack to become part of the family and ease your responsibilities. Jack slips into your life more smoothly than you could have imagined and you plan to marry soon.

In Option C, you're forced to deal with your own physical needs. You plan to reschedule your OB/GYN appointment, because you know at this point in your life you should get a complete physical exam with all of the extra blood tests. You look into alternative remedies others say have worked well for them. You check out information about vitamins and herbs at the health food store and avoid remedies that you don't feel comfortable using. You purchase a multivitamin and mineral supplement and start adding more fresh vegetables and exercise to your daily routine. At your physical your OB/GYN encourages you to keep up your new health routine in order to avoid estrogen replacement drugs. You feel better and handle your commitments with less stress.

Though you don't take any direct action or make any specific decisions in Option D, you learn an important lesson from those around you. At the podiatrist's office you receive information about a service that could drive your mother to doctors, and you meet a less fortunate woman in a similar situation. You count your own blessings and resolve to maintain a positive and appreciative attitude. When you decide you need to get away to refresh yourself, Jack notices the tension in your voice and you both decide to take the trip to Mexico when your schedule lightens. You're pleased with Jack's understanding nature.

What positive lessons can you take from this adventure?

DO:

1. Know you have choices concerning your personal time, even when everyone depends on you.
2. Keep your personal priorities straight.
3. List your blessings.
4. Compare the most annoying aspects of your life with the benefits they also provide.
5. Pay attention to those who offer unexpected lessons about living a full life.
6. Remain realistic about what you expect of yourself, and what you're willing to give up.
7. Research your options for assistance in the areas where you need it.
8. Consider paying for assistance when you need it.
9. Take care of your health.
10. Remind yourself of the value of an optimistic and positive outlook.

Assessing Your Own Situation

When requests for your time seem endless and overwhelming, ask yourself some important questions.

1. Have you tried to see yourself handling your schedule differently? Ask, "If I could change one thing, what would it be?"
2. Two years from now, might you wish you had done anything differently? Ask, "If I had only two years to live, what would I do during that time?" "Who would I want to spend that time with?" "What is really important to me?"
3. Do you seek time for yourself, or do you just complain about it? Ask, "Who am I trying to impress by keeping myself terribly busy?" "Have I added three things I want to do for myself to my schedule?"
4. Have you looked for the good in your life? Ask, "Have I listed what I enjoy most about everyone in my life?" "Do I pay attention to the small things they do for me?" "Have I ignored the positive because of my overwhelming schedule?"
5. If you can't find personal time, have you created special time with people? Ask, "If I am simply running errands with my children, do I make it fun or do I just anticipate checking it off my list?" "Have I spent special time with my family, or just 'dutiful' time?"
6. If you don't hire help once in a while, why not? Ask, "Will I feel guilty if someone else does something instead of me?" "Have I devalued my own time, by thinking I can't hire someone to help?"
7. Have you communicated with loved ones clearly? Ask, "Have I discussed my concerns with others?" "Would my family get upset with me if I took a few days to relax?"

8. Ask yourself, "What's most important to me?" "What can I learn by listing ten things I love to do and noting when I last did them?"

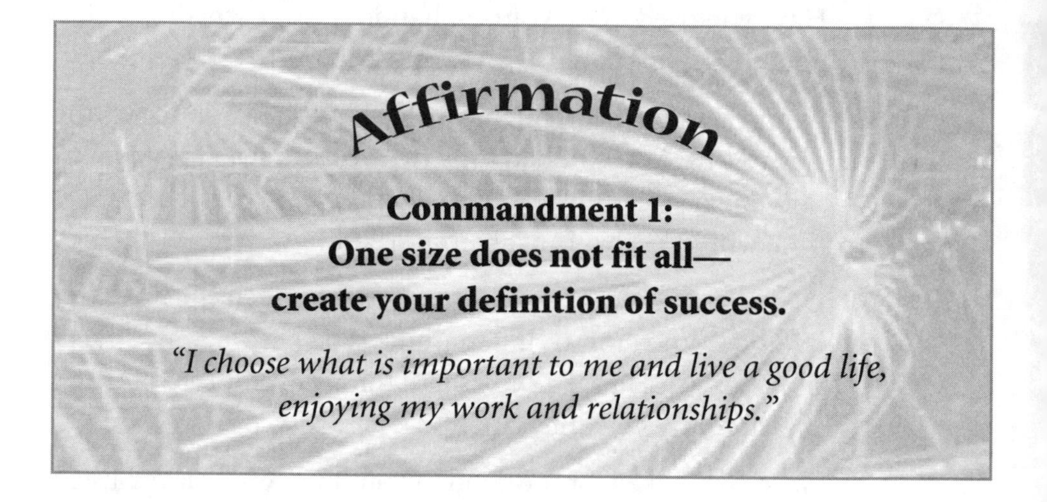

INDEX

A

B

C

D

E

F

G

H

I

J

L

M

N

O

P

R

S

T

U

W